SAGA OF AFRICAN UNDERDEVELOPMENT

SAGA OF AFRICAN UNDERDEVELOPMENT

A Viable Approach for Africa's Sustainable Development in the 21st Century

TETTEH A. KOFI & ASAYEHGN DESTA

Africa World Press, Inc.

P.O. Box 1892
Trenton, NJ 08607

P.O. Box 48
Asmara, ERITREA

Africa World Press, Inc.

P.O. Box 1892
Trenton, NJ 08607

P.O. Box 48
Asmara, ERITREA

Book design: Aliya Books
Cover design: Ashraful Haq

Library of Congress Cataloging-in-Publication Data

Kofi, Tetteh A.
Saga of African underdevelopment : a viable approach for Africa's sustainable development in the 21st century / by Tetteh A. Kofi and Asayehgn Desta.
    p. cm.
Includes bibliographical references and index.
ISBN 1-59221-582-3 (hard cover) -- ISBN 1-59221-583-1 (pbk.)
1. Sustainable development--Africa. 2. Africa--Economic conditions--1961- 3. Economic development--Environmental aspects--Africa. I. Desta, Asayehgn. II. Title.

HC800.Z9E5475 2007
338.96'07--dc22

2007026301

DEDICATION

To Dr. Judy Wosfy and my family, who helped me in many ways to concentrate my energy on completing this book.

Tetteh Kofi

To my daughters, Elda, Hararta, Sunny, and Hierete, my son Adeda, my mother, Woizero Worku Redda, and especially to my wife, Elsa Berhe, my friends Zemam Berhe and Michael Beyene, for their challenge, affection, patience, and support during the book's very long gestation and somewhat painful labor.

Asayehgn Desta

CONTENTS

ACKNOWLEDGMENTS

Three names deserve special mention as key catalysts for the birth of this book. The first is Walter Rodney, who, through his incredible knowledge of the political history of Africa, presented in his book entitled *How Europe Underdeveloped Africa* directed us to understand the political and economic history of Africa. The second is the Abibirim development strategy that, in the 1960s, explicitly recognized that the initiated economic models in Africa couldn't materialize because they were ethnocentric; and thus there was a mismatch between the transplanted Western institutions and indigenous social systems. Last but not least, we need to mention that despite our disagreements with the basic tenants of the New Partnership for Africa's Development (NEPAD), it is worth mentioning that it provided us the critical impetus that Africans need to be the future architects of their own sustainable development models. Thus, contrary to NEPAD, which is based on western capitalist models transplanted by apostles of external agencies, we have proposed that Africa's sustainable economic development model must be largely based on integrated, environmentally sensitive, cooperative agriculture; human capital; and domestic and foreign investments. Thus our paradigm emphasizes that an integrated agroinvestment and educational development strategy, rooted in harmony with the objective conditions of Africa, would achieve growth with equity. It could also collectively empower the African people to fully participate in the design and management of long-lasting development models.

This book has benefited greatly from the generous support and assistance of the Council for Development of Social Science Research in Africa (CODESRIA) and the Third World Network (TWN-Africa). Research funding was provided by the Compton Foundation, San Francisco State University, School of Business. Specifically, we would like to thank Dr. Edward Kujawa, the then Dean, School of Business, Education, and Leadership, Dominican University of California, for the financial support, that he rendered us to present versions of our work at a number of conferences and seminars. We would like to acknowledge that we have benefited from the insightful comments of the seminars and conference participants.

Special thanks also go to Jason Frazier whose unflagging efforts—proofreading, editing, indexing, and assembling the manuscript—made an invaluable contribution to the final product and helped us meet an otherwise impossible deadline. Our students provided wonderful feedback that affected the book in very significant ways. We are indebted to Kassahun Checole, publisher of Africa World Press, and The Red Sea Press, for detailed comments and suggestions. Also from Africa World Press and The Red Sea Press, we would like to thank Damola Ifaturoti, Senior Editor and Editorial Coordinator, and K. Chase, Copyeditor, for their hard work and dedication. We also benefited from the anonymous readers for giving us detailed reviews and their support in guiding this manuscript to its completion. We owe a special debt of gratitude to Dr. Tesfay Teklu and Iyasu Gorfu, who read through the whole text at an early stage and made constructive criticisms and invaluable comments and suggestions.

Grateful acknowledgement is made to the authors and publications listed below for kind permission to quote passages from the following works:

Samir Amin, "Underdevelopment and Dependence in Back Africa: Origins and Contemporary Forms," in *Journal of Modern African Studies*, No. 4, 1972, pp. 503—521.

V. DeLancey, "Understanding the Economies of Africa," in *Understanding Contemporary Africa*, 2nd ed., Editor, A. A. Gordon and D. L. Gordon, Boulder, CO: Lynne Rienner, 1996, p. 91 and p. 127.

Jacques Diouf, "The Challenge of Agricultural Development in Africa," in *World Bank Online*, Washington, D.C., November 2, 1989.

Carl Eicher, "Institutions and the African Farmer, Issues in Agriculture 14," in *World Bank Online*, Consulting Group on International Agricultural Research (CGIAR), Washington, D.C., September 1999.

D. L. Gordon, "African Politics," in *Understanding Contemporary Africa*, 2nd ed., Editor, A. A. Gordon and D. L. Gordon, Boulder, CO: Lynne Rienner, 1996, p. 55 and p. 151.

Tetteh Kofi, "Development and Stagnation in Ghana: An 'Abibirim' Approach," in *Universitas: An Inter-Faculty Journal*, University of Ghana, pp. 12—36, 1974—1975.

Tetteh Kofi, "Structural Adjustment in Africa: A Performance Review of World Bank Policies Under Uncertainty in Commodity Price Trends," in *World Institute for Development Economics Research (UNN-WIDER)*, Helsinki, 1994.

Walter Rodney, *How Europe Underdeveloped Africa*, Washington, D.C., Howard University Press, 1974, p. 36 and p. 76.

INTRODUCTION

There is a specter haunting the world. Global capitalism, under World Trade Organization (WTO) rules and the economic power of the Atlantic world, is attempting to revolutionize the Third World economic structures and institutions to deeper depths than the Industrial Revolution had manifested. African economies were ill prepared to face the "free trade imperialism" of the 1850s, and even more unprepared *now* to survive in the new global economic order. For instance, though Africa is the home of mankind, the cradle of civilization, and one of the richest continents in terms of natural resources, it is a paradox to note that Africa is the least developed continent. In aggregate terms, sub-Saharan Africa enters the twenty-first century with half of its population (or about 340 million people) living on less than US$1 per day. The mortality rate of children under five years of age is 140 per 1,000. Life expectancy at birth is only

54 years. Only 58 percent of the population has access to safe water. The rate of illiteracy for people over 15 years of age is greater than 40 percent. There are only 18 mainline telephones per 1,000 people in Africa, compared with 146 for the world as a whole and 567 for high-income countries.[1]

It is a tragedy that a continent with immense natural resources should, in the twenty-first century, become the home of human suffering. On the global stage, the economic conditions of Africa have deteriorated. For example, it stands in danger of being excluded from up-to-date information technology. Its share of exports in traditional primary products has been declining and Africa faces adverse terms of trade. In the 1990s, Africa's share of world trade was less than 1 percent. It has hardly diversified into new lines of business. It is faced with a massive flight of capital and loss of skills to other regions. About 70 percent of Africa's private wealth is being invested outside the continent.[2] Africa is in danger of losing its soul. The entire human civilization is at stake.

Various explanations have been rendered for Africa's underdevelopment. The New Partnership for Africa's Development and the World Bank generally assume the problem is a malaise endemic to Africa. Therefore, they suggest Africa would have developed if it strictly adhered to the footpaths of the Anglo-Saxon and neoliberal Washington Consensus model. Contrary to Africa's social values, these ethnocentric models place heavy emphasis on free markets, deregulation, privatization, and the limited role the state has to play in the development process.[3]

Following the methods of historical materialism, others attribute Africa's poverty and underdevelopment to its economic dependence on capitalist, industrialized countries. To prove their point, they show how Africa's previous economic models are not rooted in the African system of thought. In addition, they demonstrate why the Western models have failed to transform the African economies on a path of sustained growth and empower the African people to fully participate in the design and management of long-lasting development paradigms in harmony with the objective conditions of Africa. They expose how the various economic models, which Africa has followed for the last 50 years, have not been people-centered and were transplanted by apostles of external agencies. Finally, they persuasively argue that the externally generated economic solutions imposed on Africa have created more economic problems than they have solved.[4]

Given these diametrically opposed viewpoints, the central questions studied in this book include:

1. Have the economic models been compatible with the needs of the continent, given that colonial rulers imposed them on Africa?

2. Was the transition from colonial state to independent nation-state carried out optimally to assure viable economic growth?

3. If the various economic paradigms that Africa has pursued in the past have been compatible with its needs, then why is the African continent still facing serious economic stagnation, devastation of public health, and continuing ecological crises?

4. What other sustainable strategies can be proposed to repair the damage and help Africa's economy catch up and rejuvenate?

To answer some of these questions and draw up an alternative development strategy to enhance development and growth in Africa, we will have to examine the colonial and postcolonial experience—in order to identify problems that hindered growth and development, and will evaluate the empirical evidence to find out what went wrong and examine what it would take to jump-start the African economies.

Chapter 1 analyzes Africa's economic condition before its contact with a number of European countries. It also maps out how Africa provided increasing amounts of gold to help the European economy to expand. Furthermore, it shows how Africa became economically dependent and retrogressed during the colonial and postcolonial periods.

Chapter 2 describes why, during the First Development Decade, the then politically independent African states mechanically followed the Anglo-Saxon paradigm and implemented W. Arthur Lewis' "two-sector economic growth model" (unlimited surplus-labor).[5] Lewis' model assumed that industrialization would act as the engine of growth and would provide the means to develop infrastructure and restructure the agricultural sector of Africa. Following the footsteps of Lewis' model, Kwame Nkrumah's Ghana (the first country in Africa to gain independence), persuasively argued Africa's economic transformation and the termination of its economic dependence was possible if the surplus labor available at subsistence wages in the rural areas was transformed to work in the urban industries. This was the key to achieve an industrialized pan-African unity, similar to the United States. When implemented, however, Lewis' two-sector economic model, which was based on the concept of "industrialization by invitation," failed miserably because it was incompatible with Africa's economic structure, social values, and institutions. To demonstrate the economic effect of Lewis' model, we present an empirical study of pre-1970s Ghana.

Chapter 3 analyzes the Second Development Decade of the 1970s as well as the import substitution model, which a number of African countries experimented with when "industrialization by invitation" failed during the First Development Decade. In the 1970s, import substitution (or inward-looking development policy) was tried in Africa to reduce economic dependence by producing previously imported goods. Though import substitution raised the learning curve of a number of

African countries that went through it, the overall analysis is that it neither produced forward and backward linkages, nor did it improve the economies of Africa. African countries were disenchanted with the trickle-down theory of economic growth of the 1960s and the inward-looking model of the 1970s, so they experimented with the basic needs development model. However, a number of African countries failed to implement the basic needs model because of external shocks such as the oil crises of 1973–1974 and 1979, and the ensuing global economic slowdown of the 1980s.

Given the natural disasters, famine, ethnic conflicts, and the economic recession of the early 1980s, African countries stepped up the need for the reassessment of their development strategies. During the Third Development Decade, African countries initiated the Monrovia Declaration of 1979, followed by the Lagos Plan of Action (LPA) of April 1980. The LPA endorsed self-sufficiency and the democratization of Africa's development process, and pressed for subregional economic integration. However, instead of endorsing the LPA, the World Bank in 1981 commissioned Professor Elliot Berg to prepare another plan for Africa, which was entitled "Accelerated Development in Sub-Saharan Africa: An Agenda for Action" also called the Washington Consensus Model. The Berg Report argued that pricing policies, overvalued exchange rates, and excessive state intervention in the economy were Africa's cardinal problems. To have access to financial credit from the International Monetary Fund and the World Bank, the African countries agreed to focus on market-oriented reforms, export promotion, privatization, and direct foreign investments. Chapter 4 highlights the lessons learned from the Washington Consensus Model using economic development status in Mauritius.

Chapter 5 presents some of the environmentally sustainable economic development programs launched in Africa during the Fourth Development Decade. Given the internalization of environmental issues in the development process and the adoption of sustainable development as the agenda for the twenty-first century, the results of sustainable economic development in Africa are analyzed by comparing Mauritius and Costa Rica.

Chapter 6 critically assesses the limitations of both the NEPAD model, initiated by African heads of states, and the World Bank's model, initiated under the title: *Can Africa Claim the 21ˢᵗ Century?*

The last four chapters discuss how to catch up, repair the damage to, and transform Africa's economy in the twenty-first century, while protecting the poor. Chapter 7 proposes an environmentally sustainable agricultural development policy for Africa using a Ghanaian, people-centered development case study. Then Chapter 8 outlines an environmentally sustainable educational program. Chapter 9 suggests some environmentally sustainable cooperative small-business investment models that could transform Africa's economy in this century. Finally, we come to Chapter 10, which: (1) presents a brief summary of African history and addresses a critical analysis of some of the most significant development paradigms it undertook in the past 50 years, and (2) suggests an outline of pragmatic strategic imperatives, in which the people-centered approach is integrated with agricultural, educational, and cooperative small-business investments. These imperatives can rescue the African continent from some of the malaise of conspicuous development it is currently facing.

Chapter 1

AN ECONOMIC HISTORY OF AFRICA
An Overview

[P]olitical economy has to be studied within a wider framework of culture; and this becomes of special importance when culture are as different as those of African and European peoples. Agronomists from the North have had to learn that agricultural techniques appropriate to Northern soils and climates are not necessarily at all appropriate in Africa, and that African resistance to changing traditional techniques is often soundly based…Economists and political scientists have [to] adopt a similar humility before criticizing African approaches to political economy and proposing their own solutions to problems as if these were of universal application. This is all the more necessary because educated Africans have themselves been brainwashed by European education into devaluing their peoples' culture.

— Michael Barratt Brown[1]

> To see Africa in its historical context is to grasp the complexity of
> the continent and to appreciate the ingenuity and dynamism of
> its people as they responded to the challenges posed by history.
> —Thomas O'Toole, "The Historical Context"[2]

The first part of this chapter will briefly review the historical background of Africa, to discount the myths of a "dark continent" without history until the coming of the Europeans. Then, we will chronicle past economic systems to help facilitate an understanding of the various economic models presented in the subsequent chapters.

THE PRE-EUROPEAN ECONOMIC HISTORY OF AFRICA

It has been affirmed by archaeological, anthropological, and genetic studies that Africa is the ancestral homeland of humanity from whose roots the rest of the people of the world sprang forth. Our oldest known direct descendants (*Homo sapiens*) originated in Africa about 400,000 years ago and then migrated to the other parts of the globe. As discussed by Albert Churchward

> Human ancestors appeared first ...on the African continent, then
> from the region of the Great Lakes (around Kenya, Tanzania,
> and Uganda) they spread over the entire continent. Bands of
> these early human beings wandered along the Nile valley to
> present-day Egypt, and later, dispersed themselves to all parts
> of the world.[3]

Africa is not only the origin of humanity, but it is the cradle of civilization—from which some of the most essential elements of human society and human growth were derived. Egyptian civilization, built by black Africans, is an extension of the more ancient Ethiopian (Kush) civilization.[4]

African achievements "[stand] as contributions to man's heritage of beautiful creation. The art of Egypt, the Sudan, and Ethiopia, was known to the rest of the world at an early date."[5] For example, the archaeological evidence from East Africa clearly demonstrates that upright-walking ancestors existed in Africa more than 4 million years ago. By approximately 2.5 million years ago—that is, by the Stone Age period—African ancestors were involved in making stone tools in order to satisfy their daily conditions.[6] For example, the earliest archaeological sites with stone artifacts are found in Ethiopia and Kenya.

The history of Africa passed from one generation to the next through artifacts and narrative oral history. Elders would pass the oral history to the young generation through memorization and recitation. An example is the *griots* of West Africa, who would recite to the accompaniment of stringed instruments. In parts of Africa where writing systems existed, traditions were transformed from generation to generation through written records. For instance, the history of the Egyptian civilization was chronicled using systems of hieroglyphics dating back to 3000 B.C. From these sources we have a detailed and vivid picture of this extraordinary place for over three millennia. Further south, in and around the ancient city of Meroe, the Kushitic civilization had its own form of writing in place at least five centuries before the birth of Christ. And in Ethiopia, Ge'ez—the classical language of ancient Axum—had become a written language by the fourth century A.D.[7]

Creativity, adaptation, change, and continuity distinguish the African history, from the earliest times.[8] During the later Stone Age, hunting and gathering subsistence was combined with the reliance on stone technology. In K. D. Schick's words, "Other distinct trends in the later Stone Age include the widespread appearance of well-made bone tools, and also body ornaments such as pendants and beads of shells, bone, and ostrich eggshells."[9] Thus, "making and using stone tools is one of the hall-marks of the emergence of humanity in Africa, and this technology has served various needs for strong, sharp, and durable tools for most of African history."[10]

In most areas of Africa, the later Stone Age industries were replaced by new technologies. For instance, "[s]everal parts of Africa passed through this ...sequence of technological development, but many areas moved from the middle Stone Age into a latter Stone Age, when highly sophisticated stone tools were manufactured, then directly into the Iron Age, usually entering this latter stage between about 500 B.C. and A.D. 500."[11]

The history of the many societies and cultures formed in Africa begins, to a large extent, with the discovery of agriculture and its spread to various parts of the continent. As enumerated in E. J. Murphy

> There were only four regions of Africa where the conditions of fertile soil, adequate rainfall or water supplies, and potentially domesticable [sic] wild grains or tubers encouraged the development of agriculture by early man: the middle and lower Nile valley; the highland plateau of northern Ethiopia; the grasslands of the far western Sudan; ...and the highland plateaus in the central Sahara.[12]

Before the fifteenth century, Africa passed from reliance on stone technology to the domestication of plants and animals, farming, and food production to the use of copper, bronze, and iron tools. As stated by Kathy Schick

> Over the ensuing centuries ...the archaeological record shows larger, more permanent villages and more complex farming. Concentration of wealth and power and other social complexities are sometimes suggested by evidence, such as large homesteads with large cattle herds, the appearance of crafts (sometimes including clay cattle figurines), or accumulation of trade goods such as gold, glass beads, ivory.[13]

Based on claims of descent from a paternal or maternal common ancestor, every African was entitled to have access to the means of production. The predominant factors of production (land and labor) in Africa were founded on communalism where reciprocity, kinship bonds, equal access to land, and equality in distribution reigned. Before the fifteenth century, the family in communal Africa, therefore, had full control over land, labor, and the distribution of goods and services. According to Walter Rodney

> In Africa, before the fifteenth century, the predominant principle of social relations was that of family and kinship associated with communalism. Every member of an African society had his position defined in terms of relatives on his mother's side and on his father's side. Some societies placed greater importance on matrilineal ties and others on patrilineal ties.[14]

Similarly, as discussed by J. C. McCall, "In most African communities in which descent plays an important role, either the paternal or the maternal descent group is predominantly responsible for the land tenure."[15] In communally owned land, every person, based on an age-grades system, is assigned to plow and farm for the entire tribal group or ethnic stock. Walter Rodney comments that

> [a] single family or household would till its own plots and it would also be available to share certain joint farming activities with other members of the extended family or clan. Annual hunts and river fishing were also organized by a whole extended family or village community. ...Having been produced on land that was family property and through family labor, the resultant crops and other goods were distributed on the basis of kinship ties. If a man's crops were destroyed by some sudden calamity, relatives in his own village helped him. If the whole community was in distress, people moved to live with their kinsmen in another area where food was not scarce.[16]

In the centuries before the contact with Europeans, large portions of African societies operated by primordial bonds of kinship and affinity. The dominant activities in Africa were hunting, gathering, fishing, and agriculture. Everybody had access to land, and ownership was in the hands of various kinds of collectivities.

> In all the settled agricultural communities, people observed the peculiarities of their own environment and tried to find techniques for dealing with it in a rational manner. Advanced methods were used in some area, such as terracing, crop rotation,

green manuring, mixed farming, and regulated swamp farming.[17]

The communal villages farmed, hunted, fished, and looked after themselves. To fulfill some of their needs, they got involved in bartering. They exchanged food crops, livestock, and household and farming equipment with their neighbors. In later years, however, salt, cloth, iron, hoes, and cowry shells were also used as a form of money to buy different products.

Until the fifteenth century, Africa had minimal contact with Europe. But around 1415, the story of African and European interaction began when Henry the Navigator, a Portuguese prince, began sponsoring voyages in which he established direct trade (especially in gold) with West Africa.[18] With the internationalization of trade in the fifteenth century, Europeans took the initiative and went to other parts of the world. Walter Rodney comments:

> Europeans used the superiority of their ships and cannon[s] to gain control of all the world's waterways, starting with the western Mediterranean and the Atlantic coast of North Africa. From 1415, when the Portuguese captured Ceuta, near Gibraltar, they maintained the offensive against the Maghreb. Within the next sixty years, they seized ports such as Arzila, El-Ksar-es-Seghir, and Tangier, and fortified them. By the second half of the fifteenth century, the Portuguese controlled the Atlantic coast of [Morocco] and used its economic and strategic advantages to prepare for further navigations which eventually carried their ships round the Cape of Good Hope in 1495. After reaching the Indian Ocean, the Portuguese sought with some success to replace Arabs as the merchants who tied East Africa to India and the rest of Asia. ...Therefore by control of the seas, Europe took the first steps towards transforming the several parts of Africa and Asia into economic satellites.[19]

Stated differently, Africa's contact with Europe from 1400 to 1600 was almost entirely through Portugal, and the Portuguese confined themselves to trading along the coast. Nonetheless, before 1600 Europeans accepted Africa as different but equal. By the late sixteenth century, however, Spain, Holland, France, and England sent ships to Africa, the New World, and the Far East in search of trade and territories that had been denied them by the primacy of Portugal.[20]

By the mid-1500s, the Dutch, English, French, and other European maritime powers started replacing the Portuguese in Africa. During this period, ivory, timber, wax, and gold were the stable exports of Africa. However, in the first half of the seventeenth century, the Portuguese, Dutch, Spanish, French, and English started exchanging slaves from Africa to mine gold in Central and South America. Part of the gold from the Americas was then used to buy spices and silks from the Far East. However, the demand for slaves from Africa predominantly arose with development of European-owned sugar plantations. By the middle of the seventeenth century, the transatlantic slave trade was in full swing and manpower as a commodity began to drive out all other commodities in the African trade. More important than African commodities, the Europeans became interested in trading slaves from Africa. It has been estimated that between 1450 and 1889

> roughly twelve million Africans, torn from homes and families from Senegal to Angola reached [America] as slaves, countless others, perhaps millions, died either during the course of enslavement in Africa or en route to the America. Most slaves were taken to the plantation and mining regions of the Caribbean and South America.[21]

The opening of sugar plantations (and later tobacco, coffee, and cotton) in South America and the Caribbean required large amounts of labor. Plantation owners could not meet the demand with native American workers because of their high mortality rates when exposed to European disease and their prolonged resistance to incorporation into the colonial workforce. European workers also had high mortality rates due to tropical disease, and their numbers were not sufficient to meet the demand for plantation labor. Africans, on the other hand, had some immunity to tropical diseases, and they also had some resistance to European disease as a result of ancient contacts across the Saharan Desert and Indian Ocean. Over time a business partnership developed between European traders and African middlemen who delivered slaves captured in the interior. On the Atlantic side the severest drain in population came in the eighteenth century, when Africa lost perhaps 10 million people, and in the nineteenth century, when as many as 4 million died or were transported overseas.[22]

It needs to be noted that African societies had practiced a form of slavery before their contact with Europe, but this form of owning slaves was substantially different than the chattel slavery that was carried over the Atlantic Ocean. Most of the African "slaves" were more properly serfs or vassals. They were conquered people who lived within a kingdom or empire and who were regarded as different from and on a slightly lower level than the people of the conquering group. These serfs were required to perform labor in the fields as well as in various crafts. Serfs were generally not sold and were protected by custom from capricious treatment by the ruler. Gradually, the slaves melded into the capturing society, and were frequently used as soldiers, palace guards, personal servants, and artisans for the king. They often rose to positions of great prominence and power.[23]

The slave trade helped the European economies to develop at a faster rate. On the other hand, the slave trade practiced by the Europeans not only depopulated Africa, but also had a disastrous and profound impact on the continent. Africa lost its status with Europe as different but equal. As discussed by Virginia DeLancey:

> The most immediate economic impact of the slave trade was the loss of an enormous source of productive human labor and the resultant redistribution of the population of the continent. The civil disruption associated with slaving also had economic effects. Many of those who were not captured died during the

raids or went into hiding to escape being caught. Agricultural production must have decreased in part because of the difficulty of farming during the raids. In addition, the strongest young men and women were forced to leave their farms, or disappeared on their own initiative until danger subsided. Health was affected as a result of new diseases such as cholera and smallpox, which were introduced by the movement of peoples through the continent. Susceptibility to disease also increased, resulting from the poor diets and reduced food consumption that occurred with the disruption of agriculture. This surely lowered productivity for physical reasons as well as for psychological reasons.[24]

In the eighteenth century, England became the workshop of the world. In 1804, Haitian slaves established the first African-ruled nation in America. Indeed, the mushrooming of the Industrial Revolution in Europe and the slave revolt created an atmosphere where the commercial slave trade was replaced by systematic exploitation and control of Africa's raw materials. These commodities were in heavy demand by European firms in the metropolis.

The slave trade eventually came to an end because the Industrial Revolution made way for a new economic role for Africa:

> Growing manufacturing interests desired larger African markets as well as cheap and plentiful African raw materials such as palm and peanut oils, rubber, beeswax, ivory, gum, and coffee. But the violence of the slave trade hindered both trade and production of non-slave products. Thus, increasingly powerful industries began to demand an end to the slave trade.[25]

The decline of the slave trade gave way to an increase in commodity trade between Africa and Europe:

> In the nineteenth-century substitution of commodity trade for slave trade, it is noteworthy that European-African relations continued to be based primarily on commerce. Tropical Africa still exported its low-priced raw materials in return for higher-priced European manufactured goods. In fact, the new trade patters, European exploration, missions, technological advances, and

other outside factors are evidence of intensification of European influence on and exploitation of the continent, and a prelude to colonialism.[26]

Thus, the European governments integrated the African states into the emerging new international capitalist system.

African territories supplied inexpensively produced agricultural commodities such as palm oil, rubber, and cotton, and such minerals and metals as copper and gold to the industries of Europe. Manufactured textiles, household goods, farm implements sold to Africans at high profit completed the integrated economic system.[27]

Before the modern world system, Africa had provided increasing amounts of gold, which helped the European economy expand, and later provided a workforce to further develop the European economy. While Europe expanded and developed, Africa retrogressed.

Fueled by their political rivalry, territorial ambition, and the economic expedience of greed the Europeans powers abolished the slave trade as illegitimate and instituted free-trade imperialism. Instead, they formally sanctioned, at the Berlin Conference of 1884—1885, to partition the African continent into colonial spheres of control by the Western powers. The whole process became known as "the Scramble for Africa." To completely amalgamate Africa into the international capitalist economic system, the European powers partitioned the African continent into their sphere of economic and political influence.

[I]nternational trade was generally oriented toward the metropole. ...[N]ationals of the metropolitan power controlled the most important sectors of the colonial export economy. ...[C]olonial development policies reflected the interest of the metropolitan banks, import-export houses, shipping firms engaged in colonial trade, mining companies which exploited the mineral resources of the colonies, and the white settler population. The colonial system provided the metropole with outlets for its manufactured goods, raw materials for its industries, and tropi-

cal products for metropolitan consumers on terms that were
advantageous to the colonizers.[28]

THE COLONIAL ERA

"The Scramble for Africa" was, to a large extent, tailored by
the European colonialists to fulfill their economic resource
needs and political ambitions. As the leading military-indus-
trial complex in Europe, Britain obtained the most valuable
colonial possessions in Africa. France was given a large number of colonies on the continent. To compensate for the provinces of Alsace and Lorraine, lost to Germany during the
Franco-Prussian War of 1870—1871, Germany was allowed
to establish colonies in German East Africa, Southwest Africa, Togo, and Cameroon. Belgium established the Congo Free
State. Portugal was given territories in Angola, Mozambique,
and Portuguese Guinea. Italy gained colonies in Libya and
Somalia. Spain acquired holdings in the Spanish Sahara and in
Equatorial Africa.

As narrated by S. Amin:

> the European powers were highly motivated to gain a foothold
> on the economic base of the African continent and link it to the
> metropolitan economy. This was the underlying motivation for
> the Scramble for Africa in 1884—1885. For example, the coastal
> territories of French and British West Africa were designed to
> satisfy the needs of European industry by producing cash crops
> such as palm oil, rubber, cotton, cocoa, and peanuts. The labor-
> ers from Malawi, Mozambique, and Upper Volta (Burkina Faso)
> were used as reservoirs of labor migrants to mines of the Bel-
> gian Congo (Zaire), Northern Rhodesia (Zambia), South Africa,
> and the white settlers plantations of sections of Kenya,
> Tanganyika (Tanzania), and South Rhodesia (Zimbabwe). The
> French colonies of Gabon, Congo, the Central African Republic,
> and the Belgian Congo (Zaire) were bestowed to concession-
> owning companies.[29]

Though there was little or no structural change in agricultural production methods for Africans

colonial rule meant the expropriation of traditional communal lands, the transformation of many Africans into an uprooted and poorly paid urban and rural proletariat, and a labor system which kept Africans at the bottom of the economic scale and prevented them from effectively competing with European farmers.[30]

The European colonizers foreclosed the possibility of organized resistance, and in collaboration with their commercial and industrial compatriots, formulated colonial policies in London, Paris, Brussels, and Lisbon to shatter and handicap Africa's economic development in the future.[31] As stated by DeLancey:

> Colonialism did not originate to assist African countries to develop economically. It originated to benefit European countries. That is not to say that African countries did not receive any benefits, but the growth or development that occurred in those countries was mainly peripheral to the growth and development of Europe.[32]

For example, in the British (Anglophone) model of "indirect rule," the African traditional tribal authorities were allowed to remain in place though they were subservient to the central British rule. In areas where there were substantial British settlers, a dual rule was developed separately to administer the British and Africans. The British colonial policy was "designed to provide a stable framework for commerce, industry, and some settlement. There was no attempt to transform all aspects of African life. Colonies were expected to pay for their administration, and education was largely entrusted to church groups and philanthropic organizations."[33]

The French (Francophone) colonial policy was direct rule. The elite Africans were forced to assimilate and accept French rules and standards. The colonies were the source of resource materials and manpower for the metropolis. The Belgians, on the other hand, ruled through private companies, which were responsible for areas of administration. Like the French, the Belgians under direct rule introduced primary education. However, the pedagogical and ideological content of the curriculum was to instill a sense of deference, serve the interest of the Belgian colonialists, and to produce semiskilled Africans to work in the mines and agricultural plantations.[34]

The Portuguese were the first to come to Africa. However, their colonial administration was haphazard and very sporadic.

> A tiny fraction of the Africans became assimilated into the *neoindigena* class (*asimilados* and Europeans), but generally speaking, scant opportunity for education, and high incidence of forced labor, and strict enforcement of the *caderneta,* a passbook system as well as generally harsh treatment, insured that few Africans ever crossed the cultural barrier.[35]

Italy was the last European power to acquire colonies in the 1880s. From 1936 to 1941 Italy occupied Ethiopia, but Italy formally colonized Eritrea, Libya, and Somalia. In exchange for the development of a physical infrastructure, the Italian colonial rulers provided raw materials and living space for the Italian immigrants. But Italy's colonial economic sphere was mainly characterized by monopolies and parasitical organizations. Most important, Italy attempted to indoctrinate the future pan-Somali leader to pursue "Greater Somalia" and integrate the heartland of Somalia with Somalis living in Ethiopia and Kenya.[36]

German colonial rule encompassed Togo, Cameroon, Southwest Africa (now Namibia), Rwanda-Burundi, and Tanganyika (now Tanzania). From 1884 until the German elections of 1906, German colonial rule in Africa was militaristic and repressive in character. "With the defeat of Germany during World War I, the German colonial areas were divided among Britain, France, Belgium and South Africa."[37]

With colonization, African communal living was dismantled. The communal lands were expropriated. The colonialists instituted private landownership and the fertile lands were mainly accorded to white settlers. Leaving the wife and family behind, rural men were dragged to work in low-paying jobs either in the mining and agricultural concessions or in the urban areas. Nonetheless, World War II heightened African aspirations for self-government and weakened the ability of the major colonial powers to maintain their overseas empires, setting the stage for the period of political decolonization that followed.[38]

In the Fifth Pan-African Congress of 1945 in Manchester, England, chaired by W.E.B. Du Bois, Africans from the continent and diaspora demanded full independence for Africa. Although well-laid plans for decolonization had not yet been mapped out by any of the colonial powers,

> immediately after the war, programs were set in motion which accelerated the rate at which the colonizers moved toward self-government. France was confronted with increasing pressures for independence in its colonies in Indochina and North Africa; Britain was being similarly challenged in the Middle East and on the Indian subcontinent. Belgium was racked by internal political turmoil involving liberals and conservatives, clerks, and anti clerics; the status of the Belgian Congo was the central issue in these disputes. Throughout Europe, the mood in the immediate postwar period with regard to the colonial experiment was one of reflection and doubt.[39]

In the 1960s and 1970s, a number of African countries achieved political independence from colonial rule. Though politically independent, these African countries were heavily locked up in a dependent economic system. As discussed by Kofi, "African economies gained independence from colonial rule in the 1960s without modern agricultural production methods and without an industrial sector to speak of."[40] To achieve what had been heralded as Africa's development decade, the independent African states fully followed Lewis' economic model sponsored by the United Nations to achieve their economic growth development plan.

The model of industrialization by invitation failed to work in Africa as planned during the so-called First Development

Decade. Therefore, a number of African countries switched from their peripheral position in the global economy to using inward-looking industrialization strategies, eventually attempting to apply the basic needs and participatory growth development model. Further complications appeared during the 1970s and 1980s, when many African economies weakened due to oil shocks, political turmoil, and drought, and began to suffer declining standards of living. For example:

> The rate of growth of gross domestic product (GDP) in sub-Saharan Africa fell from 4.2 percent per annum in the period 1965–1980, to only 2.1 percent in the years 1980–1990, while agricultural production, long the mainstay of African economic output and the source of livelihood for the majority of the population, hovered around 2 percent per annum. Over the same period, average population growth rose from 2.7 percent in 1965–1980, to 3.1 percent per annum from 1980 to 1990.[41]

In 1981, Africa's development policy veered to the right and African governments were required to put in place structural adjustment programs designed by the International Monetary Fund (IMF) and the World Bank.

> African governments were urged to reduce or eliminate controls on foreign trade and payments, devalue their currencies, dismantle domestic price controls, decrease government spending and employment, and divest themselves of productive assets and enterprises. The IMF and the World Bank added pressure to persuasion, making both short-term balance-of-payments credits and long-term development loans "conditional" on governments' adoption of these "structural adjustment policies."[42]

After following the prescribed stabilization and structural adjustment programs, many African countries experienced little or no growth. Thus, the poor performance of the Washington Consensus Growth model in explaining the sources of long-term economic growth gave way to the Environmentally Sustainable Economic Development model of the 1990s. The purpose of the latter model is to achieve sustainable activity that meets the needs of the current generation (intragenerational equity) without depleting the future supply of resources from future generations (intergenerational equity). Since the Rio Earth Summit in 1992, various African countries have undertaken numerous environmental plans (such as National Environmental Action Plans), and the African Development Bank has conducted a number of studies. Nonetheless, because of lack of adequate financial resources and major economic distresses exacerbated by structural adjustment programs, so far environmental needs have not been systematically incorporated into Africa's economic development paradigms. A decade after the Rio Earth Summit, the situation still appeared bleak in many areas.

The various economic models, which a number of African countries have implemented within the past few decades, have condemned these states to marginality instead of fostering the externally envisaged economic growth. To reverse five decades of economic decline, a number of African leaders have recently designed a plan to eradicate poverty and help the continent to participate actively in the emerging global order of the twenty-first century. Though instructive, NEPAD does not present an economic model for Africa's development. Rather, it presents a strategy to obtain funds or loans from industrialized countries (G8) in the name of Africa. Therefore, chapters 2 through 6 present a critical review of the "failed" models of development. Chapters 7, 8, 9, and 10 put forward environmentally sustainable agricultural, educational, and foreign investment models that could reconcile indigenous and endogenous strategies for helping Africa to reclaim its own development in this new century.

CHAPTER 2

THE TWO-SECTOR ECONOMIC GROWTH MODEL

The various economic models, which a number of African countries have implemented within the last five decades, have condemned these states to marginality instead of fostering the externally envisaged economic growth. To reverse five decades of economic decline, a number of African leaders have recently implemented a plan to transform the Organization of African Unity into the African Union and thereby have formed the New Partnership for Africa's Development.[1] NEPAD (created at the October 23, 2001, meeting of the Head of State Implementation Committee in Abuja, Nigeria) is a merger of the Millennium Partnership for Africa's Recovery Program and the Omega Plan for

Africa, which used to be called the New African Initiative. Briefly stated, NEPAD was designed to eradicate poverty and help the continent to participate actively in the emerging global order of the twenty-first century.

In order to rationalize the call for NEPAD as a means of ensuring Africa's sustainable economic development, it is worth reviewing the prevailing economic models, which a number of African countries (consciously or not) have tried since the establishment of the Bretton Woods Institutions (the World Bank, the International Monetary Fund) and the United Nations. In this chapter, we discuss the dominant paradigm of Africa's development strategies in the 1950s—the Arthur Lewis two-sector growth model.

THE GENESIS AND ANALYSIS OF LEWIS' TWO-SECTOR MODEL OF DEVELOPMENT

Economic development as an academic discipline is of recent origin, having evolved at the close of World War II. Before then, it was believed that the developing countries would follow the footsteps of the developed countries. For example, when developing issues first surfaced in the international debates in the 1950s, the then politically independent nations of Africa attempted to mechanically transform the Anglo-Saxon development models. Based on the application of Keynesian demand management, the reconstruction following World War II led to the establishment of the Marshall Plan in Europe, and the industrialization of the Soviet Union based on five-year plans.

For the Third World countries, Professor (now Sir) Arthur Lewis was approached to develop a strategy to industrialize the Caribbean countries, and the Third World countries in general. Thus, African countries heavily relied on Lewis' two-sector economic growth model (surplus-labor) to structure their economies. Furthermore, "there were the African leaders' keen sense of the waste of the peoples' human potential under colonialism and the ambition to catch up with the industrial countries, by taking advantage of their technology and of the aid that was expected to flow from them in growing amounts."[2]

Since Lewis' economic growth model was heavily endorsed by the United Nations (the First Development Decade of the 1960s and 1970s) and various funding agencies, it was accepted as the general theory of development for Third World nations, when the tide of independence was surging. Thus, the politically independent African countries wholeheartedly attempted to industrialize by instituting massive capital formation (industrialization, urbanization, technological transformation of the agriculture sector). Ghana's President Nkrumah, for example, persuasively argued that the key to Africa's economic transformation and the termination of its economic dependence was through industrialization, and he employed Lewis as his advisor in Ghana's structural endeavors. Stated in his own words:

> Every time we import goods that we could manufacture if all the conditions were available, we are continuing our economic dependence and delaying our industrial growth. It is just these conditions that we are planning to provide …to build up our knowledge, techniques and skills, to make us more self-confident and self-sufficient, to push toward our economic independence.[3]

Thus, Sir Arthur, as an economic adviser to the Nkrumah regime, had a profound effect on the economic development strategy of that regime. His influence on subsequent regimes was equally strong. It is intended here to reconstruct the evolution of the economic development philosophy in order to evaluate its limitations.

It is hypothesized that Sir Arthur's philosophy was molded and influenced by the cultural experience of his native country, the British West Indies, and by the post-World War II Puerto Rican development strategy. These two facts underlie the basis for his two articles entitled "Industrial Development in Puerto Rico"[4] and "The Industrialization of the British West Indies."[5] The two articles and the *Report on Industrialization and the Gold Coast*[6] perhaps formed the empirical basis of his much-celebrated theoretical paper on dualism, "Economic Development with Unlimited Supplies of Labor."[7]

An analysis of the development strategy that Sir Arthur recommended for the Gold Coast should therefore be prefaced with: (1) an understanding of the society (Puerto Rico) which he investigated empirically and which influenced his basic philosophy of economic development, and (2) the history and operations of the Caribbean Commission which represented the policies and interest of the imperial powers in the Caribbean area.

PUERTO RICO: THE LIMITATIONS OF THE SPECIAL CASE

Puerto Rico became a United States colony in 1898 when the island was occupied by U.S. troops and Spanish rule was brought to an end. For a year and a half the U.S. Army governed the island. A rush of U.S. capital, the most important being that of sugar investors, followed this occupation. The United States instituted a civil government under the Foraker Act, which ruled Puerto Rico form 1900 to 1917. In March 1917 President Woodrow Wilson signed the Jones Act, which provided the Puerto Ricans a greater degree of local autonomy. They became citizens of the United States and were given a Bill of Rights, although the U.S. Constitution still did not apply fully to the island.[8] Thus, since the turn of the twentieth century, Puerto Rico has had a special association with the United States. In 1952, Puerto Rico became a "free associated state" within the United States of America. Under the above conditions, capital flowed from the United States to the island.

In 1942, the Industrial Development Agency was set up on the island to push industrialization. The first development plans visualized government ownership and operation of manufacturing enterprises, and several enterprises were established. Perhaps this was in response to the general civil unrest in the Caribbean just preceding World War II. After the war, it became evident that the government, through the Industrial Development Agency, did not have enough capital to build all the factories to absorb the unemployed. The industries were sold to private operators (as Ghana was to do in 1966) and a massive effort was mounted to attract the kinds of industry that Puerto Rico wanted—by a combination of temporary exemption from taxation and research and advisory services provided to potential investors. The new policy was crystallized in a "tax holiday" law of 1947 and the creation of the Economic Development Administration in 1950. The policy met with amazing success. Thus the private investors who were invited or attracted to the island actually came with the capital.[9] This strategy of development is known as industrialization by invitation (IBI).[10] Note that the seeming success of this strategy is due, in large part, to the associated status of Puerto Rico to the U.S. mainland. Puerto Rico, with a per capita gross national product that stood at $1,340 in 1968, was the seventeenth richest country in the world, according to World Bank figures for that year. However, this index for measuring relative development may be disputed because it says nothing about income distribution.

THE CARIBBEAN COMMISSION

The other set of historical facts we need to know about the Caribbean before we can understand Sir Arthur's development strategy concerns the operations of the Caribbean Commission. R. D. Crassweller[11] claims that formal association of casual groupings were familiar in the Caribbean in the early nineteenth century.

> But a certain type of organization, new in its direct (although at times hesitant) approach to economic affairs, came into existence during World War II, in the aftermath of the agreement to trade American destroyers to England for naval bases in the Caribbean. The first of the new-style bodies was the *Anglo-American Caribbean Commission* established in 1942 to encourage social and economic cooperation between the United Kingdom, the British colonies in the Caribbean, and the U.S. and its possessions and bases. ...The *Anglo-American Caribbean Commission* was revised and enlarged in October 1946, when it evolved into a successor organization—*The Caribbean Commission*.[12]

The enlarged group included France, the Netherlands, and their possessions.

For our purposes, we are interested only in the economic research aspect of the Caribbean Commission's work. At its seventh meeting held in Guadeloupe in December 1948, the Commission took action on a secretariat proposal which read as follows: "The Commission recognizes the need for an economic periodical and feels that such a publication could be extremely helpful in keeping up to date its trade statistics ...and in serving as a general source of information."[13] Eric Williams (then the prime minister of Trinidad) in a foreword to the first issue of *The Caribbean Economic Review*, December 1949, supported the idea and pointed out, "it can be said that the Caribbean area needs, and does not possess, a journal devoted to economic matters in general, under the specific guidance of some organization which, like the Caribbean Commission, takes a regional viewpoint and exists for the purposes for which the Commission has been created."[14] *The Caribbean Economic Review*, which was discontinued in 1954, published the previously mentioned two important articles by Sir Arthur Lewis, which formed the basis for his development policy for the Gold Coast. For the most part, it published articles on policies and strategies for development. It may be said that the function of the

Caribbean Commission's economic periodical was to legitimize, academically, the development policies proposed for the area.[15]

This introductory analysis of the Caribbean Commission and the history of Puerto Rico is essential in order for us to fully comprehend the ideology and the direct and indirect intertwined forces of the powers behind the development strategy suggested for the Gold Coast. As Joan Robinson has pointed out, economics itself (that is, the subject as it is taught in universities and evening classes and pronounced in leading articles) has always been partly a vehicle for the ruling ideology of each period as well as partly a method of scientific investigation.[16] Whether or not ideology can be eliminated from the world of thought in the social sciences, it is certainly indispensable in the world of action in social life. A society cannot exist unless its members have common feelings about what is the proper way of conducting its affairs, and these common feelings are expressed as an ideology. Therefore, it seems that the imperial powers of the Caribbean Commission expressed their common feelings in an ideology, which was in turn legitimized via the newly created *Caribbean Economic Review*. The resulting economic policy was implemented in the Caribbean and in the African colonies. It was the vehicle of the "ruling ideology."

INDUSTRIALIZATION POLICIES IN PUERTO RICO

The first issue of *The Caribbean Economic Review* featured an empirical study by Lewis of the Puerto Rican industrialization strategy. This study showed a short-lived, supposedly unworkable independent development strategy—"Operation Bootstrap"—which was quickly replaced by a colonial-type dependent development strategy and labeled as IBI. "Three distinct phases may be observed in the industrial development policy. In the first stage, the government built plants and operated them itself. In the next stage, it built factories, which it leased to private manufacturers on favorable terms. In the third stage, now operating, both these policies have ceased, and the emphasis is on offering aids and incentives to private capital."[17] The first and second stages of the above strategy had their problems—the losses on the government plants were blamed partly on the initial difficulties of establishing market connections. The other reasons were the small size of its market and the lack of local entrepreneurship, technical "know-how," and capital. The Puerto Rican Industrial Development Company which was created in 1942 to pursue the "Operation Bootstrap" strategy, was later entrusted with the power to pursue the third strategy of development which is best explained in Lewis' own words:

> The company is taking the initiative in trying to persuade manufacturers to come to Puerto Rico. It is, of course, equally anxious that local capital should be invested in industry, and some local capital is coming forward. But most local capitalists are shy of industry. They have not the "know-how"; and even more important (since "know-how" can be hired), they have not the market connections which are essential to profit. Success on a big scale therefore depends on persuading established U.S. manufacturers to come to Puerto Rico.[18]

Thus, because of the initial "infant industry" problems facing a small, "latecomer" country, a case was established for an IBI strategy of development for Puerto Rico. Lewis ended the empirical study by endorsing the IBI strategy. He said in part that

> [t]he people may congratulate themselves that the program has begun well and is meeting response with an inflow of new industries. Those who direct this program, and who are in touch with potential newcomers, report that the flow is still well-maintained. The energy, initiative, and intelligence with which the island is making this effort deserves the fullest reward.[19]

Immediately following the Puerto Rican study, Lewis did a study for industrialization of the British West Indies. The empirical part of the study was based on an analysis of all potentially viable commodities manufactured in the West Indies. The strategy suggested, after an in-depth theoretical and empirical analysis, was the Puerto Rican IBI. It is right to say that his later work was heavily influenced by his endorsement of the Puerto Rican prescription.

A DEVELOPMENT MODEL AND POLICY: BRITISH WEST INDIES

Lewis' paper on "The Industrialization of the British West Indies" is indeed a classic, based on sound economic analysis. However, the realism and relevance of the assumptions upon which the analyses and policies were based may be questioned. The work begins with an analysis of the need for industrialization in the West Indies to absorb the unemployed. The theoretical formulation is in the classical economic doctrine in that it is concerned with the harnessing of unemployed resources—surplus labor.

> The case for rapid industrialization in the West Indies rests chiefly on over-population. The islands already carry a larger population than agriculture can absorb, and populations are growing at rates of from 1.5 to 2.0 per cent per annum. It is, therefore, urgent to create new opportunities for employment off the land.[20]

The overpopulation issue is analyzed and supported empirically for all the islands and it found that unemployment had become endemic. Lewis assumed implicitly that there is disguised unemployment or underemployment. These unemployed masses must be employed somewhere via industrialization. The assumption of surplus labor is critically important for "classical" type theories of development because they assume that the rural surplus labor can be removed without reducing the total agricultural output. This is so because the marginal product of some laborers may be zero. Thus the capitalist sector can develop by obtaining increasing supplies of labor at the existing wage rate. The capitalist sector can expand indefinitely at a constant wage rate for unskilled labor so long as there is disguised unemployment.

Under the above assumptions pertaining to the West Indian economies, the stage was set to analyze the ingredients and mechanism of industrialization. A case is made for the improvement of agriculture: "If industry is to be developed, then agriculture must give a higher standard of living, in order to provide a demand for manufactures."[21] Thus a basic condition has been established for industrialization. The next problem is to ensure profitability and marketability of the industrial goods. "How is it possible for newly industrialized countries to contemplate producing and exporting manufactures in competition with old and established rivals?" He offered an answer:

> Manufactures are not one commodity, but several hundred commodities, and …the conditions necessary for successful manufacture vary widely from one commodity to another …The secret of success, for any country, is to specialize in those to which its resources are most appropriate, and to avoid the others.[22]

The classical economic doctrine of the concept of "comparative advantage" was invoked to answer the question. The next problem is to determine the requirements of each industry in order to judge its suitability for establishment on the island.

The manufacturing experiences in the United Kingdom and the United States provided the solution to the above problem: "We are fortunate in being able to obtain from the Censuses of Production taken at frequent intervals in the United Kingdom, the United States, and elsewhere, much information about the varying requirements of each industry, which we can use to judge its suitability for establishment in the islands."[23] Information was gathered on 137 industries. The establishments selected had over 10 persons working in them. Eight indexes were devised to analyze the data and to show in which trade the island had a comparative advantage. The eight indexes were:

(1) The ratio of wages to gross output, (2) the ratio of wages to net output, (3) the net output per person employed, (4) the amount of mechanical horse power in use per operative, (5) the consumption of fuel per operative, (6) the weight of materials used per operative, (7) the average size of establishment, and (8) the localization co-efficient of the industry.[24]

On the basis of the empirical results of these indexes the industries were grouped into most favorable to least favorable.

There are important questions that arise concerning the methodology for selecting profitable industries for the Caribbean. The criteria for technological choice was based on the United Kingdom and the United States, where the capital stock and labor conditions were quite different from the Caribbean. It seems that Lewis assumed away the essential problem of "choice of techniques of production" for a developing country.[25] This question becomes important when the same model is used to recommend policies for the Gold Coast where the sociocultural milieu is much different from either the British West Indies, the United Kingdom, or the United States, and where a traditional economy exists.

After having selected the industries where the Caribbean area would have a comparative advantage, it remained to find capital to establish these industries and make them viable. The Puerto Rican experience provided answers. Essentially, the Caribbean faced the same problems that Puerto Rico faced: lack of size, capital, know-how, and "market connections."[26]

Breaking into a market (says Lewis) involves great expenditure on sales promotion, to establish new trade channels, and this will hardly be worthwhile for the limited amount of trade that the islands would do. The moral of this is that what should rather be done is to try to persuade existing suppliers, with established distribution channels in Latin America, to open factories in the islands to supply their trade. It is this that Puerto Rico is doing, in its invasion of the U.S. market, and it is one of the outstanding lessons of Puerto Rican experience.[27]

It is clear that Lewis is prescribing the Puerto Rican medicine (IBI) for the British West Indies. The strategy for industrialization is now complete. The next problem was to send the invitation and get the invitees to come to the British West Indies. Lewis justified his strategy thus:

> [T]he industrialization of a new country cannot just be left to the ordinary forces of the market, but demands very positive and very intelligent action by governments. This action is of two kinds; the creation of a special agency, and the offer of special incentives to overcome the handicaps of starting. ...The first step (after establishing a customs union, which is almost a *sine qua non*) is to set up a special Industrial Development Corporation would need to have offices in London and New York, in order to make and follow up contacts with potential clients.[28]

The corporations had to be persuaded to come by giving them tax holidays similar to the Puerto Rican tax holiday law of 1947, among other incentives.

> The proclamation of a tax holiday is another incentive, and both Jamaica and Trinidad have already passed legislation to this effect. The remission of taxes on imported raw materials and machinery goes without saying. No intelligent government taxes such things, even in advanced industrial countries. So such a "concession" amounts to very little.[29]

This strategy of development by invitation as set forth by Sir Arthur will not sound that naïve if one looks at the political and economic conditions prevailing on the island at that time. These conditions together with Puerto Rico's seeming success at solving its problems surely influenced Sir Arthur's choice of strategy:

> The much more serious difficulty is, where is the drive to come from? A visit to the British West Indian islands at the present moment is a depressing experience. Everyone seems to be waiting for something to happen, but the traveler is never quite able to discover what it is that they are waiting for. Some key is needed to open the door behind which the dynamic energies of the

West Indian People are at present confined. The key has obviously been found in Puerto Rico, where the drive and enthusiasm of a people hitherto as lethargic as the British West Indians, warms the heart, and inspires confidence in the future.[30]

We have quoted Lewis profusely because, as far as Third World countries are concerned, this model for development outlined above has influenced their lives a great deal. Next, an attempt is made to show that the IBI strategy was recommended for the Gold Coast by Lewis without due regard to the problem of the choice of production techniques. For the Gold Coast, unlike the Caribbean, has traditional economic institutions rooted in a culture that has survived Western colonialism. In the Caribbean, on the other hand, plantation-type economy destroyed the West African culture and institutions that the slaves brought with them. Second, the problem of market size that the Caribbean faces is not a limiting factor as far as the African continent is concerned.

SUMMARY

Put simply, according to Arthur Lewis, the prerequisites for economic growth include: (1) the efforts to economize: taking risk, mobility, specialization, and freedom of expression, and replacing African traditional value systems by imported structures and foreign beliefs; (2) the increase and application of human capital and skilled knowledge; and (3) hard work and capital formation.[31] More specifically, Lewis argued that if the surplus labor available at subsistence wages in the rural areas were transferred to the urban areas, it could enhance capitalistic development. For economic growth to be achieved, Lewis proposed a structural transformation of a subsistence-based agricultural economy into a modern industrial economy.

The significance of Lewis' model rests on the assumption that growth takes place as a result of structural change. That is, the subsistent agricultural sector needs to be transformed into a predominantly modern (capitalist) sector. As the capitalist sector grows as a result of the process of labor transfer, the growth of output and employment in the modern sector will achieve self-sustaining growth.[32] Furthermore, Lewis assumed that industrialization: (1) would act as the engine of growth, (2) would provide the means to develop infrastructure and restructure the agricultural sector, and (3) would provide the opportunity to capitalize on the migration of people from rural to urban areas by providing secure employment in the growth industries.[33]

Lewis' model assumes that Third World countries need to follow the experience of the West in order to develop. In addition, the model assumes that the foreign investors would reinvest their profits in the newly independent countries rather than sending their profits to their mother countries. Lewis' two-sector model contributed the following problems to Africa's experience with the industrialization process:

1. Agriculture and local knowledge, which were the mainstay of Africa's economy, were given less importance by the two-sector economic model as a viable means of achieving Africa's industrialization. It was suggested that the rural economy should perform a secondary role as an outlet for capital products (producing food for consumption and to production for export currency earning) and be a supplier of manpower.[34]

2. By emphasizing the perpetuation of capitalist infusion as a major means of Africa's development, Lewis' model contributed to insufficient agricultural investment, which resulted in the rising of food imports and the failure of export earnings to grow fast enough to provide the needed industrial inputs.

3. In the African countries that tried Lewis' model, industrialization was very disappointing both in its inability to absorb the large numbers of workers it had attracted to

urban areas and in its limited contribution to development outside the principal urban areas.[35]

4.   Finally, Lewis' model of development mainly concentrated on output and failed to take into account income distribution, welfare, and human satisfaction.[36]

As summarized by Michael Todaro:

When one takes into account the labor-saving bias of most modern technological transfer, the existence of substantial capital flight, the widespread nonexistence of rural surplus labor, the growing prevalence of urban surplus labor, and the tendency for modern-sector wages to rise rapidly even where substantial open unemployment exists, the Lewis two-sector model— though extremely valuable as an early conceptual portrayal of the development process of sectoral interaction and structural change—requires considerable modification in assumptions and analysis to fit the reality of contemporary Third World nation.[37]

Nonetheless, as shown in Table 2.1, Lewis' development model desperately failed in Africa because it "sought to apply linear and similar development models that were incompatible with African economic structure, social values, and institutions."[38]

Table 2.1:
Lewis' Economic Development Paradigm

Paradigm	Explanation	Major Limitations
Arthur Lewis' two-sector economic growth or structural-change model (1950s)	Economic growth would be achieved through capital formation (industrialization, urbanization, technological transformation of agriculture)	(1) This model neglected agriculture, the backbone of Africa's economy, as a strategy for development; (2) it neglected African knowledge assets and experience in its design; (3) it contributed to the massive migration of rural people into urban sectors

Case Study: Industrialization by Invitation for the Gold Coast (Ghana)

Ghana gained political independence in 1957. Under a nationalistic government, it tried to accelerate its economic growth and ran into difficulties. Ghana's development experience since 1957 shows that structural inflation and balance-of-payments problems are part and parcel of its underdevelopment. Ghana's experience with structural inflation and underdevelopment may be categorized under two basic periods: (1) era of controlled structural inflation: a colonial monetary strategy, 1900 to 1957; (2) controlled structural inflation—financing capital formation out of foreign exchange reserves: a postcolonial strategy, 1957 to 1961.

Controlled Inflation Under Colonial Regimes: 1900 to 1957

Structural inflation was controlled by the colonial regimes in Ghana and other colonial areas by keeping growth rates and institutional changes at low levels. The modern sector was expanded slowly. The precapitalist sector, which earned foreign exchange through exports of cash crops, was able to produce and finance the consumption needs of the modern sector.

The Lord Lugard (1908) strategy of indirect rule reinforced dualism by slowing down the interaction between the "modern" market institutions and the precapitalist African institutions and modes of production. The colonial economic policies were consciously or unconsciously designed to keep structural equilibrium in the "modern sector," that is, the import-export economy. This was done through monetary arrangements between the sterling exchange standard and the colonial Currency Boards. The Currency Boards were required to maintain a 100 percent cover of their currency liabilities. This tied the money in circulation to the balance of payments.

West African sterling was issued only against the exchange of British sterling. Such issues, and counterparts redemption, took place on an automatic basis. Under the above conditions, the threat of inflation normally originated from the fact that export receipts tended to be bigger than import expenditures.

The colonial monetary policy was able to keep inflation in check. A balance was sought between export earnings (which commanded the purchasing power) and the imported merchandise available in Ghana. At times, there was congestion at ports and the volume of imported merchandise was limited. In such a situation, the money supply (purchasing power) was reduced to keep inflation in check.

Under the colonial monetary policy, economic development was stifled because the West African Currency Board used capital formation financed out of credit creation. Thus, the colonies were denied a strategy to accelerate development based on credit creation by the central banks.

The colonial policies encouraged the production of agricultural products to be exchanged for manufactured goods. These policies created structural disequilibria and disarticulated the production matrix in Ghana. The potential for industrial development was nipped in the bud. Expansion of agriculture did not lead to the development of linkages to initiate other sectors of the economy.

In 1952, the structural disarticulation in the economy was complete, but the national income of Ghana depended solely on one cash crop—cocoa. Since the 1920s, cocoa had accounted for over two thirds of the export receipts; the diamond and gold mining enterprises and exports of timber and lumber accounted for the rest. Marketing of cocoa was under a statutory marketing board that was set up in the 1947—1948 season. Marketing of imported items was under the control of expatriate merchant firms—United Africa Company (Unilever subsidiary) was by far the biggest merchant firm. Under the above structure of production and distribution, the successive colonial administrations were able to contain inflation by managing the incomes of cocoa farmers (purchasing power) to equal the value of imports by the merchant firms; government expenditures were financed mainly out of modest taxation on imports, company profits, and exports.

The colonial development policy constrained capital formation and growth to a modest level because of its deflationary policies. The deflationary monetary policies succeeded in building up large international reserves, which stood at 145 million pounds in 1952, and in 1955 attained its highest level of 208 million pounds. This was possible because of the Korean boom and high prices of cocoa.

Controlled Inflation: Financing Capital Formation out of Reserves, 1957 to 1961

Ghana attained internal self-government in 1954 and its independence from colonial rule in 1957. It immediately embarked on an ambitious program to accelerate its growth, which had been anything but modest under the colonial regime before 1954. What were the development strategies available to Nkrumah and his party, the Convention Peoples Party (CPP)?

The cold war atmosphere in the 1950s seems to have forced the Nkrumah regime to follow the development plans and strategies bequeathed it by the colonial regime as propounded in the following documents:

√   "The Ten-Year Plan of Development and Welfare of 1951" (colonial plan)[39]

√   D. Seers and C. Ross, "Financial and Physical Problems of Development in the Gold Coast"[40]

√   W. Arthur Lewis, Report on Industrialization and the Gold Coast[41]

All the documents laid heavy emphasis on the need to build the infrastructure—this was made more explicit in Lewis' report and in the Ten-Year Colonial Plan. Thus in 1952, K. A. Gbedemah, minister of commerce and industry, commissioned Sir Arthur Lewis to write a report on industrialization and economic policy for the Gold Coast. Perhaps it was the Colonial Office that recommended Lewis to Mr. Gbedemah. He visited the Gold Coast from December 15, 1952, to January 4, 1953. During the 21-day visit, which included the Christmas holiday season, Lewis traveled extensively, covering 1,800 miles by air and road. He then went back to the University of Manchester and produced a document, *Report on Industrialization and the Gold Coast*, which was presented to the Ministry in June 1953.

As pointed out, the Report was an extension of his two previous works on the British West Indies and Puerto Rico. There were minor modifications in methodology but the strategy for development devised for the British colonies was the same. It is important to present a summary analysis of the Report before it is assessed.

As indicated in *Report on Industrialization and the Gold Coast*, the basic question that Sir Arthur sought to answer was "which manufacturing industries are most likely to succeed in the Gold Coast, having regard to markets and to raw materials?" (31).[42] Unlike the British West Indian case, the criteria for choosing the industries were through a qualitative rather than quantitative analysis. The comparative advantage criteria for processing materials for export were based on (a) low labor cost, based on low wages; and (b) an advantage in transport cost, if the material loses weight in the course of processing. For commodities destined for home consumption the procedure used to suggest home production was "to pick out from the Import List those commodities which have a *prima facie* case for further examination, or in which Gold Coast opinion had expressed special interest" (46). By looking at the amount of the commodity imported and the amount of money spent on it coupled with an analysis of United Kingdom productivity patterns, a decision was made as to the profitability of producing that commodity in the Gold Coast. There were no cost computations nor demand and supply projections nor choice of technique analyses. Industries so analyzed were designated as "favorable," "marginal," or "unfavorable." It may be emphasized that the proposed industries were viewed as United Kingdom factories with the United Kingdom's level of capital-intensive mode of production. Later on, when an alternative strategy of development is presented, a criticism will be leveled against the industrialization by invitation strategy for neglecting to build on some traditional industries that could be viable under labor-intensive modes of production, and that could have been transformed later into capital-intensive industries, through a process of investing savings and learning by doing.

The analysis resulted in a classification of a short list of 11 "favorable" industries: oil expressing, canned fruits and vegetables, salt, beer, bricks and tiles, cement, glass, lime, industrial alcohol, miscellaneous chemicals, and wood products. Among the 15 marginal industries were biscuits, soap, cigarettes, confectionary, jute bags, foundry products, and candles.

The next step in Lewis' now well-known methodology is to make a case for "industrialization by invitation." The point is made that "African entrepreneurship is deficient in technical knowledge, in managerial capacity, and in capital" (145). The market size constraint on producing for home consumption is stressed (15). The capital constraint on industrialization is analyzed (95—100). The point is made that the proposed Ten-Year Development Plan will need about 38 million pounds sterling for implementation, which cannot be footed by the government alone. "The alternative is to rely, instead, to a considerable extent on foreign capital" (99). "In any country," Lewis pointed out, "the early stages of industrialization are usually the work of foreigners, because usually only they have the knowledge and the capital" (93).

After a case has been made to have foreigners come to industrialize a Third World economy, the next issue is to discuss the "terms on which they come in and how much of their own capital they must invest" (94). Lewis of course assumes that the foreign entrepreneurs will accept the invitation and that conditions can be negotiated so that the two groups could benefit mutually. On this point, Sir Arthur assured Ghanaians that "many foreign capitalists automatically reinvest their profits in the country, and indeed there is no reason why they should not do so if the country continues to offer opportunities for economic expansion. It is probable that a very large proportion of the foreign-owned capital now in the Gold Coast consists simply of profits made there and reinvested" (103). Sir Arthur seems to have been too optimistic about the growth-generating potential of foreign capital under any condition: "Even when foreigners make large profits they are still contributing to development, not only by means of the wages, taxes, and other expenses that they incur, but also because they train labour and impart commercial experience to the general population" (106).

The last condition remaining, according to the IBI model, is to create an atmosphere in the Gold Coast to induce foreign entrepreneurs to come. The recommendations ranged from building infrastructure to senior civil servants befriending industrialists. The recommendations fall into two categories: (a) creating favorable internal conditions, and (b) creating inducement mechanism for foreigners to come. On the first point, Lewis points out that "the best way to promote industrialization is to have an agricultural policy which raises output and income per head, then the next best way is to have an adequate framework of public services" (180). The infrastructure includes the building of industrial estates (206). Also, Gold Coast managers must be trained abroad, and technical schools should be expanded. The second set of recommendations includes generous tax holidays, and exemption from payment of import duties on capital equipment and raw materials imported for manufacturing purposes and also on raw materials to be worked upon in any industrial establishment. Lewis was also worried about the comforts of the entrepreneurs. "The minimum that the Gold Coast Government ought to do is to guarantee the capital and interest on a first class hotel in Accra. Such a hotel is absolutely necessary if a good flow of highly placed business people is to be attracted into the country. This is one of the cheapest ways in which the Government might contribute to industrialization" (178). It is also necessary that industrialists have special "native" friends to aid them in negotiations: "All countries that are anxious to stimulate industrialization appoint a senior public official, whose duty it is to be the friend of industrialists in their negotiations with government departments, and to ensure that these departments take full account of the priority which the government attaches to industrial expansion" (183). This was indeed a strategy of Industrialization by Invitation.

The industrialization strategy that Sir Arthur recommended for the British West Indies and the Gold Coast were the same. The only trouble with the strategy was that the capitalist invitees did not show up in large numbers in these countries as envisaged. Perhaps with the exception of Puerto Rico, the strategy has been a failure everywhere else.[43]

Part of the reason for this failure is due to the heavy reliance on foreign capitalists to both save and reinvest the surplus into productive capital assets. This did not happen in Africa or the Caribbean. Second, the model was also insensitive to the subsistence and neotraditional sectors. The peasants, wage earners, landlords, and members of the indigenous sector were not induced to engage in capital formation. Third, empirical evidence has shown that wages rise long before the surplus labor from the subsistence sector has been absorbed in the industrial sector. The capacity of the industrial sector to absorb labor has turned out to be small, indeed.[44]

In the case of the Gold Coast, it is correct to say that the colonial regime and the postindependence Nkrumah regime followed Lewis' strategy of development from 1953 until the early 1960s, when it was clear that the "invitees" were not going to come, despite the fact that the infrastructure was being built rapidly.

CHAPTER 3

THE WASHINGTON CONSENSUS ECONOMIC DEVELOPMENT MODEL

Africa countries that experimented with the import substitution strategy, which was very predominant in the 1960s,[1] were convinced that be cause of the secular decline in the value of their exports of agricultural products to their imports of manufactured products, their terms of trade were declining. (That is, export prices declined relative to import prices.) For instance, in Ghana, Nkrumah clearly understood that industrialization as advocated by Arthur Lewis did not reduce Ghana's dependence on foreign capital and did not improve its terms of trade. Mali and Kenya looked at industrialization in terms of cost savings from local production, instead of the high-cost imports from abroad. Similarly, other African countries seriously questioned why they should have to import manufactured goods based on the raw materials they exported.[2] Thus, it became very essential for some African countries (for example, Ethiopia, Nigeria, Ghana, Kenya, Mali, and Zambia) to pursue import substitution (IS) industrialization strategies in the 1960s. They argued strongly against primary-product export expansion, and instead moved toward producing manufactured products at home. As discussed by Todaro, advocates of import substitution (inward-looking development policy) believe that less developed countries (LDCs)

> [s]hould initially substitute domestic production of preciously imported simple consumer goods (first-stage IS) and then substitute through domestic production for a wider range of more sophisticated manufactured items (second-stage IS)—all behind the protection of high tariffs and quotas on these imports. In the long run, IS advocates cite the benefits of greater domestic industrial diversification and the ultimate ability to export previously protected manufactured goods as economies of scale, low labor costs, and the positive externalities of learning by doing cause domestic prices to become more competitive with world prices.[3]

Import substitution industrialization strategy raised the learning curve of the African countries that went through it. Furthermore, it had the following limitations:

1. Import substitution's products were noncompetitive and very expensive, due to security behind protective tariff walls.
2. Import substitution's main beneficiaries were the owners of foreign direct investments.
3. The imported capital-good inputs and intermediate products that come under government subsidies contributed

not only to heavy debt burden but also balance-of-payments deficits.

4.   Import substitution industrialization policy negatively affected the exportation of traditional primary products because the exchange rates of some of the African countries were artificially overvalued in order to raise the prices of exports and lower the prices of imports.

5.   Import substitution, which was created in order to stimulate infant industry growth and self-sustained industrialization by creating forward and backward linkages with the rest of the economy, has inhibited the industrialization process.[4]

In short, economic practices of the 1960s and 1970s in Africa were consistent with the development models initiated by the United Nations for those decades. Nonetheless, "more than four-fifths of the sub-Saharan African countries still fell in the low-income category of developing countries (with annual per capita incomes of less than US$360 in 1978), and their average rate of growth per capita of 0.9% over the two decades was the lowest of all the regions of the Third World."[5] Although politically independent, "control of the import-export trade and the financial sector and ownership of major production capacity in the export and industrial sectors remained in foreign hands (industries were owned and managed by Europeans or third-country nationals)."[6] In short, African countries were economically dependent on the West for their (1) technology and capital goods industries, (2) managerial skills, (3) finance, and (4) marketing skills.

Disenchanted with the trickle-down theory of economic growth of the 1960s, in the 1970s international agencies (for example, the International Labor Organization and the World Bank), while not threatening conventional orthodoxy, began to question the efficacy and effectiveness of their component strategies. As part of that movement—"redistribution with growth," "the basic needs approach," "the basic services approach," a focus on "the informal sector," and the idea of empowerment and grassroots approaches all began to emerge as development practice.[7] As discussed by Tade Akin Aina:

> Each of these strategies was an expression of concern over the limited impact that the development process was having on the lives of the majority of the citizens of the developing countries. They represented a recognition of the need for the majority of the people to be involved in the process and to be *enabled* to be involved in a meaningful way in terms of activities and contributions.[8]

While "growth with equity" and "development through empowerment" were regarded as progressive ideas and were being entertained by some elements of the African leadership as a viable development option, a number of African countries failed to implement them. The chief causes of this were: (1) the ensuing deep recession that Africa underwent (despite the fact that gross domestic product for sub-Saharan Africa grew in real terms by 6 percent during 1965—1973) as a result of the oil crisis of 1973—1974, (2) subsequent oil crises of 1979, (3) a global economic slowdown, and (4) the fact that African governments did not implement a consistent set of policy tools to deal with the crisis at a much earlier stage. Thus, natural disasters, famine, ethnic conflicts, and the economic recession of the early 1980s strongly contributed to "the end of development planning and the return of neoclassical theorizing in the form, for example, of supply-side economics in the early part of the 1980s and neo-liberalism at the beginning of the 1990s."[9]

Neoclassical Economic Paradigm of the 1980s (or Washington Consensus)

As a result of the global economic recessions of the early and late 1970s, African countries stepped up the need for the reassessment of development strategies. For example, in 1970, they developed the Monrovia Strategy for the Economic Development of Africa.

> It was realized that the development performance of most African states had been disappointing over the past decade and, more importantly, that the prospects for the future were gloomy. Furthermore, the failure of the demands for a New International Economic Order (NIEO) implied that the solution to the African problem—indeed to that of most of the Third World—did not lie in a restructured international economic system.[10]

The acute nature of the economic crisis, as clearly demonstrated by the Monrovia Strategy, necessitated immediate action.

> The first economic summit of the Organization of African Unity in Lagos in April 1980 convened to devise a plan for the implementation of the Strategy. It was this economic summit that produced the Lagos Plan of Action (LPA). The chief elements of LPA centered around its endorsement of the African objective of attaining a more self-reliant and more economically integrated continent by the year 2000. Being a complete departure from the past and the substitution of an inward-looking development strategy, according to Adebayo, the five main pillars on which the Monrovia Strategy and the Lagos Plan of Action were based [included]:

1. the deliberate promotion of an increasing measure of national self-reliance;
2. the acceleration of internally located and relatively autonomous processes of growth and diversification and achievement of a self-sustained development process;
3. the democratization of the development process;
4. the progressive eradication of mass poverty and unemployment and fair and just distribution of income and the benefits of development among the populace;
5. the acceleration of the process of regional economic integration through cooperation.[11]

Instead of endorsing the Lagos Plan of Action (which also became an integral part of the International Development Strategy for the Third United Nations Development Decade) and helping the African nations to design appropriate strategies, the World Bank (under the request of the African governor of the bank), one year after the adoption of the Lagos Plan, commissioned Professor Elliot Berg to prepare an opposing plan entitled "Accelerated Development in Sub-Saharan Africa: An Agenda for Action" (the Berg Report and also known as the Washington Consensus Model). The central argument of this neoclassical theorist attributes the heart of the crisis in sub-Saharan Africa to unrealistic domestic policy issues such as pricing policies, overvalued exchange rates, and excessive state intervention in the economy (see Table 3.1). Thus, Berg's report focused on how Africa's growth could be accelerated and how the resources to achieve long-term growth could be realized with the support of the international community. As discussed by Adebayo Adedeji, the Berg Agenda was diametrically opposed to the Lagos Plan in the following ways:

1. Where the *Lagos Plan* emphasizes self-reliance and self-sustaining growth based on integrated and dynamic national, sub-regional, and regional markets, the Bank's *Agenda* puts the emphasis on external markets and on the continuation of the colonial export-oriented economies inherited at independence.

2. While the *Agenda* identifies agricultural exports as the motor for African development, the *Lagos Plan* recognizes that the motor in each country will depend on the nature of its natural resource endowment.

3. The *Agenda* goes on to draw the mistaken conclusion that it is poor export performance rather than the worsening external economic environment (which manifested itself

in the collapse of the commodity market) that is responsible for Africa's poor overall economic performance.

4. Whereas the *Lagos Plan* emphasized the unlinking of Africa, the *Agenda* was regarded as the World Bank's vision of how the global economy should be ordered and how it would like to see that Africa remains the storehouse of natural resources necessary for the maintenance of the West's industrial power and leadership—hegemony. It was felt that too much orthodox Marxist thinking must be counteracted if Africa is to show economic growth.[12]

To have access to financial credit from the International Monetary Fund and the World Bank, African countries were forced to undertake structural adjustment programs (SAPs). Among other things, under the SAPs, the development policies in Africa had to focus on market-oriented reforms, export-promotion, and the *laissez-faire* system. These new forms of reform arose because political changes in the West triggered an ideological shift to the right, especially in Washington, London, and West Germany. In contradiction to the existing thinking, there was economic growth in the newly industrializing countries (NICs) of Asia because the state played a major role in designing and implementing the development agenda (dirigiste development path).[13]

Reviewing the shortcomings and consequences of SAPs in African countries, the United Nations Economic Commission for Africa (ECA) prepared the African Alternative Framework to Structural Adjustment Programmes for Socio-Economic Recovery and Transformation (AAF-SAP). Criticizing the omission of regional economic cooperation and integration in the SAP program, the AAF-SAP recommended inter-country cooperation in the designing, implementation, and monitoring of national programs so that African countries could attain "collective self-reliance." Realizing that regional integration and cooperation were very indispensable for

Table 3.1

Comparing the Structural Institutionalism, Growth-with-Equity, and Washington Consensus Economic Growth Paradigms

Economic Growth Paradigm	Cause	Effect
Structural Institutionalism (Prebisch-Singer Thesis of the 1960s)	There was a secular decline in the terms of trade between agricultural and industrial commodities, and the desire to reduce economic dependence led to a development strategy that favored import-substitution or inward-looking development policy.	A number of African countries that developed an inward-looking industrialization strategy experienced heavy balance-of-payments deficits. In addition, incentives favoring capital, high effective protection to assembly-type industries, and direct controls over prices and foreign exchange have tended to introduce distortions and to support inefficient industries while discouraging agricultural and export production.[a]
Growth-with-Equity Basic needs approach, participatory development	(1970s)Satisfaction of basic needs and growth with equity (for example, GDP per capita was replaced by Physical Quality of Life Index—literacy, life expectancy and infant mortality). The proponents of this development approach focused on agriculture-first development and new international economic order, and viewed grassroots participation as means of poverty reduction and self-actualization.	Though favored by some progressive leaders of Africa, it could not be implemented because of the oil crisis of the 1970s and the subsequent world recessions. This mostly hurt the non-oil-producing countries of Africa, because although prices of some products (for example, cocoa and coffee) increased, this was offset by the high oil prices. However, the deep recession in the first half of the 1980s was due to rising oil prices, the Sahelian drought, and the higher cost of external borrowing.[b]

Neoclassical (market-friendly) Paradigm led by the World Bank (1980s), and the **New Growth (endogenous) Theory** of Paul Romer and Robert Lucas (1990s)	Neoclassical theorists argued that lack of economic growth in the Third World was due to poor resource allocation and state intervention. Hence the central tenets of development policy in the 1980s shifted to the adoption of the following strategies: (1) implementation of competitive free markets, (2) privatization of state-owned enterprises, (3) promotion of nontraditional agricultural products for exports, and (4) the creation of conducive environments for foreign direct investments. Thus, to borrow funds for internal and external macroeconomic balance from the IMF and the World Bank, sub-Saharan African countries were required to undergo structural adjustment programs. After following the prescribed stabilization and SAPs, many African countries experienced little or no growth. Thus, the poor performance of neoclassical theories in explaining the sources of long-term economic growth led to the concept of endogenous growth of the new growth theory. "Models of endogenous growth suggest an active role for public policy (unlike the neoclassical theory it advocates for government intervention) in promoting economic development through direct and indirect investments in human capital formation and the encouragement of foreign private investments in knowledge-intensive industries (for example, Finland and Ireland achieved tremendous growth because they focused on high-tech industries and intellectual development) such as computer software and telecommunications."[c]	Though SAPs were to restore macroeconomic stability and eventually generate sustained economic growth, from 1980 to 1985 "the real per capita GDP for the sub-Saharan Africa region declined nearly 20 percent; export earnings dropped by about 40 percent; import purchases fell by about 40 percent; and the region's external debt, which stood at US$6 billion in 1970, reached an alarming figure of more than US$120 billion. The economic crisis confronting these countries included crumbling roads, impoverished health facilities, falling educational standards, idle factories, growing unemployment, and falling nutritional intakes." Though challenged by the United Nations Economic Commission for Africa, the World Bank, and the Regional Bureau for Africa the United Nations Development Program concluded that, from 1985 to 1990, those sub-Saharan Africa regions that implemented SAPs were doing better than countries that didn't in terms of growth in the short run (but the growth dissipates quickly, doesn't increase domestic savings, and didn't protect the poor from bearing undue hardships).[d]

[a] William F. Steel and Jonathan W. Evans, Industrialization in Sub-Saharan Africa: Strategies and Performance (Washington, DC: World Bank, 1985), v.
[b] Lual Acuek Lual Deng, *Rethinking African Development: toward a framework for social integration and ecological harmony* (Trenton, N.J.: Africa World Press, 1998), 34.
[c] Ibid., 53.
[d] Ibid., 49—50.

Africa's long-term sustainable growth, a workshop on regional integration and cooperation was organized by the World Bank in 1988 as part of a conference entitled The Long-Term Perspective Study of Sub-Saharan Africa.

Nonetheless, the SAPs designed to restore internal and external macroeconomic stability did not bring about the expected growth in sub-Saharan countries because they tended to

> [i]gnore the social fabric and objective conditions of the African society, and to this extent they are inconsistent with African thought and culture. Moreover, those who designed adjustment programs assumed that institutions of the market economy (without legal foundations of exchange and contract) could easily be transferred and adapted to the African situation. In addition, the African State has not been able to establish itself as an agent of development as was/is the case for its counterpart in East Asia.[14]

Thus, as articulated by I. Elbadawi, sub-Saharan Africa was the only developing region of the world that experienced zero average per capita growth over the last 30 years and only 0.35 percent growth during the structural adjustment period. In his words:

> Structural adjustment programs in Sub-Saharan Africa have not significantly improved growth in the second half of the 1980s, and they have hurt investment. They have significantly improved export performance but the perceived increases in export competitiveness and in the efficiency of investment have not been sufficient to counterbalance the decline in investment and to restore economic growth.[15]

What is more fundamental, "many African governments did not really internalize and/or own the adjustment programs. The internationalization of policies and programs was weak because African governments depended heavily on the international donor community and foreign consultants for analytical work on which key policy decisions had been based."[16]

Moreover, the now economically advanced countries don't seem to realize their historical development and are "kicking away the ladder" by which they climbed to achieve economic growth. Instead, they are imposing on today's developing countries certain institutions, which had not been used by them at comparable stages of development. For example, as argued by Ha-Joon Chang, the multilateral conditions, which were imposed by the IMF-World Bank (Fund-Bank) on the developing countries as parts of the "good governance" package, were in fact the results, rather than the causes, of economic development of the newly developed countries (NDCs). In this sense, it is not clear how many of them are indeed "necessary" for today's developing countries.[17]

In Africa, the IMF and World Bank stabilization programs tend to negate hard-won national sovereignty by imposing conditions on the sovereignty of each country. This conditionality has turned African countries into mere "adjustment states"—where world imperialism demands adjusting their economies, and indeed their whole countries, for better exploitation. The IMF and World Bank programs encourage the militarization of the political arena that lead to repressive authoritarian regimes. These programs encourage the negation of basic democratic and human rights. Therefore, all austerity programs create different degrees of economic and political repression.[18]

In addition, the stabilization policies produced catastrophic results on workers, peasants, women, and children:

> There were uniformly gruesome tales of sudden mass retrenchment of 30 percent of a national workforce without benefits, that often affected both husband and wife; of suicides; of rising infant and child mortality rates after the declines of the previous two decades; the re-emergences of epidemics of mea[s]les, tuberculosis, kwashiorkor, as well as outright starvation.[19]

CASE STUDY 1: COMMODITY PRICE TRENDS IN GHANA

The main purpose of this chapter is to argue that Ghana's economic recovery under its structural adjustment program would have been much brighter if policy makers had not made some obvious errors in the application of the theory of "comparative advantage" and in the selection, timing, and sequencing of commodities for export. Agriculture is the dominant sector of the Ghanaian economy. It generates 43 percent of GDP, over 50 percent of export earnings, and provides 70 percent of employment. As a result, any policy lapse in this sector is bound to affect economic performance negatively. This chapter draws attention to a critical evaluation of agricultural sector policies. Specifically, it argues that cocoa sector policies and implementation priorities were misplaced, thus compromising economic recovery.

It is suggested that Ghana's economic recovery would have been much brighter if policy makers had been able to predict the cocoa price slump of the 1980s and 1990s and had sought to diversify the commodity export base of the economy away from cocoa exports. It is suggested, further, that diversification of the export base should be taken seriously so that the economy can move away from dependence on cocoa exports. In the past, violent fluctuations in cocoa export earnings created problems of economic instability for Ghana, which, in turn, led to political instability, economic chaos, and a virtual collapse of the economy in 1981. Diversification would go a long way to stabilize commodity export earnings and secure stable economic growth. Diversification by itself is not enough if supply response and institutional development in the rural sectors are low. Economic and noneconomic factors should therefore be included in designing models for economic recovery.

It is recognized that commodity diversification by itself is not enough to do the trick. Recent research by institutional economists has shown that the most important variable for economic growth is institutional innovations brought about by superior political organization and administrative competence in government. It is suggested that for Ghana (and thus, Africa) to solve the problem of low supply response in agriculture, it must find a way to develop efficient institutions, for example, by lowering transaction costs. The study provides empirical examples of institutional innovations and growth.

The suggestions developed in this chapter—that is, to ensure a viable SAP with the help of government intervention—may be summarized as follows: (1) a superstructure of an agrarian development strategy "with an institutional development face," for example, a cooperative movement must be put in place, and (2) an agriculture-led growth strategy "with an equity face" must be followed before rapid industrialization begins. The internal terms of trade are biased toward the agrarian sector.

THE CONSEQUENCES OF THE WASHINGTON CONSENSUS MODEL ON GHANA

The *Financial Times* of London reviewed economic conditions in Africa in a special issue on September 1, 1993. The newspaper provided facts to tell its own story:

> After a dozen years of structural adjustment and more than $170bn in net development assistance, the sub-Saharan economy is still falling behind. Incomes per head fell by an average 1.1% a year between 1982 and 1992 compared to an average rise of 0.8% a year in all developing countries and 6.4% in the east Asian developing countries.[20]

On the other hand, the World Bank reminds us that some of the African countries, which have taken structural adjustment advice to heart, have been singled out for praise as success stories. Using microeconomic commodity price trends in Ghana, the case study given below critically evaluates the lessons learned from the Washington Consensus Model.

COMMODITY PRICE TRENDS IN GHANA

Since Ghana's adjustment program began, its gross domestic product has grown by an average of 4.9 percent a year, over twice the sub-Saharan average of 2.1 percent.[21] But there are economists and international agencies that do not believe in the Ghanaian success story. The skeptics believe that the cost of the SAP has been severe on some social groups in Ghana. They point to high rates of inflation averaging over 30 percent per annum between 1984 and 1992; a high dependence on a few commodities for export (principally cocoa and gold); low rates of domestic saving; and a strikingly low level of private investment.

The main purpose of this case study is to argue that Ghana's economic recovery under the SAP would have been more significant if policy makers had not made some obvious errors in the sector selection of the Ghanaian economy. Because cocoa provides 70 percent of employment; produces over 50 percent of export earnings; and generates 43 of percent GDP, it is argued that Ghana's economic recovery would have been much brighter if policy makers had predicted the cocoa price slump and seriously diversified its commodities, as suggested above.

Violent fluctuations in past cocoa export earnings created problems of economic instability for Ghana and prevented secular increase in per capita income. This, in turn, led to political instability, economic chaos, and eventual collapse of the economy in 1981. Diversification of the export base would go a long way to stabilize commodity export earnings and secure stable growth.

In the sections that follow, Part I presents a brief discussion of the controversy over the success or failure of SAPs in Africa, and especially in Ghana. Part II reviews SAP and economic recovery program (ERP) policy reforms, then explains how they were implemented in Ghana from 1983 to 1993. Part III provides an evaluation of how the theories behind agricultural sector policies were misplaced. Part IV argues that Ghana's economic recovery performance would have been better had mistakes in the agricultural sector been avoided and policy implementation improved.

PART I: CONTROVERSY OVER SUCCESS OR FAILURE OF THE SAP

Several African countries and international agencies are watching the SAP experiment in Ghana with a great deal of interest. If the experiment is successful, then the World Bank will continue to try to implement such strategies in other African countries. So far, opinion is divided over the success of the SAP program in Ghana. There are those, including the World Bank, the *Financial Times* of London, and the *New York Times*, who think that the program has succeeded. On the other hand, there are those, including the United Nations Economic Commission for Africa (UNECA), who feel that the exercise in Africa is bound to fail. The controversy over the failure or success of the SAP program in Ghana, or in Africa in general, is just beginning.

The World Bank's own studies and other studies they commissioned seem to claim that the SAPs have been a success not only in Ghana but in Africa as a whole.[22] The Economic Commission of Africa issued two reports challenging the conclusions of the World Bank study. The first report was entitled: *Statistics and Policies ECA Preliminary Observations on the World Bank Report: Africa's Adjustment and Growth in the 1980s.* This report was presented before the ECA Conference of Ministers, which met in Addis Ababa from April 1 to April 6, 1989. A resolution was passed condemning the World Bank reports. The resolution praised the work of the secretary-general of the United Nations on the midterm review of the United Nations Program of Action for Africa Economic Recovery and Development (UN-PAAERD) as reflecting the true economic situation in Africa and that the World Bank reports contained statistical inaccuracies and misinterpretations of the real situation in Africa. The UNECA issued another report in 1989 outlining an alternative strategy of development: *African Alternative Framework to Structural Adjustment Programmes for Socio-Economic Recovery and Transportation* (AAF-SAP).

The United States Congress commissioned a report on the performance of SAPs in some African countries. The report found that

> [i]n both Ghana and Senegal structural adjustment has contributed to the first real sustained per capita economic growth in many years and to an improved framework for future growth. ...structural adjustment has produced little enduring poverty-alleviation, and certain policies have worked against the poor.[23]

Thus the Congress report sees some positive results as well as some negative aspects of SAPs. International newspapers including the *New York Times* have evaluated the impact of the SAP on the Ghana economy. The *New York Times*, on January 3, 1989, in a lead article, reported favorably on the impact of the SAP on the Ghanaian economy under the title "In Western Eyes," where Ghana is regarded as the African model:

> More than five years ago, when the World Bank decided to make the state-dominated economy here a model for free market innovation in Africa, Ghana was in the grip of stagnation. Since then, Ghana has boasted Africa's highest consistent growth rate, an average of 6% a year since 1983.

Some Ghanaian government officials are quite satisfied with the performance of the economy under the SAP. Dr. Joe

Abbey, one of the architects of the SAP and current ambassador to Washington, was invited to give the 1989 IMP Per Jacobson lecture. He spoke highly of the impact of the SAP on the Ghanaian economy. Dr. Abbey argued that

> [t]hroughout the seventies, the Ghanaian economy stagnated, exhibiting negative growth rates in real per capita income. The low point was reached in 1983. Since then real output has expanded by about 40%; real per capita income by more than 20%; the inflation rate, while still bothersome, has been dramatically reduced; the balance of payment is in surplus and the initial large stock of external arrears has been virtually eliminated. ...[How] was this success achieved? ...[To] answer this question we have to look to the strategy of adjustment that was pursued in the context of three successful standby arrangements with the Fund, which has now been succeeded by an enhanced structural adjustment facility arrangement, and the support provided by the various adjustment loans from the World Bank.[24]

Abbey was so impressed with the Ghanaian performance that he wanted Ghana to share its experience with other countries. To do this, he wanted the IMF to develop an institute that could be set up on an interim basis for promoting growth-oriented adjustment.[25] Some economists will challenge the methodology used by Dr. Abbey to assess the impact of the SAP on the performance of the economy. The obvious criticism is the choice of the base year of 1983. Using this lowest point of the crisis as a basis for comparisons with succeeding years will tend to exaggerate the performance of the SAP.

Professor John Loxley, in a study commissioned by the North South Institute, a Canadian nonprofit corporation, evaluated the performance of the SAP by examining the 13 objectives that the Ghanaian government had set for itself. Loxley added four other criteria, which he thought were extremely important to ordinary Ghanaians. Loxley's methodology is different from that of Abbey. He evaluated the performance of the economy under the SAP by comparing the relative performance of specific targets or objectives set out at the beginning of the program and at a later date. Loxley concluded: "To this point in time, on the basis of the criteria outlined the adjustment programme in Ghana has been remarkably successful and has been a classic example of adjustment with growth."[26]

There have been a few studies that focus on specific sectors and on social groups in evaluating the performance of the SAP. The International Fund for Agricultural Development (IFAD) did one such study. The report consists of a comprehensive summary and a main report.[27] The IFAD report seems to suggest that some specific groups have not fared too well under the SAP.

An interesting inference can be drawn from studies done by several people, reported above, on the impact of the SAP on the Ghanaian economy:

1. The researchers who based their analyses on specific sectors of the economy seem to conclude that the SAP failed and/or had an adverse impact on that sector.[28]
2. The researchers who based their analyses on examining aggregate macroeconomic variables over time claimed that the SAP was a remarkable success.[29]

Do we have a methodological and/or aggregation problem here? Studies based on specific sector analyses may be more appropriate than those based on aggregate macroeconomic variables. Oscar Morgenstern has discussed these issues.[30]

To shed light on the issues raised above, this case study evaluates the impact of a major policy designed and implemented in the agricultural sector in Ghana. To do this, we must first analyze policy reforms designed and implemented under the SAP.

Part II: Description of SAP (Policy Reforms)—Mix, Timing, and Sequencing of Policies

This section of the case study draws heavily on the 1984 World Bank country study entitled *Ghana Policies and Programme for Adjustment*.[31] The SAP is divided into three phases: the Stabilization phase; the Rehabilitation phase; and the Liberalization and Growth phase. Each phase has a set of objectives to be achieved. It is necessary to identify these objectives before impact studies can be undertaken or evaluated.

Stabilization Phase

The main function of this phase was to reduce price distortions in the economy. Basically, the Stabilization phase sought to: (1) correct structural imbalances; (2) realign relative prices in favor of production and export sectors; (3) reduce the governments' budget deficit; (4) reduce inflation; and (5) stimulate aggregate domestic supply and reduce imbalances in external and fiscal accounts. It was recognized that a quick disbursement of assistance, to finance the inflow of supplies—such as food, fuel, and other imports—would be necessary to ensure the success of the program. This was considered as a precondition for the success of the currency devaluation exercise.

Rehabilitation Phase

The main objective in this phase was to improve the capacity utilization of existing assets. This phase called for the rehabilitation of the road, port, railway, and transport infrastructure. It also envisaged the provision of essential raw materials and imported inputs to the productive sectors, with particular emphasis on exports. The general macroeconomic policies carried out under this phase included programs: (1) to maintain the incentive structure; (2) to provide an appropriate exchange rate; (3) to streamline the import licensing system; (4) to ensure an adequate foreign exchange budgeting system; (5) to realign the interest rate structure; and (6) to minimize the use of price and distribution control systems.

The policies carried out in this phase included what needed to be done at the sectored levels. The agricultural sector policies and programs are presented below.

COCOA PRODUCTION POLICIES

The policies, which were to be implemented in the production sector, are the following: (1) inefficient operation of Cocoa Marketing Board to be studied and corrected; (2) increase in real producer prices to maintain them at incentive levels; (3) increase cocoa production from 180,000 in 1979/80 to 300,000 by 1986; and (4) long-term plans for new plantings.

AGRICULTURAL SECTOR PERFORMANCE

The reasons for poor agricultural performance are many. The major problems to be resolved are: (1) the deterioration in transport services – roads, ports, and the like; (2) unavailability of inputs like fertilizer, seeds, skilled labor; (3) inadequate producer prices for industrial crops; and (4) unsatisfactory marketing arrangements.

REFORMS TO BE UNDERTAKEN BY THE GOVERNMENT

The government needs to pay attention to: (1) foreign exchange allocations for agricultural inputs and transport; (2) frequent readjustments in output pricing policies; (3) greater competition in the marketing and distribution of agricultural produce and input supplies; and (4) increased supplies of incentive goods in rural areas.

Policy for the Forestry Sector

The forestry sector offers the greatest immediate potential for growth and foreign exchange earnings. According to the World Bank, this sector has been plagued by poor managerial performance, inappropriate organizational arrangements, shortage of imported equipment and spare parts, and an unrealistic exchange rate. The policies to be undertaken in this sector include: (1) exchange rate adjustments (recently undertaken) to make exports of logs and timber products attractive; (2) massive infusion of spare parts and logging equipment with the intention of earning quick foreign exchange; and (3) the exploration of vertical integration when the industry returns to normal, that is, to benefit from higher value added in the channels.

External Capital Needs

External capital needs for the program were worked out for the period covering the Three Year Investment Program (TYIP) under two alternative scenarios: low and high. The low case assumes that the import program will equal export earnings, net aid flows from existing commitments, IMF standby, and new credits from the International Development Association (IDA). The high case includes some bilateral assistance. External financing for the three years of the TYIP was projected to be US$156 million, US$248 million, and US$316 million for 1984, 1985, and 1986 respectively. It was hoped that under the above conditions, the external financing gap would be reduced to US$152 million, or about 5 percent of imports by 1993. Some of these projections have not been met.

Liberalization and Growth Phase

After successful implementation of the first two phases, the Liberalization and Growth phase would be implemented. The policies to be undertaken are spelled out below: (1) liberalizing trade and payment controls; (2) reducing domestic price controls; (3) introducing competition in the public sector and removing rigidities, barriers, and distortions in the economy; (4) removing barriers that inhibit production and growth; and (5) upgrading management and technical efficiency in individual enterprises.

We have presented above the outlines of the SAP or the economic recovery program. Next we present an analysis of SAP in practice.

THE SAP IN PRACTICE: MACROECONOMIC STABILIZATION PHASE (1984 TO 1986)

The Ghanaian military seized power in December 1981 and took the name of Provisional National Defense Council (PNDC). It took about one year for the new regime to set up the machinery to govern the country. At first, it tried to implement a populist strategy for development. The PNDC populist program was announced on radio and television in November 1982, but it was dropped four months later. An IMF/World Bank economic recovery program was announced in April 1983 and put into operation.

Why did the regime drop the populist recovery program in favor of an IMF/World Bank-supported program? There was a disagreement between advisers to the PNDC regime over where and how to generate funds to finance the economic recovery exercise. It was argued that the populist program would fail because it would take too long to produce any tangible results. It was argued further that the economic crisis could be solved quickly by borrowing money from the IMF and the World Bank to finance the recovery exercise.

There was a group of economists who had written papers on how to resolve the economic crisis facing the regime without depending solely on seeking financial assistance from the IMF and the World Bank. See, for example, papers written by Tetteh Kofi and others, including Samir Amin, a former professor at the Institute for Economic Development and Planning (IDEP), Dakar, Senegal.[32] Those who argued for the IMF/World Bank-assisted recovery program won the day. The supporters of this view included Dr. Joe Abbey, who became ambassador to Washington, and Dr. Kevesi Botchway, who became the minister of finance.

The major objectives of the IMF/World Bank-assisted ERP were to: (1) shift relative prices in favor of production (particularly for export) and efficient import substitution; (2) restore fiscal and monetary discipline; (3) initiate the rehabilitation of the country's productive base along with its economic and social infrastructure; and (4) encourage private investment. How were the above programs carried out in practice? We present below a general outline of how the ERP was implemented, followed by a detailed analysis of policies in the agricultural sector.

Loans from IMF and Bank Sources

The Ghanaian government developed the ERP in close coordination with the IMF and the World Bank. The first order of business was to negotiate for cash to support the program:

1. Two IMF Standby Arrangements totaling SDR (special drawing rights) 419 million were negotiated.
2. The Compensatory Financing Facility (CFF) provided SDR 179 million, on account of a shortfall in merchandise exports, to pay for imports including an excess in the cost of cereal imports.
3. Two IDA Export Rehabilitation and two Import Reconstruction Credits totaling SDR 187 million were negotiated. These loans improved the financial situation of the country.

TOWARD A REALISTIC EXCHANGE RATE AND A REALIGNMENT OF PRICE DISTORTIONS

Apart from loans negotiated to pay for imports, the most important measure taken was the decision to devalue the overvalued currency toward a more realistic exchange rate. The cedi was devalued from 2.75 = $1.00 in April 1983 to 90 = $1.00 by January 1986. Throughout this period attempts were made to adjust administered prices to reflect changes in the exchange rate. For example, cocoa and petroleum prices were adjusted to reflect exchange rate movements. Cocoa producer prices were almost doubled in May 1985 and then raised by 50 percent more in May 1986.

Price controls for a wide range of commodities were dismantled. In April 1983, the Prices and Incomes Board administered 23 items. By 1985, the Board was administering only eight "essential commodities": textiles, soap and detergents, matches, machetes/cutlasses, drugs, cement, beer, and cigarettes. Interest rates were raised gradually to the point that they became positive in real terms in 1985.

FISCAL POLICY—STABILIZATION PHASE

In the area of fiscal policy, the Stabilization phase of the ERP concentrated on eliminating subsidies, raising consumption taxes and charges on selected commodities, and improving tax-collection measures, thereby increasing the revenue base of the government.

The devaluation of the currency resulted in the erosion of real incomes. Public-sector salaries and wages, along with statutory minimum wages, were raised to offset part of the loss in real income. The government made some improvements in public expenditure in such areas as public administration, health, and education.

It became clear at the beginning of the ERP exercise that Ghana would need substantial loans over the years to rehabilitate the economy. Thus following the announcement of the ERP, the Bank, in consultation with the Ghana government, decided to reactivate the Ghana Consultation Group, which had not met for the previous 13 years. The Group met in Paris in November 1983 and the prospective donors endorsed the program. Initial commitments in 1984 amounted to US$478 million. This commitment played a role in defining the subsequent ERP and SAP strategy. Beginning in 1986, the government prepared a rolling, three-year investment program. It made provisions for rehabilitation programs in key sectors: cocoa, timber, gold mining, and transport infrastructure. What was done at the sector levels during the stabilization phase? Only the agricultural sector will be analyzed in this chapter.

SAP IN PRACTICE: THE AGRICULTURAL SECTOR IN THE STABILIZATION PHASE

The Ministry of Agriculture (MOA) prepared an agricultural development strategy in support of the economic recovery program. The document was entitled *Ghana Agricultural Policy— Action Plans and Strategies 1984-86*.[33] The document defined long-term and short-term objectives for the period 1984 to 1986. The aims of the short-term agricultural program for that period were: (1) satisfying 80 percent of maize and 60 percent of rice requirements while maintaining self-sufficiency in cassava production; (2) satisfying 50 percent of fish and 53 percent of meat requirements; and (3) maintaining reasonable production levels for other cereals, starchy staples, nuts, oil seeds, fruits, vegetables, and industrial crops.

In the crop subsector, the government's strategy was to emphasize maize, rice, and cassava production during the three-year period. Output was to be increased by improving yields in selected high-potential areas including irrigation project zones. Attempts to modernize the agricultural sector in Ghana had been emphasized by several governments. The PNDC government was no exception. The emphasis of the PNDC under the SAP was on irrigation. No strategy was developed to improve yields on either peasant farms or traditional farms. The area of irrigated farms was estimated to be 4,600 hectares (ha), which was about 0.2 percent of the country's non-cocoa-growing acreage. The MOA document targets for the period 1984 to 1986 were 3,900 ha for rice, 400 ha for maize, and 300 ha for vegetables, totaling 4,600 ha, the total available irrigated acreage. There were plans for a further 4,600 ha under various stages of development for irrigation to be completed by the end of 1986. There were further plans to develop 23,500 ha by 1988 and 180,400 ha by 1993.

These were some of the strategies to be used to increase productivity in the agricultural sector. It was estimated that it cost US$1,500 to develop a hectare of irrigated land, using a large-scale dam, for agricultural production in Ghana. Thus capital expenditure on 23,500 ha and 180,400 ha would be about $35.2 and $271 million respectively. This capital-intensive strategy of agricultural development may be technically efficient but not price efficient. It seems that the emphasis on modern production methods at the expense of the traditional and "peasant" systems of production was inappropriate.

The MOA action plan did not articulate a strategy for the traditional sector or peasants to increase productivity. The action plan talked in general terms about increasing extension staff density and effective distribution of inputs. Additionally, it spoke of establishing rural service centers for the provision of inputs, credit, storage facilities, and processing equipment.

The general objectives of the MOA document were as follows:

1. There should be self-sufficiency in the production of cereals, starchy staples, and animal protein to ensure adequate nutrition for every Ghanaian.

2. Maintenance of adequate levels of buffer stocks of grains, particularly maize and rice, were to ensure: (a) availability of food during the lean season (March to July); (b) price stability; and (c) provision of maximum food security against unforeseen crop failure and other natural hazards.

3. Self-sufficiency was needed in the production of industrial raw materials, such as cotton, palm oil, tobacco, and groundnuts to feed current and future agro-based industries.

4. There should be promotion of increased production of exportable agricultural crops, including cocoa, pineapple, coffee, shea nuts, ginger, and kola.

5. Finally, there should be promotion and provision of improved storage, processing, and distribution systems to minimize port-harvest losses.

Which of the above objectives have been met? In reality, the answer is very few. Before an analysis of the impact of the SAP on the agricultural sector is undertaken, it will be necessary to examine and evaluate: (1) how agricultural policy prescriptions were sequenced; and (2) the criteria used to determine agricultural decisions and their sequencing.

PART III: THE THEORY OF COMPARATIVE ADVANTAGE AND THE RECOVERY MODEL

World Bank consultants helped to design the Ghanaian government's strategy for agricultural sector rehabilitation and growth. The strategy was based on a modified theory of comparative advantage, which was developed by Israeli economists including Michael Bruno.[34] The domestic resource cost

(DRC) compares value-added in domestic and world prices. The domestic value-added factors of production are measured in terms of the actual value to society—the opportunity cost or shadow prices of these factors:

$$\text{DRC ratio} = \frac{\text{Domestic resources and nontraded inputs valued at opportunity costs or shadow price}}{\text{Net foreign exchange earned or saved by producing the goods domestically}}$$

The DRC ratio, as defined above by Isabella Tsakok, becomes a measure of domestic costs of earning or saving foreign exchange.[35] World Bank consultants explained how the DRC ratio could be used for policy analysis:

> An analysis of comparative advantage of Ghana in major tradable crops using different techniques of production and an analysis of the incentive framework was undertaken. The comparative advantage was assessed by calculating [the] Domestic Resource Cost Coefficients (DRCs), which measure the cost of domestic resources (land, labor, materials, etc.) used to save or earn a net unit of foreign exchange. The lower the DRC coefficient, the more efficient the activity; a DRC less than or equal to one (using shadow prices for land, labor, capital, and foreign exchange) indicates comparative advantage in a particular commodity and technique. The analysis of the incentive framework was undertaken both in terms of financial returns to land and labor and nominal and effective rates of protection.[36]

The operational aspects of the model as described above were developed for the World Bank. The consultants included S. Pearson and J. D. Stryker of Stanford and Tufts universities respectively. The model was used "to review the feasibility of the Government strategy mentioned above and provide a basis for policy recommendations on promotion of specific crops, cropping patterns, and techniques."[37]

The World Bank consultants believed that the DRC measurement could be used to make decisions on the serialization of investments in commodity production in an African-type economy. The World Bank DRC calculation shows Ghana's strong comparative advantage in tree crops, viz., cocoa, oil, palm, rubber, and coconut (copra) ...DRCs for tree crops remain favorable in a variety of scenarios including projected declines in world prices in real terms for cocoa, oil palm, and copra. ...The DRCs are also attractive for other industrial crops such as tobacco and cotton, except for irrigated cotton.[38]

It seems that the DRC results are biased against domestic food crops. Export commodities seem to have a stronger comparative advantage compared with local food items. The farmers had been switching over to domestic food crops from export crops. Despite this fact, the World Bank consultants concluded that "as for food crops, except for rice, which appears extremely uneconomic owing primarily to low yields, all other commodities are borderline cases."[39]

Can we interpret the DRC ratios as measures of comparative advantage? How much faith should we put in the results? Is the theory behind the concept of comparative advantage realistic? Did the consultants adapt the theory of comparative advantage properly so that it can be used to rank commodities in order of comparative advantage? We will discuss these questions below.

PROBLEMS WITH THE RECOVERY MODEL—DRC RATIOS

William Brainard and Richard Cooper discussed some of the questions raised above.[40] They argue that trade theory, which is based on the Ricardian concept of comparative advantage, is a theoretical concept. It can be argued that the model, which was used to design the agricultural sector policy, was inappropriate. The theory behind the "decision making model" was based on economics of certainty. It should be based on economics of uncertainty as Brainard and Cooper suggested several years ago:

Classical trade theory fails to recognize the implications of risk aversion for the profitability of specialization and foreign trade.

A few writers on trade theory have acknowledged in passing that uncertainty will influence the degree of specialization, but the formal theory has proceeded on the assumption that production costs and trading possibilities are known with certainty—or, alternatively, that there is no lapse of time between investment for production of a given product and its exchange for imports of foreign goods. Specialization in a product often involves investment in production facilities a substantial period of time before actual production takes place. Investment decisions today affect future output, not present output, and they must be based on some estimate of (uncertain) future prices. The presence of uncertainty modifies the descriptive and normative conclusions of neo-classical trade theory.[41]

To adapt the classical trade theory so that it can be used for empirical work is a difficult task because of the problems involved in predicting the future. Bruno and others adapted the trade model for policy analysis. According to Bruno, one of the originators of the DRC methodology,

the concept of DRC relates to a measure of real opportunity cost in terms of total domestic resources, of producing (or saving) a net marginal unit of foreign exchange. By comparing it with some measure of the economy's real or accounting exchange rate, it can be used as an investment criterion, just as the internal rate of return of a product is compared with some of the real rate of interest. The concept bears a close relationship with basic international trade consideration of comparative advantage.[42]

The last sentence in the quote above refers to the Ricardian doctrine of comparative advantage. The World Bank consultants seem to assume that the DRC concept can be used as a criterion to measure comparative advantage in the Ricardian sense. The Ricardian model is an abstract one. To use the comparative advantage model for policy analyses requires some more work. The restrictive assumptions must be removed in order to make the model operational. The basic problem with the model is that it is not based on economics of uncertainty. Brainard and Cooper have explained this point as follows:

The pure theory of international trade has not incorporated uncertainty about prices at which trade will take place (or the quantities which will actually be available for exchange); it rests on assumption concerning the mobility of resources and knowledge about the future which reduce the questions of uncertainty to negligible importance. In the real world, however, lack of perfect knowledge about the future combined with a time lag between investment and returns to investment give uncertainty a very great importance in influencing economic behavior.[43]

It is always difficult to bridge the gap between trade theory and applications of the theory. The exercise involves structuring and solving a well-posed problem: How well was the theory adapted and applied to meet SAP agricultural sector objectives? We shall evaluate the performance of the model in Part IV, the empirical section of this chapter.

Some economists find the DRC approach inadequate for measuring comparative advantage in the sense used by Ricardo. Other economists, like Raul Prebisch, feel that development should not be looked at from the point of view of the allocation of real resources but from the balance-of-payments point of view. The different approaches lead to different results. Real cocoa prices were projected to fall. Despite this fact, the consultants put cocoa at the top of the list of DRC measures of comparative advantage. The priority given to rehabilitation of the cocoa industry in all phases of the SAP was justified by the static DRC studies.

It may be argued that the margin of error that may be incurred in measuring the DRC variable is high. This makes dependence on DRC ratios suspect in the ranking of commodities. The World Bank study underscored difficulties in measuring variables:

Though the utmost effort was made to refine data and cross-check those from several sources, particularly large cost items such as labour cost, complete data accuracy cannot be claimed. ...Precise estimates of shadow exchange rate (SER) and opportunity cost of capital (OCC) are not available for Ghana. ...Given this uncertainty as to the SER estimation of the shadow wage rate (SWR), which requires valuation of the marginal product of labor in alternative activities at border prices was difficult.[44]

The margin of error in measuring these variables is high in African-type economies, which are not full-fledged market economies. In many ways they are precapitalist in nature. For example, how do we value family labor when there is no wage sector? The problem is compounded when peasant farmers engage in double cropping. Thus it is difficult to apportion labor time to specific crops being produced. How do we find "shadow prices" for land, labor, and other variables in a semiindustrialized economy?

Another problem is the use of the "marginal rule" in valuing DRC variables in a sector without market relations, let alone perfect competition. Microeconomic theory shows that resources are optimally allocated when under perfect competition each factor of production is employed up to the point where its marginal product is equal to its price. For the allocation problem at hand, it means that efficiency will be maximized when no agricultural commodity will be produced if it can be imported at a lower cost compared with the resources that would have to be sacrificed to produce it domestically.

Looking at it from this point of view, the use of DRC to rank commodities and to apply the doctrine of comparative advantage becomes a dangerous numbers game as far as resource allocation is concerned. This is so because the variables cannot be measured under perfect competition market conditions. There are other drawbacks with the application of the marginal pricing principle:

1. The marginal rule is a static criterion. Thus the maximization of present levels of output may not be the best for the society in the future.

2. The marginal principle is blind to external economies and increasing returns to scale. There is no way to quantify these dynamic variables or account for them.

3. The application of the marginal principle does not automatically ensure "optimal" distribution of income.

Thus, Pareto optimality may be involved. The question that needs to be answered is this: Can the DRC measure be used as an investment criterion in semi-industrialized or in agrarian economies? Bruno and others believe that DRC can be used as an investment criterion if we can measure an economy's real or accounting exchange rate:

> Domestic resource cost has a relatively long history of practical use in at least one country, Israel, where it was being applied quite extensively by government planners ever since the early 1950s as a means of project evaluation under conditions in which the official rate of exchange and the prices of tradable [goods] were distorted. It can be rationalized analytically in an input-output or linear-programming general equilibrium framework.[45]

It would be unwise to use the DRC measure as an investment criterion in an economy like that of Ghana. We do not have the data to construct an "input-output" model for Ghana or use linear-programming techniques to calculate optimal shadow prices. Second, unlike Israel, government officials have not applied the DRC method for a long time, so that the results could be tested and validated. It may be argued that it was a mistake for the Ghanaian economists and the World Bank consultants to use the DRC ratios as investment criteria for the reasons explained above. Third, the stakes were too high for the DRC model to be used to make major investment decisions, which would impact heavily on the recovery effort of a whole economy or a whole country.

AN EVALUATION OF THE INCENTIVE STRATEGY

The World Bank report claims to have developed an "incentive strategy" to support the DRC-inspired selection of commodities for production. According to the World Bank's Agricultural Sector Review,

> the comparative advantage analysis was undertaken to provide a basis for the formulation of an investment strategy, given extreme shortages of resources in Ghana at present and the need to concentrate these resources on crops and techniques which promise to be the most efficient. This was combined with analysis of incentive framework in order to determine whether the prevailing incentive was conducive to a successive implementation of the investment strategy resulting from the comparative advantage analysis. The incentive structure is at present highly distorted with high net taxation of some crops with a clear comparative advantage (cocoa, rubber, tobacco, and cotton) and high net protection to crops with a clear comparative disadvantage (rice). ...The overvaluation of the exchange rate over most of the 1970s and early 1980s discouraged export industries, including agricultural exports such as cocoa and timber.[46]

The emphasis was placed on realigning the overvalued exchange rate. It turns out that the "incentive structure" is nothing more than restoring the price distortions brought about by the overvalued exchange rate. No attempt was made to suggest any structural changes, such as land reform, to boost production. It is not clear why rubber, tobacco, and cotton were selected for the DRC study and why incentive strategies were developed for these crops. Ghana does not export these crops. They are not important in domestic or international trade.

The DRC comparative advantage measures were used as the basis to advise the Ghanaian government to pay more attention to the development of export crops and/or industrial crops. The agricultural review had little or nothing to say about the development of food crops because DRC ratios for these items were too high. The emphasis on tree crops, especially cocoa, might have been misplaced, for several reasons. The world cocoa economy was poised for a long period of large surpluses: Brazil and Côte d'Ivoire took policy decisions to expand output in the 1970s, both intensively and extensively. Both countries had large tracts of cocoa-growing land. Thus, bringing more land into cultivation increased output. Second, the planting of the newly developed Amazon hybrid variety of cocoa increased productivity. As a result, cocoa prices have been depressed since the early 1980s because of overproduction arising from bringing more land into cultivation and the use of high-yielding varieties. It was therefore bad policy for Ghana to rehabilitate its industry and expand output under the SAP. Third, if foreign exchange is considered as a scarce commodity and growth is constrained by balance of payments, then it might be unwise to develop activities to expand the production of commodities like cocoa, with a low price and income elasticity of demand in the world markets. Low price elasticity of demand and supply can cause violent fluctuations in export earnings with supply shifts and cause the terms of trade to move adversely when output is increased. This problem has been behind political instability and the collapse of several governments in Ghana since 1966. The Nkrumah, Kofi Abrefa Busia, and Ignatius Kutu Acheampong regimes collapsed with military takeovers, due to shortfalls in cocoa incomes, as a result of price and income fluctuations.[47]

In the next phase of the SAP sequence, the cocoa sector was singled out for favors, even though the world market price for cocoa was declining because of overproduction. The policies, which were designed for the second phase of SAP, are described below.

ERP II Policies—Growth and Development Phase, 1987 to 1993

The Stabilization phase had been completed by 1986/87 with some degree of success. International agencies and donors commended Ghana for the achievements of the economic recovery program from 1983 to 1986. Fiscal and monetary stability had been restored and external arrears had been reduced. At the same time, it was recognized that the economy faced difficult structural problems. Public resources were not well managed. Banks were weak and inefficient. The rate of domestic savings and the level of private investment were strikingly low. These problems were not important as long as external finances were available from the World Bank. The time had come to move from the Stabilization phase of the ERP to the Growth and Development phase.

ERP II phase was described as the structural adjustment and development phase. The first phase of the structural adjustment program (SAP I) covered the period 1987—1988. The second phase, SAP II, covered the period 1989—1990. The third phase, SAP III, was to cover the period 1991—1993.

ERP II: GENERAL POLICIES

In the context of the general aim of laying a firm base for sustainable self-reliant growth and long-term balance-of-payments viability, the specific goals of ERP II are the following, as spelled out in the National Program for Economic Development: (1) to ensure sustainable growth at between five to 5.5 percent per year over the medium term; (2) to increase the level of public investment from about 10 percent of national income to about 25 percent by the end of this decade; (3) to increase domestic savings from about seven percent at the end of ERP I to about 15 percent by the end of the decade; (4) to further improve the management of resources in the public sector; and (5) to effectively mobilize the resources thus generated to improve the social and overall well-being of the people of Ghana, particularly the under-privileged, deprived, and vulnerable.[48]

The main objective of ERP I was trade and exchange rate reform. The reforms were continued under SAP I and II. In September 1986, auction exchange rate systems were introduced to help reach a market-determined exchange rate. On February 20, 1987, the official and auction rates were unified so that all foreign exchange transactions were conducted at the auction rate.[49]

In February 1988, plans were started to improve the exchange rate system by bringing the parallel market rate in line with the auction rate. To do this, the government authorized the establishment of private foreign exchange bureaus—a de facto recognition of the existence of the parallel market for currency dealings. In 1989, the foreign exchange bureau rate was about 40 percent above the auction rate. In 1990, there was improvement toward unification of the two rates but the discrepancy was still large. The rates will be unified only when demand for and supply of foreign exchange are equal.

ERP II: AGRICULTURAL SECTOR COCOA POLICIES

In 1987 the balance-of-payments position showed a surplus of US$140 million despite relatively lower cocoa prices. Export earnings, led by timber and gold, rose by 10 percent. Agricultural sector policies favored increased investments in timber production. Environmentalists would argue that the balance-of-payments surpluses were achieved by increased investment in capital equipment to cut the timber trees. As a result, the environment was damaged by high rates of deforestation. In this study, our focus is on cocoa not on timber.

ERP policies have favored the cocoa farmer. For the 1986—1987 main crops, the producer price was raised by 65 percent. This brought the farmers' share of the world price to 33 percent in 1987—1988. The farmers' share of the FOB price was increased to 46 percent in 1988—1989. These were some policies and incentive programs designed for the cocoa sector, with the ultimate goal to improve Ghana's foreign exchange earning position through the sales of increased cocoa output. In developing countries like Ghana, the level of foreign exchange earnings underpins the development process. It is clear that a lot of preparation went into the design of the SAP agricultural policies. It is not intended to evaluate all these policies. In this chapter, attempts will be made to evaluate the policies with regard to the cocoa sector, which is the most important sector in Ghanaian economy from the point of view of income and employment generation. This is why the ERP I and ERP II policies were designed to shift the internal terms of trade in favor of cocoa producers. Were these cocoa policies the right policies to undertake to achieve a faster rate of economic recovery and lay the foundations for viable growth in the future? This question will be discussed in the next section of this study.

PART IV: IMPACT OF THE SAP COCOA-SECTOR POLICIES ON GHANA'S GROWTH PERFORMANCE

It may be hypothesized that economic recovery in Ghana from 1983 to 1993 would have been much brighter had policy makers taken steps to diversify Ghana's agricultural export base rather than intensifying Ghana's dependence on cocoa production and exports in a market facing declining prices. This section presents analyses to support the above hypothesis. The study argues that the World Bank's inspired policy to use the cocoa sector as the "growth pole" to rehabilitate the Ghanaian economy was misplaced. We present arguments based on our knowledge of the world cocoa industry to explain this situation.

WERE POLICIES FAVORABLE TO COCOA SECTOR MISPLACED?

The policy makers and their consultants failed to critically analyze future trends in cocoa prices. A sensitive student of the international cocoa market would have seen that in the 1970s Brazil, Côte d'Ivoire, and Malaysia were poised to expand output both extensively by clearing new forests and intensively by the use of newly discovered hybrid varieties of cocoa. Cocoa producers all over the world began using the hybrid varieties of cocoa in the 1970s. Robert Evenson and Yuav Kislev undertook a survey and concluded that "increased productivity of agriculture is due to improved technology inputs. Many of the new techniques of production were created by agricultural research."[50] Research aimed at producing improved cocoa planting materials began in the 1930s in several countries including Ghana, Nigeria, and Trinidad. Most cocoa-producing countries developed their own breeding programs. R. A. Lass and G. A. R. Wood report that

> the national cocoa breeding programs tend to have different aims and cannot be of much assistance to each other. ...One of the side effects of the Ghana breeding program has been the common use of Upper Amazon types in other countries, resulting in new plantings with greater vigour than the previously used West African Amelondado and Trinitario material.[51]

It will be shown later that the use of the hybrid materials resulted in increased output, which can be attributed, in part, to increased productivity. In fact, these countries purposefully developed and implemented policies to expand cocoa output. As a result, the supply curve for cocoa began to shift to the right, after the normal gestation period. Because the demand curve did not shift that much, the prices of cocoa began to fall under the regime of oversupply. Cocoa prices have been registering record lows in real terms since 1983—1984.

It is against this backdrop that the World Bank policy to expand cocoa production to resuscitate the Ghanaian economy must be viewed. The point, discussed above, could be made clearer by reviewing the policies that were undertaken by Brazil, Côte d'Ivoire, Malaysia, and Indonesia to expand their output of cocoa production in the late 1970s.

BRAZIL'S COCOA POLICY IN THE 1970S

According to a study commissioned by the International Cocoa Organization, the Brazilian government played a major role in directing activities in the cocoa economy:

> The Brazilian policy for the cocoa sector during the 1970s was characterized by several objectives. The major ones were: to increase export earnings from cocoa beans and cocoa products; to define and create new production areas in the country; to promote the diversification of traditional cocoa-producing regions by introducing alternative agro-industrial activities; to develop the infrastructure of cocoa areas; and to raise the country's share of the world cocoa output. Within this framework, Comisau Executiva de Plano de Lavoura Cacaueira (CEPLAC) was given the responsibilities of implementing national production policies, assisting in the marketing area and participating in the decisions regarding the International Cocoa Agreement.[52]

The Brazilian decision to expand production was based on the assumption that the demand curve would shift to the right and also new markets would open up in traditionally low- or nonconsuming countries. Thus, high world equilibrium prices would be maintained to ensure continuous expansion of supply. This assumption turned out to be wrong because supply expanded too rapidly in other countries as well; whereas the demand curve did not shift that fast to the right.

Brazil's policy of expanded cocoa production in the 1970s was so successful that the policy was reversed in 1981. How was this achieved? The role of the state was very important in this regard. In the history of cocoa production in Brazil, two semigovernmental institutions were established to guide farmers to increase output via the provision of extension services, credit, rural infrastructure, and marketing services: (1) Institute de Cacau da Bahia (ICB) was established in 1931; and (2) in 1957 CEPLAC was established and given a bigger mandate than the ICB.

Two more programs were established in the 1970s in order to implement government policies. In 1971, the Land Redistribution Program (PROTERRA) was established within CEPLAC. CEPLAC was given the mandate to supervise all credit given to farmers for cocoa production through the Banco do Brasil. In 1976, the Centro de Pesquisa da Cacau (PROCACAU) program was established with the aim of expanding production of cocoa up to 1985. It is the activities of the PROCACAU program and the results it achieved that concern us here.

The PROCACAU program was established under the assumption that cocoa production in West Africa, especially Ghana, would remain stagnant. Given the fact that demand was rising, Brazil could expand its output and benefit from the prevailing high prices. Brazil, however, underestimated Côte d'Ivoire's potential to increase output. The initial target of the PROCACAU program was to increase cocoa plantings by 300,000 hectares. It was estimated that by 1990 when the new trees were fully productive, output would reach 700,000 tons, compared with fewer than 200,000 in 1975.

According to the ICCO study, "the results achieved during the first five years of the program were impressive. Production grew by 41% in relation to the six-year average of the period prior to the program, while average yields rose by more than 30%. Average national cocoa earnings increased by more than US$500 million during the same period."[53]

By 1981, it was clear that the PROCACAU program needed revision. Other countries, notably Côte d'Ivoire, Malaysia, and Indonesia, had expanded output. As a result, prices began to decline due to overproduction. Second, domestic costs of cocoa production had increased, including increased cost of credit. As a result only 66 percent of the initial target, set in 1976, was achieved at the end of the project in 1985.

As shown in Table 3.2, Cote d'Ivoire, Indonesia, and Malaysia had the best potential to expand cocoa output. The spectacular increases in output were achieved in part due to high productivity as a result of the use of hybrid varieties of cocoa.

Table 3.2
Fastest Cocoa Growing Countries: 1970—1988

Production in 1,000s of tons	Year					
	1970-71	1974-75	1980-81	1984-85	1987-88	1988-98
Côte d'Ivoire	180	242	403	565	665	850
Brazil	182	273	349	412	402	324
Malaysia	4	13	43	93	222	243
Indonesia	1	2	12	31	58	93

Source: ICCO (data).

CÔTE D'IVOIRE'S COCOA POLICY IN THE 1970S

Now we turn to an explanation of the institutional changes and price incentives used by Côte d'Ivoire to expand output in response to high prices in the 1970s. Côte d'Ivoire was able to expand cocoa output from 180,000 tons in 1970 to 849,000 tons in 1988/89 due, in part, to the work of Societe d'Assistance Technique pour la Modernisation de l'Agriculture en Cted'Ivoire (SATMACI). SATMACI made the hybrid high-yielding variety of cocoa available to cocoa farmers through the extension services. SATMACI launched a program to expand cocoa output in 1971. By 1979, 138,000 hectares of new farms had been created, and as a result output doubled in 10 years.[54] In 1977—1978 producer prices were increased from 180 francs per kilo to 250. This incentive given to farmers allowed them to expand their cocoa farms. As a result, the area planted with hybrid farms expanded in five years from 221,000 hectares in 1977—1978 to 544,000 hectares in 1982—1983. By 1992—1993 the area planted with hybrid cocoa had increased 751,000 hectares (see Table 3.3). This represented over one-half of the total area planted with cocoa in Côte d'Ivoire. Given the fact that hybrid trees produce yields three times that of normal cocoa trees, it is clear that productivity increases accounted for a large part of the increased output.

Côte d'Ivoire, like Brazil, decided to expand cocoa production because Ghana's output had been decreasing over the years. This was part of the policies outlined in the Five-Year Development Plan of 1976—1980.[55] The policy was so successful that in 1978, Côte d'Ivoire became the leading producer of cocoa in the world. Plans were made to increase output further in the 1981—1985 Five-Year Development Plan. The objective was to increase cocoa production from 320,000 tons in 1980 to 450,000 tons by 1985 and to 500,000 tons in 1990. This target was surpassed.[56]

The cocoa expansion program undertaken by SATMACI since 1971 outstripped planners' expectations. In the 1981 to 1985 Five Year Development Plan, attempts were made to slow down the growth rate in output and produce 500,000 in 1990 but this could not be done. Farmers continued to plant the hybrid cocoa. The revolution in cocoa production in Côte d'Ivoire was achieved because optimal pricing policies were undertaken to provide incentives to producers and at the same time land tenure policies were changed to make land easily available to prospective cocoa farmers, especially the Mossi migrant farmers: *La terre appartient à celui qui la travaille.* This law, which says that the land belongs to the one who tills it, created, to some extent, a land tenure reform in Côte d'Ivoire. The modalities of this law have yet to be worked out. The Mossi, who are from Burkina Faso, are regarded as "strangers" and are forced to pay rent by some Ivorian chiefs.

THE IVORIAN MIRACLE IN COCOA EXPANSION

Cocoa production in West Africa has been dependent on migrant labor. Polly Hill, an anthropologist, proved this hypoth-

Table 3.3

Evolution of Land Areas Planted with Traditional and Hybrid Cocoa in Major Producing Countries, 1970—1971 to 1982—1983

	1970-71	71-72	72-73	73-74	74-75	75-76	76-77	77-78	78-79	79-80	80-81	81-82	82-83
Traditional													
Brazil	407	406	404	402	400	398	396	394	392	390	388	386	384
Ghana	1,286	1,285	1,280	1,275	1,249	1,218	1,183	1,145	1,107	1,067	1,028	991	904
Côte d'Ivoire	632	656	677	693	704	751	780	816	826	836	844	851	855
Hybrid													
Brazil	11	14	21	30	45	60	80	109	147	189	242	283	305
Ghana	3	3	5	9	16	28	48	69	90	113	135	159	151
Indonesia	12	13	14	15	16	18	20	24	27	32	37	43	49
Côte d'Ivoire	2	5	13	25	42	84	137	221	278	347	415	487	544
Malaysia	7	12	18	23	29	35	41	49	61	89	124	159	209
Total													
Brazil	418	420	425	432	445	458	476	503	539	579	630	669	689
Ghana	1,289	1,288	1,285	1,284	1,265	1,246	1,231	1,214	1,197	1,180	1,163	1,150	1,055
Indonesia	12	13	14	15	16	18	20	24	27	32	37	43	49
Côte d'Ivoire	634	661	690	718	746	835	917	1037	1104	1183	1259	1338	1399
Malaysia	7	12	18	23	29	35	41	49	61	89	124	159	209

Source: ICCO Quarterly Bulletin of Cocoa Statistics (several issues).

esis empirically in her classic study on the system of cocoa farming in Ghana.[57] These migrants, mostly from Burkina Faso, provided the cheap labor, which helped Ghana to develop its cocoa industry. Ghana was the leading producer of cocoa in the world from 1911 until 1978. From the turn of the century until the 1960s, economic activity was more buoyant and real wages were higher in Ghana than in neighboring Côte d'Ivoire. As a result, the migrants from Sahelian regions preferred to come to Ghana rather than go to the Côte d'Ivoire. By 1970, the migrants preferred to go to Côte d'Ivoire where wage levels had risen relative to wage levels in Ghana due to the overvaluation of Ghanaian currency. Second, in 1969, Ghana expelled these migrants. Third, the new Ivorian law, making it possible for the one who tills the land to claim its fruits, made migration to Côte d'Ivoire much more attractive. These are some of the institutional reasons that created a new production culture and made increased cocoa production in Côte d'Ivoire possible and enabled it to become the leading world producer.

MALAYSIAN AND INDONESIAN COCOA POLICIES IN THE 1970s

High cocoa prices in the 1970s, together with the breeding and use of the Amazon hybrid variety, have made cocoa production attractive in Malaysia and Indonesia. In Malaysia, several attempts had been made to produce cocoa in the twentieth century but without much success until the 1970s. Production rose from 7,000 tons in 1970 to 344,000 tons in 1987. In Indonesia, cocoa production was insignificant until the hybrid variety came on the scene. Between 1980—1981 and 1988—1989 cocoa output increased from 12,000 tons to 93,000 tons respectively (see Table 3.2).

Production increases in Malaysia and Indonesia have been spectacular because the yields per hectare are relatively higher compared with the average yield in other countries. The reason is that Malaysian and Indonesian farms are relatively new, post-1970. All the tree stock is of the Amazon hybrid variety. Thus Malaysia and Indonesia are the beneficiaries of scientific selection and development of a high yielding cocoa tree stock. Second, Malaysia has been favored by good local climate and soil. Third, Malaysia and Indonesia are entering a market where a new product (Amazon hybrid) is suitable for the plantation system of production as opposed to traditional or "peasant" forms of production. It is assumed that under the plantation system of production, scientific farming practices, including application of fertilizers, are implemented properly to ensure optimal yields from the farm. In Malaysia, three quarters of production is from estates. This may account for the high yields registered on Malaysian farms.

F. Ruf has argued that it is possible that Indonesia can become the world's biggest producer in a few years' time.[58] Small families, who find current cocoa prices attractive, produce more than two-thirds of Indonesia's output. There are many of these farmers around. At the same time there is plenty of land available. Indonesia produced about 200,000 tons of cocoa in 1992—1993 compared with 93,000 tons in 1988—1989. Currently, Indonesia is the fifth largest cocoa producer in the world.

As regards future prospects, if such a boom was limited only by disappearance of the Indonesian forest, all other producers might as well abandon cocoa, as this tropical giant is composed of 180,000 km² under a humid tropical climate, 100,000 km² of which are still officially under forest. Million of families are still ready to clear them.[59]

Cocoa production and expansion in Malaysia and Indonesia, as in Côte d'Ivoire and Brazil, have been aided by government policies. The governments have funded research and development, have enforced bean grading standards, and have taken steps to regulate the markets.[60]

The development of the Amazon hybrid variety of cocoa and its use in the 1970s, together with positive government policies in Brazil, Côte d'Ivoire, Indonesia, and Malaysia, have all contributed to create a revolution on the supply side of the world cocoa industry since 1970. The supply curve has been shifting to the right. The demand curve, however, has not shifted that much. What are the implications of these shifts in the demand and supply schedules on world cocoa prices? What are the optimal policies available to an old cocoa-producing country? What should this country do if it has a high percentage of "nonhybrid" stocks of cocoa trees? The main purpose of this study is to provide insights and answers to some of these questions, as well as show that the World Bank made a mistake with regard to SAP cocoa policies in Ghana. To do this, we must first examine the impact of production decisions on cocoa prices in the 1980s and 1990s.

COCOA: REVOLUTIONARY EXPANSION IN THE 1970S AND PRICE TRENDS IN THE 1980S AND 1990S

As discussed before, the record of high prices of cocoa registered in the 1970s provided an incentive for farmers, at times with government support, to increase plantings in the 1970s and early 1980s. This was followed by increased output, which in turn led to the price downturn in the 1980s and 1990s. This downturn in prices was written on the wall for all market analysts to see for the following reasons:

1. Farmers all over the world began new plantings with the Amazon hybrid variety.
2. This Amazon hybrid variety has a potential yield of two or three times that of the traditional cocoa varieties.
3. Governments in several cocoa-producing countries undertook policies to increase output. As a result, the world supply curve of cocoa shifted to the right. It could be

hypothesized that the shift of the supply curve represented the biggest structural change in the history of the world cocoa industry.

Table 3.3 shows the evolution of land areas planted with traditional hybrid varieties in the major producing countries. In 1970, very little or no hybrid cocoa was planted by the major producers. In late 1980s, over one half of cocoa land areas in Brazil and Côte d'Ivoire had been farmed with the Amazon hybrid plant. In Malaysia and Indonesia, only the Amazon hybrid variety has been used in developing the cocoa industry. The cocoa industry in these countries began practically in the 1970s. In Ghana, where cocoa farming lands have been used up, old farms have been rehabilitated, to a large extent, with the use of hybrid varieties. As acreages of old farms fall, hybrid farm acreages rise. The use of hybrid varieties has been slow relative to the other countries.

As explained above, the Brazilian government began to take steps in 1981 to control the expansion of cocoa production. In the case of Côte d'Ivoire, it was pointed out that the government was not able to control the expansion of output, which began in the 1970s. It seems, however, that output has begun to stabilize since 1989. Indonesia and Malaysia show an increased upward trend. Ghana shows a noticeable upward trend in 1988 and 1989. Output seems to have taken a downward trend since 1989.

Given the "yield time" function of a hybrid variety for Malaysia and Côte d'Ivoire, it may be assumed that the shift in the supply curve represents a structural change that will ensure high output of cocoa for 20 to 30 years. Prices will therefore remain low for a long time, discounting short-term price instability, until the demand schedule shifts to the right to pull up the equilibrium prices, and/or policy changes slow down shifts in the supply curve to the right.

It is against this backdrop that we must evaluate the performance of cocoa sector policies in Ghana under the World Bank/IMF-sponsored structural adjustment programs.

POLICY PERFORMANCE REVIEW—COCOA-SECTOR POLICIES

Structural changes in the cocoa industry in the 1970s should have indicated to policy makers that international prices for cocoa would be very low by the 1990s. It was clear that supply was going to outstrip demand in the near future. It is now clear that low cocoa prices in the world markets today are not short-term phenomena. During the 1930s depression when prices collapsed, they were followed by output declines and prices rebounded after three years. The situation is now different. See Alfred Maizels for a full analysis of the factors behind this phenomenon.[61] The commodity price collapse of the 1980s continued into the 1990s, yet output has not declined. In fact, it has increased. In the case of cocoa, the increase in output is clearly due to the use of the hybrid variety. Kofi and Fry have characterized this as the "new commodity problem."[62] Thus, the Ghana SAP policy makers have made a serious mistake because they looked only at one side of the equation. They used the DRC results, assuming that the estimates were correct, to make a policy. Then they ignored the long-run downward trends in cocoa prices, due to the new commodity problem, which the market fundamentals were pointing at. Why would policy makers decide to allocate more resources to prop up a waning cocoa industry, which then exports into a market where cocoa prices are declining? If the objective of cocoa sector policy was to increase foreign exchange earnings, then it has failed miserably.

The Ghana cocoa industry was in decline in the 1970s because of the overvaluation of the local currency, which made investment in cocoa production unattractive to farmers. Second, as explained above, Ghana had lost to Côte d'Ivoire the source of cheap labor, which had come from Burkina Faso. Other sources of labor for the cocoa industry had dried up. For example, cheap peasant family labor is no longer readily available, because the children now go to school and prefer nonfarm jobs. In short, urbanization and exogenous forces had destroyed the "culture of cocoa production" in Ghana. Thus, there were exogenous and endogenous reasons why the Ghana cocoa industry was in decline other than exchange-rate distortions. Under these conditions, it is argued that it was not economically sound to save the declining cocoa industry in Ghana.

The glaring fact that Ghana has lost its comparative advantage to producers like Malaysia and Indonesia did not bother the policy makers. The controversial low DRC estimates for tree crops in Ghana, especially for cocoa, blinded the policy makers to the prospects for world cocoa prices in the future before they made the decision to increase investments in cocoa production in Ghana.

The local farmers knew better, and they have proved that the DRC measures were wrong because they were getting higher returns for crops competing with cocoa for their labor and capital. As we have pointed out, these farmers have been cutting down cocoa trees and have been using the land to produce other crops. This policy mistake has cost Ghana dearly. This chapter does not attempt to quantify the cost of the policy mistake. We may hypothesize that this policy had made the economic recovery time period longer than necessary. Next, we provide further evidence for this hypothesis. It is also necessary to show that the policy mistake described above was a serious one.

WHY SUPPORT AN INDUSTRY WHOSE GOLDEN AGE HAS PASSED?

The rapid expansion of cocoa production and trade in the world, from the turn of the century until the mid-1960s, was mainly the result of the rapid growth of production in Ghana. In 1890, Ghana exported 80 pounds of cocoa beans. In 1911, Ghana exported 40,000 tons of cocoa beans and became the major exporter of cocoa in the world, surpassing Brazil in output. In 1922—1923, Ghana exported over 200,000 tons of cocoa. This output represented 44 percent of cocoa in the world market. In 1964—1965, Ghana produced 566,000 tons of cocoa. This output was about one-third of world production. The British economic historian Allan McPhee had characterized commodity production and trade in West Africa in the 1960s as an economic revolution.[63]

Cocoa accounted for over three-quarters of Ghana's foreign exchange earnings from the 1920s until the mid-1970s when the cocoa industry began to falter. From the peak in 1964—1965, production declined to 394,000 tons in 1976, and then dropped to 179,000 tons in 1983. The reason for the decreased production is not difficult to find. Since the statutory Cocoa Marketing Board was set up in the 1947—1948 season, farmers had been taxed progressively until they protested by not investing in cocoa production. From the turn of the century until the 1950s, farmers received 80 percent of the world price.[64] In the 1970s, Ghanaian farmers were receiving about 26 percent of the world cocoa prices. Ghana faced economic crises from the mid-1960s onward because of the progressive collapse of the cocoa economy. From 1979 to 1982 Ghana's terms of trade deteriorated by about 12 percent per year. The drought of 1981 to 1983 severely reduced agricultural production. In 1981, the military overthrew the democratically elected government. In 1983, Ghana agreed to accept help from the Bretton Woods institutions and an SAP was designed and implemented.

It has been pointed out that agriculture is still the dominant sector in the Ghanaian economy, representing 50 percent of GDP and employing over 70 percent of the labor force. Agriculture is the leading sector in the Ghanaian economy from the point of view of employment creation and foreign exchange income, which underpins the development process. Thus to turn the Ghana economy around, agricultural policy must be taken seriously.

WHAT TYPE OF AGRICULTURAL POLICY HAS GHANA PURSUED UNDER THE SAP?

Under the conditions described above, should Ghana have emphasized cocoa production? Should Ghana have made cocoa production the leading sector for economic recovery? The answers are no. Given the evolving structure of the world cocoa economy, it was clear that prices were going to fall in the 1980s, 1990s, and perhaps beyond. The shift of supply schedules to the right was not going to be matched by shifts of the demand curve to the right. The empirical evidence shows that the above description of probable price behavior was what happened.

The world cocoa prices started to fall in the early 1980s, just as the SAP's economic recovery program was implemented in 1983. Prices have not recovered—falling more than 50 percent since 1986. As world prices fell steeply, Ghana's output rose by about 100,000 tons in 1988—1989. The supply response in agriculture during the SAP period was disappointing, raising serious doubts about the usefulness of the SAP exercise. It was a mistake to base the economic recovery effort on rehabilitating the cocoa sector.

Table 3.4 shows export earnings of major cocoa producers from 1983 to 1990. The data seem to support the concern

Table 3.4

Value (in 100s of dollars) and Production Volume (tons) of Cocoa Beans by Major Producing Countries: 1983 to 1990

	1983	1984	1985	1986	1987	1988	1989	1990
Value								
Brazil	554,588	661,734	778,856	630,612	584,297	518,729	333,591	340,761
Cameroon	151,070	184,326	160,951	213,360	237,310	219,601	181,348	168,978
Ghana	268,600	383,356	399,264	497,984	530,189	470,035	413,251	393,781
Côte d'Ivoire	525,656	1,073,854	1,093,390	1,211,877	1,222,400	840,861	1,151,492	952,682
Malaysia	120,019	195,577	218,564	248,710	340,750	340,109	260,045	269,059
Nigeria	361,112	294,719	268,045	320,914	195,900	346,679	144,065	145,965
Volume								
Brazil	360	330	431	459	329	392	393	355
Cameroon	109	121	119	123	133	129	126	99
Ghana	168	167	194	226	205	247	300	295

of many development economists: that the expansion of exports, by many producers, at the same time, is likely to decrease their export revenues and real incomes. The empirical evidence shows that this is what has happened in the case of cocoa exporters. For example, Côte d'Ivoire expanded cocoa production from 555,000 tons in 1985 to 849,000 tons in 1988, an increase of over 30 percent, and current incomes fell from $1,093,390 to $840,861, a decrease of over 20 percent in revenues. In the case of Ghana, output increased from 205,000 tons in 1987 to 300,000 in 1989, and current incomes decreased from $530,189 to $413,251. We can also note from Table 3.4 that, in the case of Ghana, output increased progressively from 1987 to 1990 and at the same time, current incomes followed a downward trend. This history has been repeated several times. For example, overproduction in the 1964—1965 cocoa crop year resulted in record low prices. Although exports increased, revenues fell drastically. To solve this problem, an International Cocoa Agreement was ratified in 1963.[65] In an econometric simulation exercise, Kofi showed that "had producers and consumers ratified the 1963 Draft Agreement for three years or more, producing countries would have been better off in terms of earnings by about $185 million, net of costs of running the stabilization scheme."[66] The violent fluctuations in prices and incomes of agricultural products have caused political instabilities in monoeconomies, like Ghana.[67]

The empirical data presented, which show an inverse relationship between output expansion and income, confirm what economic theory teaches us. The central problem faced by agricultural commodity exporters is that world demand for this export is both income-inelastic and price-inelastic. As a result, growth in real incomes in the importing countries brings in relatively little growth in consumption. Whereas expansion of supplies results in lower prices and lower export earnings, because of low elasticity. Thus increasing supply tends to be self-defeating. Another problem is that the low price elasticities of demand, together with low short-term price elasticities of supply for agricultural commodities, result in violent short-term fluctuations in world prices.

Table 3.5 shows the long-run and short-run income and price elasticities of demand, which are less than one. Table 3.6 shows the long-run elasticities of supply. Given the low income and price elasticities of demand shown in Table 3.6, the spectacular increases in cocoa supply in the 1980s resulted in low cocoa prices and low producer revenues.

M. Godfrey has demonstrated this point using African cocoa and coffee data. He found that an increase of 1 percent in cocoa exports led to a 2.17 percent fall in world prices.[68] For coffee, a 1 percent increase in exports led to a 1.14 percent decline in world prices. Godfrey concluded that it is mistake for SAP policy makers to suggest export expansion to African commodity producers. Rather, African governments should diversify their commodity export base and produce commodities with a high income elasticity of demand. Ghana should have been given such policy advice at the time when the Economic Recovery Program was implemented in 1983.

BANK SUPPORT FOR AGRICULTURAL EXPORTS—A QUERY

The fears of the "export pessimists" are justified in the case of Ghana's experience. Arvind Panagariya and Maurice Schiff report that "export pessimists" have raised this issue, in the context of World Bank-supported adjustment policies in Africa, in the German parliament. As a result, a query was sent to the chief economist of the World Bank for Africa. The query read as follows:

> In the framework of structural adjustment programs, many African countries endeavor to increase their exports of agricultural products. An increased supply of goods may soon lead to

Table 3.5
Estimated Demand Elasticity Coefficients

	Types of Models	Standard Error	Price Short-Run	Price Long-Run	Income Short-Run	Income Long-Run
Western Europe						
France	Log	4.4	-0.093	-0.168 ***	0.504	0.908**
Germany	Log	6.8	-0.120	-0.292***	0.231	0.561*
United Kingdom	Log	6.1	-0.302	-0.436***	0.205	0.296**
USSR	Lin	18.6	ns	ns	0.257	0.427
Eastern Europe	^Log	11.4	ns	ns	0.782	0.553**
America/Canada/	Log	8.6	-0.183	-0.279	0.210	0.321
United States	Log	8.3	-0.199	-0.295***	0.426	0.632***
Middle East/ Asia/Oceania/Japan	Log	9.4	-0.257	-0.413***	0.329	0.529**
World Models						
Conventional Global Model	Log	2.6	-0.103	-0.199***	0.255	0.493***
Different model with price						
Level effects	^ Log (S)	2.8	-0.091***	—	-.647***	

Source: ICCO

Notes:

Log = Log Linear

Lin = Linear

^ Log = Log difference model (i.e., annual change in value on the logarithmic scale

(S) = Static; the regression model does not include the lagged dependent variable.

* = significant at 5 per cent (p<0.05)

** = significant at 1 percent (p<0.01)

*** = significant at o.1 percent (p<0.001)

Table 3.6
Estimated Long-Run Supply Elasticities for Cocoa

	Behrman (1946-64)	Akiyama & Duncan (1965-80)	Groenendaal & Vingerhoets (1955-82)
Cameroon	1.81	0.59	0.73
Côte d'Ivoire	0.80	0.59	0.82
Ghana	0.71	0.13	0.38
Nigeria	0.45	0.11	0.47
Brazil	0.95	0.54	0.29
Ecuador	0.28	0.54	——-
Dominican Republic	0.15	a	
Venezuela	0.38	a	0.28
Other Latin America & Caribbean	——-	a	——-
Papua New Guinea	——-	0.54	——-
Rest of the World	——-	0.21	0.50b
World Average	——-	0.42	0.54

Source: Alfred Maizels, Robert Bacon, and George Mavrotas, "The Potential for Supply Management of Commodities Exported by Developing Countries: The Case of Cocoa" (Mimeo) UNI/WIDER May 1992.
Notes:
a) Included in "Rest of World'
b) Asia and Oceania

> price declines of the correspondent products, so that additional revenue may not be realized. How does the World Bank justify its correspondent policy advice? What can be done to avoid the negative results?[69]

This study has advanced arguments to support the questions raised in the German parliament. Ghana has not benefited from the SAP cocoa-sector policies. The expected rehabilitation of the cocoa industry has not been successful. Supply response in agriculture has been low and cocoa export earnings have been falling.

It has been argued that the World Bank gave bad policy advice to Ghana to expand cocoa production at a time when other producers were expanding production rapidly. Ghana has not gained much from this policy advice. It is not clear what the Bank can do to correct this mistake and its impact on the

Ghanaian economy. World Bank economists continue to write papers to show that SAP was beneficial to Ghana.[70] Other Bank economists seem to express doubts about the success of the SAP.[71]

WORLD BANK RESPONSE TO THE GERMAN QUERY

A few studies have been undertaken by World Bank economists to evaluate the impact of structural adjustment cocoa policies on adjusting countries. Two studies on the subject have been produced: one by Coleman, Akiyama, and Varangis;[72] and one by Trivedi and Akiyama.[73] Coleman et al. concluded from their quantitative simulation analyses that

> the benefits of Ghana from [the] adjustment program were large. Had Ghana not implemented the program, its production would have been almost one half of what it actually was in 1989-90. Producers' welfare (measured as producer surplus) would have been substantially lower in the absence of the program and the government's budget deficit would have been at an unsustainable level.[74]

This conclusion was arrived at from simulation exercises under the counterfactual assumption that Ghana and Nigeria did not undertake any policy reforms to redress price distortions in their economy. It was assumed, in the case of Ghana, that the currency overvaluation of 1972 to 1983 was maintained throughout the rest of the 1980s. We do not think that the above assumption was a realistic one. The PNDC seized power to solve an economic crisis brought about by exchange rate distortion and overvaluation of the currency.

The relevant question to answer is this: Has the adjustment program resolved the crisis? The studies' authors do not ask this question. However, they claim that without the SAP, the 1989—1990 world cocoa prices in real terms would have been about 45 percent lower than they were in the early 1980s, compared with an actual decline of 55 percent. They also argue that SAP policies in Ghana and Nigeria had a negative effect on other countries but not adopting the policies would have been economically irrational. The study concludes that the SAP was on balance good for Ghana. This conclusion may be challenged because some of the assumptions, which were made for the simulation exercises, were unrealistic. For example, it was assumed that "the currency over-valuation of 1982—1983 was maintained through the rest of the 1980s. This assumption is unrealistic. Some countries have undertaken currency reforms on their own without World Bank assistance, including Nigeria. Japan did this exercise during the early period of the Meiji Reformation. It was called the 'Matsukata deflation.'"[75] Thus some countries can undertake policy measures to correct for domestic price distortions and exchange rate misalignment.

The study by Panagariya and Schiff examines, in part, some of the questions we have raised in this chapter. Some of the questions include the following: What is the likelihood that export expansion, resulting from better and fuller use of resources, can lead to a decline in real incomes and export revenues in African and non-African countries? For which commodities is this outcome plausible? What are the key parameters determining the impact of export expansion on the terms of trade, export earnings, and real incomes? Empirically, how important is the issue of interdependence? For instance, while considering a further tax reduction on cocoa, should Ghana pay attention to policy changes in Côte d'Ivoire and Malaysia? In which commodities, if any, does interdependence play an important role?[76]

These questions are realistic and, in fact, constitute some of the bases for the development of oligopoly theory. In the cocoa industry, the producers are not so many as to justify regarding each of them as having a negligible effect on prices. Panagariya and Schiff concluded their study by giving advice to policy makers who give advice to cocoa-producing countries: "Our findings so far seem to suggest that in providing policy advice and support of investment projects in the case of commodities such as cocoa, the donor community should take into account the effects on and possible reactions of the other producing countries."[77]

This advice raises a question: Was the agricultural-sector policy designed properly in order to achieve positive economic payoff? To answer this question, it will be necessary to examine how prices are determined in the cocoa industry.

EMPIRICAL ANALYSES OF PRICE DETERMINATION IN THE COCOA MARKET

The designers of the Ghanaian SAP failed to heed the advice of Panagariya and Schiff. They failed to look into problems of uncertainty and the implications of the strategic interactions of producers in making production and marketing decisions and their influence on world prices. It is surprising that the planners of the Ghanaian SAP failed to examine this. If the policy makers had paid closer attention to cocoa price trends on the futures market, they would have designed a better agricultural-sector policy.

First, we will examine how cocoa prices are determined in the real world. We will present empirical evidence on the performance of the price determination institutions. Next, we will explain why the World Bank consultants' decision-making model was unrealistic and why they gave bad policy advice. Their model was unrealistic because it was not based on the economics of uncertainty.

Futures markets are important institutions for determining prices of commodities. For example, the prices of the majority of agricultural commodities produced in the United States are determined on organized futures markets. It has been shown that well-established and properly regulated futures markets are superior to cash markets in price determination because they provide central market prices established in open competitive markets.

Despite the positive attributes discussed above, futures markets at times fail to determine prices optimally, especially during periods of prolonged excess supply. For example, the cocoa industry experienced a "market failure" in 1964—1965. The futures markets' prices did not respond to market signals, the fundamentals of demand and supply during this period.[78] The market failure led to disorderly marketing of cocoa by producers, which, in turn, led to further declines in world cocoa prices. It was recorded that some major producers sold tons of cocoa for as low as 9 cents per pound in 1965 compared with a record high of 72 cents a pound in 1954.[79] Middlemen and chocolate manufacturers stand to benefit when excess supplies create low prices under a market failure because their bargaining power increases in price negotiations in the actual market. Consumer bargaining power increases under a regime of market failure, because producers cannot store cocoa beans in the tropics for too long.

The problem with stocks management is a serious one for producers. In the 1960s, the president of Ghana tried to build storage silos to store cocoa beans so as to regulate sales. The silos were built but they have not been tested and used. In 1988—1989, Côte d'Ivoire experienced the same problem Ghana had in 1964—1965. After the bumper crop year of 1988—1989, Côte d'Ivoire had difficulty in selling the output systematically. A market observer explained the chaotic marketing situation as follows:

> The long rumored block sales deal with French company Sucres et Dentrees has now been confirmed by both sides and will involve the immediate sale of 200,000 tonnes on to "end users" including the Soviet Union. A further 200,000 tonnes is apparently to be stored for "two years" in Europe while an additional block sale is rumored to have been sold recently. The sales arrangement provides little relief for the cocoa market and arguably only a short-term solution to the financing problems of

Côte d'Ivoire. The uncertainty that preceded the sales deal threw the local purchasing apparatus into chaos during the fourth quarter of 1988.[80]

Cocoa producers do not receive remunerative incomes under conditions forcing them to engage in block sales. Unanticipated shortfalls in cocoa incomes generally create economic hardships in monoeconomies like Ghana and Côte d'Ivoire. In the case of Ghana, the economic hardships arising from the 1964—1965 market failure made it possible for the Ghanaian military to overthrow the Nkrumah regime in 1966.

Given the above analytical market-structure backdrop, it may be argued that it was unwise for the Ghanaian government and the Bank advisers to use the cocoa sector as the "growth pole" to pull the economy out of economic crisis. If the Ghana cocoa sector had responded positively to the correction of price distortions brought about by exchange-rate misalignment, and also responded positively to the "incentive package" and had achieved 1964—1965 levels of output, the industry would have faced a more serious market failure problem than it faces now. The market was already saturated even with the low levels of Ghana's output in the 1980s and 1990s. Thus, producer incomes would have been much lower if Ghana had been able to expand its output appreciably during the SAP period, 1983 to 1994.

Second, given the historical market-structure analyses presented above, we fail to understand why the policy makers of the Ghanaian SAP did not review seriously the price trends revealed on the cocoa futures markets in London and New York and their implications for policy reform in the agricultural sector. We pointed out earlier that if the consultants had done this, they would have suggested a different agricultural sector policy. It is important to explain this point further by using demand and supply expectations in the cocoa market between 1970 and 1980 together with futures market theory.

A Model for a Realistic Cocoa Sector Policy

"Price formation on futures markets at any point in time is the result of expert appraisal of past conditions, currently available information, and expectations on supply and demand."[81] This quotation shows us how prices are formed on the futures market. Armed with this fact, we can predict price trends by analyzing and forming realistic opinions about demand and supply expectations. The demand curve does not shift that much in the short run in the cocoa industry. Thus a good analysis of supply expectations will give us a good prediction of cocoa stock expectations and therefore the probable direction of price trends. In this study we focused on analyzing supply expectations in the cocoa market from 1970 onward. We concluded that the cocoa industry was poised for a big structural change in production. As a result of technical progress (plant breeding), high-yielding varieties were developed. Cocoa-producing countries began planting these high-yielding varieties from 1970 onward. Thus we were able to form a realistic opinion on supply conditions in the 1980s and 1990s. This then allowed us to conclude that the cocoa industry would experience a long-run downward trend in prices in the 1980s and 1990s. Furthermore, market structure analyses showed us that Ghana would not benefit from increased output of cocoa. We concluded that Ghana would earn less, not more, foreign exchange. We therefore provided evidence to support the hypothesis that it was unwise to base the recovery of the Ghanaian economy on resuscitating the cocoa industry. The reason is that if the cocoa supply response had been strong and output had increased, this would have resulted in lower prices and incomes for Ghana. It seems that the Bank consultants, who designed the cocoa-sector policy, were not students of the cocoa industry. If they were active students of the world cocoa economy, they would have advised against the policy or the strategy to rehabilitate the cocoa industry in order to earn increased foreign exchange to finance the economic recovery exercise. Thus, the DRC exercise was unnecessary. Ghana was led into a blind alley.

Next, we present the empirical evidence to show that the cocoa-sector policy was unsound by looking at what actually happened in the cocoa market from 1980 to 1990.

INCOME AND TERMS OF TRADE LOSSES TO COCOA PRODUCERS, 1980 TO 1990

The analyses carried out so far prompt us to ask the following question: Was the SAP cocoa-sector policy advice sound? We provide the empirical evidence and then show that the theoretical foundation of the policy had a flaw in it. The empirical evidence indicates that the policy advice was unsound. Cocoa, coffee, and tea prices declined in the ten years from 1980 to 1990. Cocoa prices declined by over 50 percent from 1986 to 1990. Maizels, Bacon, and Mavrotas[82] have estimated by way of simulation exercises the cumulative terms of trade loss to producers of world tropical beverages (cocoa, coffee, and tea) from 1980 to 1990. They show this loss to be over US$55 billion. This is more than three times the value of total export sales in 1980. Cocoa export earnings have been affected adversely by the fall in prices. Maizels reported that "compared with the position in 1980, export earnings were, on average, US$940 million a year lower during the succeeding decade as a result of the decline in prices, the reduced amount of earnings representing 25% of the 1980 level. Over the decade 1981 to 1990 as a whole the cumulative loss on this account (US$9.4 billion) being 2½ times the 1980 level."[83]

The foreign exchange and the terms of trade loss increased in the later half of the 1980s compared to the first half. This was due to increased supplies of cocoa on the world market as a result of bumper crop years of 1987—1988 and 1988—

1989, especially in Côte d'Ivoire. Technical progress (the use of high-yield varieties) has brought about a "scissor crisis." Maizels continued:

> As a result of this scissor squeeze, real cocoa prices (in terms of manufacturers prices) fell off sharply, causing a marked deterioration in the real foreign exchange earnings of cocoa-exporting countries. While the terms of trade effect over the period 1981—1985 had been an annual average loss of $0.10 billion (some 3% of the 1980 export value), the annual rate of loss increased in 1986—1988 to $1.86 (49%) of 1980 exports), and increased further in 1989—1990 to 3.15 billion (84% of 1980 exports).[84]

Given the conditions described above, it was clear that the objectives of the Ghanaian SAP agricultural sector policy designed to increase cocoa foreign exchange earnings were not being met in the market. Foreign exchange and terms of trade losses were increasing though the volume of exports increases, the price of purchasing decreases in the decade under study (1980 to 1990). If the DRC ratios had been updated from time to time, the policy makers would have changed the policy. As cocoa prices and earnings fell, the DRC ratios would have increased. Proper application of the DRC methodology requires that the ratios be updated and policies drawn from the ratios accordingly.

Maizels draws a conclusion from his study, which goes against the objectives of the cocoa sector policy of the Ghanaian SAP exercise:

> These losses have been particularly serious to those countries which are heavily dependent on cocoa for a major part of their export earnings. In 1989, for example, cocoa (including processed derivatives) accounted for 47% of export earnings for Ghana, 27% for Côte d'Ivoire, and 17% for Cameroon. For these countries, the movement in world prices remains a major determinant of their ability to develop their economies.[85]

Market conditions in the world cocoa economy, as described above, present a challenge to policy makers who have to design an economic recovery strategy for a monoeconomy producing a commodity for export. This is a problem in the economics of uncertainty. Did the consultants design an optimal policy? The answer is no: the empirical evidence shows that the supply response in the agricultural sector in Ghana has been sluggish. Output in the cocoa sector has remained stagnant. It seems that the consultants misapplied the theory.

Misapplication of the Theory and the Consequent Failure of Recovery

The empirical evidence, after ten years of "structural adjustment" in Ghana, shows that the agricultural-sector policy designed by the consultants has failed to achieve the principal objective. That objective was to make it possible for Ghana to develop the agricultural sector to export commodities, earn a lot of foreign exchange, and invest it to achieve economic recovery. It may be argued that the model, which was used to design the agricultural-sector policy, was misapplied. The theory behind the decision-making model was based on the economics of certainty, as we have discussed in Part III.

The theory was misapplied because the consultants used only a snapshot of costs and benefits to make their policy recommendations. Tsakok explains how the theory should be applied properly before investment recommendations are drawn from DRC ratios.[86] Two additional steps must be undertaken after the ratios are calculated:

> The first step is to compute a set of DRCs rather than relying on just one. The set should be either over time or incorporate alternative assumptions about key parameters of the DRC. These parameters are often yields and exchange rates. This set of DRCs would indicate whether there is a good case for further exploring the efficiency aspects of expanding this commodity. The second step is to undertake a full cost-benefit analysis. The role of DRCs in policy analysis is therefore to identify the efficient as opposed to the inefficient so that policy makers will have a better rationale for discouraging or promoting production of various commodities.[87]

The World Bank did not take these additional steps. There are no records of other measures of DRC ratios and of full-scale cost-benefit analyses. These steps are important because DRC is a measure of efficiency. The efficiency value will change as production and market structures change.

DRCs are snapshots and are only useful if the techniques of production, scale of output, level of demand in domestic and foreign markets, and exchange rates remain unchanged. If these factors change, the DRCs will change. Tsakok explains that it is useful to distinguish between current and future DRCs, which incorporate expected changes. To the extent that the World Bank economists did not compute and use expected DRCs in making their policy recommendation, the operational model did not incorporate uncertainty analysis.

It is clear from the above analysis why the objective of the agricultural policy was not met. The cocoa-sector policy was not changed for years although the world cocoa market faced declining prices for the entire SAP period, due to an oversupply of cocoa. As a result, export earnings declined whereas the objective was to increase foreign exchange earnings.

The consultants could be criticized from another angle; they based the recovery exercise on production and trade of a single commodity—cocoa. Thus, they exposed the economy to the disadvantages—and costs—associated with wide fluctuations in export earnings. This is what happened. See evidence provided by Maizels on the commodity terms of trade loss and loss in export earnings from 1980 to 1990 by cocoa producers. This is why exports diversification has been suggested to reduce the risk associated with violent fluctuations in income. Diversification of the export base may stabilize export earnings. Brainard and Cooper argue that

> [it] is possible to reduce the risk associated with any portfolio of investments by adding investments with returns not highly positively correlated with those already in the portfolio. Thus a coun-

try may stabilize its export earnings by diversifying into exports which have uncorrelated or (preferably) inversely correlated movements in world prices. It may even make sense for a country to invest in a low yield-high risk export industry, if its price pattern has a high negative correlation with the prices of other products.[88]

CAN EXPORT DIVERSIFICATION SOLVE THE PROBLEM FACING GHANA?

Not all the problems facing Ghana can be solved by diversification of the export base. The problem of uncertainties in commodity production and trade should be of great concern to monoeconomies like Ghana. The costs of unforeseen fluctuations in prices and incomes have been great. The economic crisis of 1983 has not ended despite a World Bank-assisted SAP. Diversification of the commodity export base has been suggested as a solution for monoeconomies to escape the heavy dependence on one product for the bulk of their export earnings and thereby avoid the costs induced by uncertainty due to sharp fluctuations in export receipts. It may be argued that the SAP policy makers could have avoided their cocoa-sector policy mistake, where the objective was to increase foreign exchange earnings, if they had opted for a diversification of the agricultural-sector export base as a policy. Thus, it may be hypothesized that if the resources that were invested in the cocoa sector under the SAP had been used to produce multiple crops for export, Ghana would have earned more foreign exchange than it received from cocoa exports alone.

At the time that Ghana was rehabilitating the cocoa industry, Colombia was investing in flower production for export. In 1986, the floral industry in Colombia earned over US$155 million in export earnings. Compare this to the Ghanaian cocoa export earnings, which was more than one-half that figure in 1983, and about one-third in 1986. The World Bank seems to endorse the "commodity diversification approach" to solve Ghana's commodity problems. In a World Bank study on Ghana, *Ghana 2000 and Beyond,* Bank officials reported favorably on the floral industry in Colombia: "in fact a 1971 study by the Colombian Government estimated that the floral industry produced 600% return per year on the initial investment."[89] Some World Bank economists seem to suggest a development strategy based on diversification of the export base in general. In a report entitled *Export Catalysts in Low Income Countries,* World Bank economists review 11 success stories of export diversification.[90] The Colombian floral industry is reported as one of the success stories.

Can Ghana's agricultural sector repeat the success story of the development of the floral industry in Colombia? This is a difficult question to answer because the supply response in agriculture under the SAP has been sluggish. We have to identify the agricultural sector problem and solve it before we can apply the "diversification" or the "export catalyst" strategy to solve agricultural development problems in Ghana.

The SAP exchange rate adjustment, together with the implementation of the cocoa sector policy and the incentive programs, has not helped to turn the cocoa sector around. The fact that the agricultural supply response is slow shows that the problem affects the entire agricultural sector, and has not been properly diagnosed. Perhaps we need to implement some institutional changes or incorporate some nonprice factors. Ghana, like most African economies, is an agrarian economy. N. Georgescu-Roegen has surmised that "agrarianism is reality without a theory."[91] To find the key to unlock the problems of underdeveloped countries, in this case the problem of a low supply response in agriculture, we must look for empirical experiences, because there is no theory for agrarian development. For those who are concerned to find strategies or models for the operation of agrarian economies, there is no substitute for concrete evidence from historical experience.

It seems that the World Bank wants to learn from historical experiences so it can develop better. To do this, the World Bank has launched a public policy research program. The Bank has published the first book in the series entitled *The East Asian Miracle*. The book extols the virtues of the East Asian Model. In the foreword to the book, Lewis Pearson, the president of the World Bank, explains the research findings as follows:

> The success of many of the economies of East Asia in achieving rapid and equitable growth, often in the context of activist public policies, raises complex questions about the relationship between government, the private sector, and the market. Understanding which policies contributed to their rapid growth, and how, is a major question for research on development policy. As reports on policy issues, we intend that they should help us to take stock of what we know and clearly identify what we do not know; they should contribute to the debate in both the academic and policy communities on appropriate public policy objectives and instruments for developing economies. The report also breaks some new ground. It concludes that in some economies, mainly those in Northeast Asia, some selective interventions contributed to growth, and it advances our understanding of the conditions required for interventions to succeed. The institutional context within which policies are implemented is as important to their success or failure as the policies themselves, and the report devotes substantial attention to the institutional bases for East Asia's rapid growth. Non-economic factors, including culture, politics, and history, are also important to the East Asian success story. Thus, there is still much to be learned about the interactions between policy choices and institutional capability and between economic and non-economic factors in development. Work in these areas will continue beyond this report (PV-VII).[92]

This quote indicates the new elements of a model that will be used by the Bank in advising developing countries. The Bank will relax its neoclassical paradigm and include institutional and noneconomical variables as well as some selective intervention in market operations by governments.

We pointed out earlier that efficient institutions are now seen as a key to economic success. There is even a new school of thought, New Institutional Economics (NIE), which propagates this view.[93] Mustapha Nabli and Jeffrey Nugent examined some Japanese institutional variables, which were responsible for unleashing the development progress in that country.[94] Harry Oshima has studied the Taiwanese model, the East Asian Miracle for rural transformation (see next section). Kofi has examined the Finnish model for an agrarian transformation called the "Pellervo Movement."[95] It was a cooperative movement, which was used successfully to transform rural sectors in Finland and lay the foundation for industrialization after World War II. Can Africa benefit from some of these historical experiences?

AGRICULTURAL TRANSFORMATION MODELS—ANY LESSONS FOR AFRICA?

Oshima explained the model used by the East Asian countries, especially Taiwan, to transform the agricultural sector and industrialize their economies.[96] Oshima claims that expanding the internal market is a prerequisite for economic growth. External forces and international trade can be of considerable importance in the short run. Second, he underscores the fact that growth with equity was necessary in the case of East Asia. This provided the power to purchase the goods produced. Through government intervention full employment in agriculture was maintained and at the same time productivity in agriculture was increased. It must be pointed out that Japanese colonial intervention contributed positively to the Taiwanese agricultural transformation exercise. This, however, was done in favor of Japanese interests.

Samuel Pao-San Ho has explained the role that Japanese colonial policy played in agricultural development in Taiwan and Korea.[97] He argues that

[w]hen Japan first began to modernize, it was able to increase agricultural productivity by exploiting internal growth potentials, thereby facilitating the transfer of resources from agriculture to the modern sector. These internal sources of agricultural progress were improvements in traditional farming methods and the transfer of better techniques (superior seeds, intensive use of fertilizer, and better farming methods) to backward areas of western and eastern Japan. By the 1910's these "indigenous" sources of growth were exhausted, and output growth in agriculture slowed, declining from an average rate of 2.38 per cent between 1897 and 1901, to 1.91 per cent from 1901 to 1917, to only 0.44 per cent between 1917 and 1931.[98]

Thus since 1897, the supply curve of agricultural output had been shifting to the right slowly or it has been stagnant. The demand curve, however, had been shifting to the right relatively faster, due to population growth and rising per capita income. As a result, food prices rose sharply and this led to riots in major cities in Japan in 1918.

Japan could have solved the food shortage problem by three methods: (1) importing food from abroad, (2) increasing food production at home, or (3) importing rice from colonies (Taiwan and Korea). Japan chose the third option. Why? To import food from outside was unattractive because Japan would become dependent on foreign sources of food supply. Japan preferred to be self-sufficient in food production for security purposes. Second, to import food from outside the empire implied that imports of capital and industrial supplies would have to be reduced. The option to increase food production in Japan was not attractive. The agricultural sector had exhausted its productivity growth, given the resources and the techniques of production. To improve productivity under these conditions would require substantial investments in research and development. This would take resources away from the modern sector.

The third alternative was more attractive. Because farming techniques were more advanced in Japan than in the colonies, agricultural productivity within the empire could be raised significantly by transferring superior Japanese farming techniques to the colonies. By selecting this third option, the Japanese determined the economic position of Korea and Taiwan in the empire: they became agricultural appendages of Japan. They were to supply inexpensive rice to prevent Japan's industrial wages from rapidly rising. These colonies also serve as markets for Japanese manufacturers. The product of this policy was that Korea and Taiwan were able to transform their agricultural sectors with the help of superior Japanese know-how. On the demand side, the colonial markets were available to buy Korean and Taiwanese agricultural produce. The circumstances were different in the case of British colonialism in Africa.

The African countries' agricultural sectors were not transformed with the help of superior farming techniques and institutional innovations of the imperial powers. African agriculture was not transformed at the end of British or French colonialism. In the case of British West Africa, Lord Lugard's "dual mandate" policy worked to retard institutional innovations in the rural sector.[99] The dual mandate allowed African chiefs to rule as before but their hands were tied. The chiefs had no power to innovate in legal areas or make substantive economic decisions.

East Asia and Africa (especially West Africa) came out of the colonial experience with different levels of agricultural development because the needs of the imperial system were different. As a result, the colonial policies were different. As far as agriculture is concerned, Africa may have very little to learn from the "East Asian miracle."

The British settled in some parts of Africa, where agricultural transformation took a different direction. The settlers developed agriculture on modern lines. In West Africa, where there were no settlers, so no agriculture was developed to exploit internal growth potentials and set the stage for transfer of resources from the agricultural to the modern sector. Thus, West Africa missed an important and essential strategy that was used by the East Asian countries to transform agriculture.

How can West Africa fill this gap, which is lost to history? The Japanese colonial strategy of agricultural development cannot be repeated. However, some elements of the model can be used. For example, elements of the Oshima explanation of the East Asian and Japanese strategies can be followed. What cannot be copied are the noneconomic factors including culture, politics, history, and the initial agrarian and institutional bases of the former Japanese colonies. Every country has its own noneconomic variables to work with. What is needed is an institutional superstructure—an ideology and a practical movement within which institutional innovations can flourish and develop. Governments in these developing countries can play a crucial role in this regard. This point is made clearly by Gustav Ranis.[100] He underscores the important role played by the Korean and Taiwanese governments in institutional development. Ranis argues that the "role of government became more important in the course of the transition process in South Korea and Taiwan, and that the critical issue is the continuous flexibility of institutional and policy change in the effort to organize society's human and natural resources most effectively rather than any absolute preference for either a pure market solution or government intervention."[101]

We have suggested above that, perhaps, the main impediment to agricultural development in the African economies is the lack of institutional innovation capable of contributing to economic efficiency. The lowering of transaction costs is an example. The empirical evidence shows that in Korea and Taiwan, the governments played a leading role to create the climate in which institutional innovations flourished and contributed positively to economic growth. Can Ghana (Africa) learn from the East Asian or similar models?

So Which Institutional Model for Ghana?

The Korean and Taiwanese rural sectors were transferred under Japanese colonialism. In the case of the African countries, British or French colonialism did not give priority to agricultural transformation. African systems of production were adequate to supply the food needs of the population. In addition, Africa had surplus labor and land to produce crops for export.

Since industrialization of the colonies was not an objective of the colonial powers, there was no pressing need to improve productivity in agriculture to release labor for industrial development. Can the ex-colonial African countries step back into history, develop their rural sectors quickly to raise productivity, and embark on the industrialization process? Did the African colonies miss the boat? Andrew Schotter has argued that "every evolutionary economic problem requires a social institution to solve it." Schotter endorses the position that institutions must be studied in a historical-evolutionary context. "Once it is recognized that observed institutions of legal-political order exist in a historical setting, the attraction of trying to analyze conceptual origins independently of historical process is severely weakened."[102]

How do we solve the African agricultural transformation problem? A solution may lie in studying the experience of other countries in a historical-evolutionary context. Looking into history, the Finnish experience seems to be the most appropriate one for an African government to study and learn from.[103]

Kofi suggests that the Finnish cooperative movement (1899 to 1939), called the Pellervo Movement by the Finns, was an agrarian strategy of development.[104] Scholars who studied the movement in the 1930s underscored this point of view. Pellervo was a national and revolutionary movement put in place to develop the country and make it strong in face of external threats. In 1899, with the rise of Panslavism, it seemed that Russia would formally colonize Finland and absorb it into the Russian empire. Thorsten Ohde observed that "in that plight co-operation proved a means of salvation whereby resistance to such annihilation might be organized and democracy rescued."[105]

Ohde records the Pellervo Society's achievements thirty years after its 1899 founding as follows:

> Cooperation in Finland ranks among the most successful applications of that principle to trade and business by an entire nation that our day can show ...Cooperative organization has exceeded all expectations in minimizing expenses for the country population and increasing their sales returns, swinging the whole of production to where it is required and therefore profitable. Finland bids fair to become a leader in Europe in smallholdings and in creamery productions. Consumer cooperative has kept down the cost of living, thus immensely strengthening competitive effectiveness in the world markets.[106]

African governments would love to implement an agrarian development strategy, which could bring about the results described by Ohde on the Finnish experience and achievement.

Henry H. Bakken, an agricultural economist who taught at the University of Wisconsin, wrote a book with an interesting title: *Cooperation to the FINNISH*. Bakken ended by explaining the achievements of the cooperative movement:

> Thus we see how during these past three decades, the farmers and workers in Finland have built up powerful institutions, which are gradually dominating finance, production and distribution. These cooperators are gradually maneuvering themselves into where they as entrepreneurs can command control in the money market, operate their own factories, manage their own distributive agencies and direct research laboratories.[107]

The Finnish Pellervo Movement was above all a social institution developed to solve an evolutionary economic problem. It solved the problem. It transformed rural Finland from a primitive low level of techniques of production to one of modern methods of production with much higher levels of agricultural productivity. Thus when the time came for Finland to begin to industrialize after World War II, it was ready.

World Bank vice president Edward V. K. Jaycox has pointed out that the missing link in African development experience is efficient evolutionary institutions, which he calls "capacity building." The concept definition is best explained in his own words:

> I've lived and worked in sub-Saharan Africa now for over 25 years. Like you, I've seen the various changes in emphasis in development strategies—from state-led growth through basic human needs to structural adjustment. These different approaches to African development have had varying levels of success and failure. But the various approaches have all lacked one ingredient: they did not incorporate, as a central feature, the building of indigenous African skills, knowledge, and institutions. Capacity building has been the missing link.[108]

The World Bank has set up an African Capacity Building Institute in Harare, Zimbabwe, with an endowment of US$100 million. This money will be distributed to African governments to "build capacity." It may be argued that only evolutionary social institutions like the Pellervo Movement can accomplish capacity building. One hundred million dollars cannot finance a Pellervo-type movement in one African country. It can be done through a revolutionary cooperative movement with minimal help from abroad.

The Finnish model seems to focus on institutional development. Perhaps Africa can learn more from the Finnish cooperative model than from the Asian model. It seems that the African SAP models need to be enriched with some aspects of the Finnish and East Asian models, among others.

CONCLUSIONS

This case study has used qualitative analyses to provide evidence to show that the SAP policy designed for the agricultural sector in Ghana was not an optimal strategy. Policy makers failed to design the policy by taking the future trends in world cocoa prices into account. As a result, a policy was designed for Ghana to increase cocoa output in a market where world prices faced a long-run downward trend. The resources devoted to rehabilitate the cocoa sector in Ghana could have been invested to produce alternative crops for export.

It is recognized that commodity diversification by itself is not enough to do the trick. Recent research by institutional economists has shown that the most important variable for economic growth is institutional innovations brought about by superior political organization and administrative competence in government. It is suggested that for Ghana (and therefore, Africa) to solve the problem of low supply response in agriculture, she must find a way to develop efficient institutions, for example, by lowering transaction costs.

The suggestions developed in this chapter to ensure a viable SAP, with the help of government intervention, may be summarized as follows:

1. The superstructure of an agrarian development strategy "with an institutional development face" must be put in place.
2. An agricultural-led growth strategy "with an equity face," where the internal terms of trade are biased towards the agrarian sector, must be followed before industrialization is begun.

This model follows the successful East Asian experience. The World Bank advises the developing countries to learn from the "East Asian miracle." This chapter suggests that the African countries can learn more from the Finnish model for agrarian transformation than from the East Asian model. The Finnish model was not directed by a colonial power, as was the case of Taiwan and Korea. Finland faced a challenge, the threat of colonization by Russia, and it responded with a movement to develop its economy. Africa faces many challenges. It has yet to respond (See Chapter 7).

CHAPTER 4

ECONOMIC DEVELOPMENT STATUS OF MAURITIUS

As indicated in Chapter 2, when some African countries were achieving their political independence in the 1960s, the prevailing paradigm in economic development centered mainly on the assumption that capital formation (industrialization, urbanization, and agricultural development for export markets) was essential for achieving economic growth.

By the 1970's, the failure of economic growth to "trickle down" to the underprivileged classes became obvious, and areas of endemic poverty remained unaffected. This observation led to new development paradigms that included the concept of economic growth with redistribution. In other words, economic growth to a large extent focused on fulfilling the basic needs (for housing, nutrition, sanitation, health services, etc.) of the poorest segments as prerequisites for achieving "growth with equity."

In the 1980s, the attention of economic development by the neoclassical economists stressed the adoption of competitive free markets, export promotion, the privatization of state-owned enterprises, and the creation of environments conducive to direct investment as fundamental for enhancing economic development.

In contrast to the capital-led model of the 1960s, the "growth with equity" paradigm of the 1970s, or the neoclassical growth model of the 1980s, in more recent years the idea of the environment as a constraint to economic growth has given way to the acceptance of the environment as part and parcel for achieving sustainable economic development in the long run. In other words, development economists increasingly have recognized that failing to take the costs of environmental damage into account will prove to be inefficient and often ineffectual in raising incomes and well-being. Similarly, environmentalists have realized that economic development can be achieved along with sound environmental policies.[1]

The internationalization of environmental issues in the development process and, in particular, the adoption of sustainable development as the agenda for the twenty-first century by the United Nations Conference on Environment and Development (the "Earth Summit," held June 3 to June 14, 1992, in Rio de Janeiro), have drawn worldwide attention to environmental problems that must be addressed in any economic growth model. In many African countries, for example, soil erosion, desertification, drought, deforestation, range degradation, urban growth, and water- and air-related diseases are just a few of the myriad challenges that must be faced. In order to reverse the cycle of destruction and integrate environmental considerations into the development process, a number of countries have begun to prepare National Environmental Action Plans and National Conservation strategies. As stated by Kevin Cleaver:

> In 1993 the World Bank launched a Capacity Building in Environmental Economics Program to support the National Environmental Action Plans (NEAPs) that are emerging across sub-Saharan Africa. With financial support from Norway and Sweden, the World Bank has initiated three activities: (1) short-term training for NEAP economists, (2) grants to fund applied studies, and (3) the development of texts for training in environmental economics.[2]

It is believed that the quality of development that will emerge in Africa in the future will greatly depend not only on the policies adopted by governments but also on the active participation and empowerment of the local people in their sustainable economic development process. For example, since deforestation, desertification, increase in population, shortage of water, and air-related diseases are to a large extent the symptoms of poverty, the poor need to be organized to formulate and implement their development strategies and ensure that their needs are fulfilled. In short, the participation of dedicated representatives of the poorest groups at the grassroots level is vital to ensuring a broad and strategic approach to environmental management and sustainable development. The question that needs to be raised is: What is the economic development status of Mauritius?

Mauritius (an island with a surface area of 1,850 square kilometers, located in the eastern part of Madagascar, southeast Africa) is saddled with substantial handicaps— cyclones, limited resources, being far from major customers, being surrounded by low-income economies. Faced with low-cost competitors, a textile worker earns about US$1.02 per day in Mauritius, compared with only $0.26 in Pakistan, $0.28 in China, $0.29 in Madagascar, $0.62 in the Philippines, $0.34 in Indonesia, and $0.36 in India. In spite of its numerous handicaps, Mauritius has achieved far-reaching economic reforms since its independence in 1968. It has successfully moved from being a monocrop agricultural economy to a newly diversified industrializing economy, driven by an expanding labor force, capital accumulation, and increased factor productivity. It has not only attracted considerable foreign investment, but has achieved one of Africa's highest per capita incomes.[3] As stated by Arvind Subramanian and Devesh Roy, instead of being a strong candidate for failure (because of being monocrop, prone to terms of trade shocks, experiencing rapid population growth rates, and being susceptible to ethnic tensions), we see that between 1973 and 1999, the "real GDP in Mauritius [as calculated by Nobel Prize winner James Mead] grew on average by 5.9 percent per year compared with 2.4 percent in Africa. In per capita terms, the corresponding numbers are 3.25 percent and 0.7 percent."[4]

Following the drought from 1999 to 2000, Mauritius' real GDP growth was projected to grow at 7.8 percent in 2000—2001 (up from 3.6 percent in 1999—2000). Aided by the nominal appreciation of the rupee and restrained monetary conditions, consumer price inflation is on a downward trend (declining to 5.3 percent in 1999—2000 from 7.9 percent in 1998—1999), and was expected to show further decreases—down to about 4.5 percent—in 2000—2001. Despite a 4.4 percent decline in the terms of trade (resulting mainly from higher oil prices), and a real effective appreciation of the Mauritian rupee of 5.6 percent, the external current account balance shifted to a surplus of 0.5 percent of GDP in 1999/2000 from a deficit of 1.6 percent of GDP in 1998/99. A resilient tourism sector and buoyant exports to the United States, both reflecting the strengths of the world economy, as well as significant sugar reinsurance receipts and strong productivity performance in the manufacturing sector, contributed to this strong external performance.[5]

Improvements in human development have been equally impressive:

> [L]ife expectancy at birth increased from 61 years in 1965 to 71 in 1996; primary enrollment increased from 93 to 107 between 1980 and 1996 compared with 78 and 75, respectively in Africa. Income inequality has also seen impressive improvements: the Gini coefficient declined from 0.5 in 1962 to 0.42 in 1975 and 0.37 in 1986–87.[6]

Mauritius has registered high rates of economic growth, despite the fact that it has: (1) large and active labor unions, (2) price controls, especially on a number of socially sensitive items, and (3) generous social security, particularly for the elderly and civil servants. Given this and that it has recorded an impressive improvement in human development, it would be useful to ask the following questions:

√ What are the sociopolitical factors that contributed to Mauritius' sustained economic growth?

√ What elements of economic policy contributed to Mauritius' economic success, and how does it compare with Costa Rica?

√ How do the social welfare distribution systems of Mauritius compare with Costa Rica?

Mauritius is being compared to Costa Rica (which covers an area of 51,100 sq. km—including 50,600 sq. km of land and 440 sq. km of water), because Costa Rica, like Mauritius, is characterized with no army but a strong democratic tradition. Also, like Mauritius, Costa Rica is regarded as a developmental "success story" among the newly industrialized countries in the twenty-first century.[7] Nonetheless, though both countries have shown economic growth, it is possible that Mauritius can learn a lot from Costa Rica on how to strategically design its environmental policies to achieve sustainable development in the twenty-first century.

This chapter is organized into three parts. The first part presents a brief historical background and assesses the degree of political stability in Mauritius. The second part describes Mauritius' economy—its determinants and the structural transformation it has undergone. The third part analyzes the social welfare status of Mauritius.

THE POLITICAL HISTORY OF MAURITIUS

Very little is known about the original natives of Mauritius, but it is assumed a number of Arab traders visited the land as early as the tenth century. As narrated by Larry Bowman, successive waves of people came to the island beginning in the sixteenth century, for a number of reasons.

> Europeans arrived as adventurers, conquerors, and agents or builders of empires. African peoples were brought to Mauritius as slaves. Indians came as indentured laborers. The Chinese arrived as free immigrants, leaving behind depressed economic conditions in China and seeking commercial opportunities throughout the Indian Ocean region.[8]

The first Europeans to have landed in the island around 1510 were the Portuguese. According to Portuguese accounts, the island of Mauritius was deserted when they first explored it in the sixteenth century. The Portuguese used the island as a victual stop on the way to Goa and Malacca, and they named the island Ilha do Cirne (Island of the Swan).

After the Portuguese left the island in 1598, the Dutch, attracted by ebony, were the next to land and renamed it Mauritius—in honor of their *stadhoulder* (governor), Prince Maurice of Nassau. Among other things, the Dutch introduced sugarcane and herds of Javanese deer. Because Mauritius was isolated from the main centers of Dutch interest at the Cape and Java, the Dutch left the island in 1710 after having destroyed the island's ebony forests.[9]

The next Europeans to arrive in Mauritius were the French. The French East India Company had occupied the island by

1721, when they renamed it Isle de France. They expanded the sugar plantations by bringing slave labor from Madagascar and the Malabar Coast. As narrated by Bowman, the French control over Mauritius can be divided into two periods:

> [T]he first, when the Company [French East India Co.] dominated, lasted from 1721 until the 1760's when the Company went bankrupt and control of Reunion and Mauritius returned to the king of France. The second period, from 1767 to 1810, began with Mauritius under the control of the French crown. ...French control [ended] (because the French were plaguing English vessels on their way to and from India) when the British conquered Mauritius and the island came under British authority (as a prize of war, the Treaty of Paris recognized the status of the island as a British colony after Napoleon's defeat in 1815. But most of the French settlers were allowed to keep their customs, religion, and laws and the name Mauritius was reinstated).[10]

British rule lasted from 1810 until Mauritius gained its independence from Great Britain in 1968. But it can be said that three major developments dominated life on Mauritius during the British era. First, slavery was formally abolished on February 1, 1835. The emancipation of slaves, who constituted about 70 percent of the population, caused a serious labor shortage. Second, starting in 1834, about 450,000 indentured (hired) laborers were brought from India to work in the sugarcane fields. The pay was approximately 5 rupees, or 10 shillings, per month. Given the increase in demand for indentured labor, the Indian proportion of the Mauritian population rose from 18 percent in 1839 to 67 percent in 1871. (At present, they constitute the majority of the Mauritian population. The local culture, however, still bears the mark of French influence.)[11] Third, Mauritius was transformed from a country based on maritime activities to a country based on an exportable monocrop of sugar. But the malaria epidemic of 1866 to 1868 drove shipping away from Port Louis, which further declined after the opening of the Suez Canal in 1869.

During World War I, the economy prospered, but the depression of the 1930s changed the situation drastically, culminating in labor unrest in 1937. After 1945, not only were economic reforms initiated, but also combative political discussions took place between the British government, the Labor Party (which consisted mainly of Mauritian Indians), and the Mauritian minorities (consisting of Franco-Mauritians and the Creoles who formed the Social Democratic Party of Mauritius [PSDM]). In addition, the Muslims founded the Muslim Action Committee.

During World War II, as the British were unable to guarantee the security of their colonial dominions, this condition encouraged the colonies' emergence of claims for independence. At the same time, U.S political and military influence increased. The inhabitants of Mauritius fought for and achieved representation within British colonial government, and in 1957 a new government structure was created, giving Mauritius its own prime minister. In 1959, the first elections with universal suffrage brought the Labor Party of Mauritius (PLM) to power, making Seewoosagur Ramgoolam (a doctor) prime minister in 1961.[12]

However, the British administration ran the islands of Rodrigues, Cargados-Carajos, and the Chagos Archipelago. Later, the United States established a major naval base on one of its islands, Diego Garcia.[13]

During the 1960s, the Indian Labor Party and the Muslim Action Party formed an alliance, which forced the British to cede independence of Mauritius within the Commonwealth of Nations on March 12, 1968. The Indian Labor groups and the Muslims together formed an alliance, and Sir Seewoosagur Ramgoolam was reelected prime minister.[14] However, a British governor general presided over parliament in the name of the British monarch from 1968 until March 12, 1992, when Mauritius declared itself a republic. Since then the president, appointed by the prime minister and ratified by the parliament, has assumed the role of the governor general.[15]

In addition to cheap resources (raw materials and competent labor), market and tax incentives, and other factors regarded as very optimal for foreign direct investments, host countries are also looked upon favorably if they: (1) are part of the capitalist system and abide by the rules of free enterprise system, (2) entertain a stable economic, social, and political condition, (3) limit the power of labor unions and income redistribution policies, and (4) avoid unpredictable alterations in the day-to-day operations, ownership, and financial conditions of the foreign firms after investment decisions have been made. Given these conditions for foreign direct investments, we must ask the following questions:

√   What is the legitimacy of the regime in power and its capacity to fulfill Mauritius' developmental plans?

√   What is the governments' official attitude toward foreign direct investment in Mauritius?[16]

The Ramgoolam Regime (1969–1982)

In 1969, the Labor Party (supported by the Hindus) and the Democratic Party of Mauritius (PSDM) formed a coalition government that was opposed to independence. However, "[i]nternally, the government was tainted by electoral fraud and trade union repression, and in foreign affairs, it established close links with Israel and South Africa. Pretoria had a free zone in Port Louis which enabled it to trade with the EEC, thus evading international sanctions."[17]

On the political side, a new opposition group, called the Militant Mauritian Movement (MMM), emerged. The MMM Party denounced the alliance between the Labor Party and the former French settlers (the PSDM Party). On the economic front, Mauritius faced high unemployment because the sugar-based economy was in decline. To redress the slowdown in the economy, the regime in power offered both domestic and foreign investors a substantial package of credit, tax, and fiscal incentives in exchange for investment export-stimulated products. Also, investors were assured that the labor force would not only be highly trained but also be inexpensive, and without trade unions to represent them.[18]

With the new investments in the Export Processing Zone (EPZ), not only were new jobs created, but also Mauritius' gross domestic product grew around 10 percent per year during the period from 1972 and the end of 1974. But, starting in February 1975, the economic boom started to decline:

> [T]he sugar, tourism, and manufacturing sectors were all in slumps. Unemployment was at 20 percent, inflation was equally high (about 30%) ...Balance of payments shortfalls led to an austerity program demanded by the International Monetary Fund (IMF). This program included cutting government spending, slowing growth of the public sector, and devaluing the Mauritian currency (by 30 percent in 1979 and by a further 20 percent in 1981).[19]

With the enduring increase in unemployment and the social unrest, the Militant Mauritian Movement in collaboration with the Socialist Party of Mauritius (PSM) came to power in 1982.

THE MILITANT MAURITIAN MOVEMENT AND THE SOCIALIST PARTY OF MAURITIUS (1982)

After the results of the 1982 election were announced, it was overwhelmingly felt in Mauritius that the new coalition group that came to power would radically restructure the Mauritian economy. As discussed by Bowman, the election

> was a powerful endorsement of the democratic process. In an open and free election, an aging elite that had run out of ideas was replaced by a much younger and basically untested group of individuals who promised new programs and new hope. It was

a democratic transformation of remarkable proportions and suggested that Mauritius was beginning to move beyond intensely communal politics. Certainly the MMM's alliance with the PSM gave it a strong base in all communities.[20]

As anticipated, the MMM-PSM Party promised to increase job opportunities and salaries, nationalize the key sectors in the economy, reduce economic links with the apartheid regime in the South Africa, and demand the return of Diego Garcia from the United States.

But the sharp increase in petroleum prices was coupled with an increase in interest rates, a drop in the price of sugar (which was the major foreign exchange earner of the country), and the decline in foreign direct investment. The MMM-PSM coalition with its socialist rhetoric had little choice but to continue the reform program suggested by the International Monetary Fund for Mauritius' structural adjustment loan.

In order to receive five standby loans from the IMF between 1979 and 1985, the Mauritian government was required to adopt austerity measures such as postponing the plan to increase salaries, cutting subsidies on basic foods, relinquishing part of its control over public expenditure, and devaluing its currency (the Mauritian rupee). But the austerity measures mandated by the IMF created dissension between the MMM and the PSM, and led to a call for early elections. Then the Mauritian Socialist Movement (MSM) created by Sir Anerood Jugnauth came to power.

THE MAURITIAN SOCIALIST MOVEMENT

The MSM included former MMM members, former PSM members, and the new Pragmatic Socialist Party led by Jugnauth.[21] In line with its political philosophy, the MSM fully compensated the low-income groups and the most vulnerable groups of society (the pensioners, the disabled, etc.) and designed a plan to reduce the income inequality in the country.[22]

Mauritius has been able to sustain a highly participative multiparty political system because the regime in power has allowed all racial, ethnic, and religious communities to flourish on an equal footing. The political environment in Mauritius since its independence in 1968 can be summarized as follows:

> [T]he Mauritian political system has maintained the multiparty democratic form that evolved during the terminal years of colonialism. Four elections have been held since independence, and power has been transferred peacefully. It seems fair to say that the acceptance of democratic procedures has brought a degree of political stability to Mauritius that is rare in the developing world.[23] A consensus exists on looking to the government as a facilitator and provider of an enabling environment for private enterprise.[24]

ECONOMIC GROWTH IN MAURITIUS

The overall economic health of a nation can be assessed in terms of the following indicators: gross domestic product, inflation, unemployment, government budget, net fixed investment, savings, and balance-of-payments status.[25] In this section, the economic health of Mauritius is compared to Costa Rica in terms of gross domestic growth, per capita income, rate of inflation, unemployment rate, investment, savings, and government budget.

Based on its GDP growth rate in the last 20 years, the economic changes that swept across Mauritius seem unprecedented in scope and speed. Mauritius' economy outperformed Costa Rica's economy between 1970 and 1997. As shown in Table 4.1, significant and rapid GDP growth did occur in Mauritius from the 1970s to the 1980s. Though not very substantial, the growth rate in Mauritius declined from the 1980s to 1997. However, when compared with Costa Rica, Mauritius' growth rate declined by only 9 percent from the 1980s to 1997, whereas the decline rate in Costa Rica was about 24 percent. In 2000, the GDP of Mauritius was estimated to have grown at 7.5 percent, whereas the GDP of Costa Rica was estimated to have grown at 3 percent because of the low prices of coffee and the overproduction of bananas.

Mauritius' per capita income was almost 1.4 times that of Costa Rica in 1998, but these figures are based on market rather than purchasing power parity (PPP) rate. However, when the data are adjusted to reflect PPP in 1998, the purchasing power per capita income of Mauritius was still 1.4 times that of Costa Rica (Table 4.2). In short, the combination of high GDP and low population growth rates in Mauritius has resulted in growth of real GDP per capita of around 3.8 percent per year.

The high economic growth rates in Mauritius have been attained as a result of macroeconomic stability. For instance, inflation declined by about 35 percent in Mauritius between 1980 and 1997. The decline of inflation in the two countries might have contributed to an increase in the purchasing power. Though not substantial, the inflation rates declined by 24 percent in Costa Rica between 1980 and 1997. In addition, a relative increase in per capita growth to achieve full employment and a substantial decline in government budget deficit were recorded in both Mauritius and Costa Rica.

In addition, the specific economic growth rate of Mauritius in contrast to Costa Rica can be better appreciated when analyzed in terms of the investment and savings rate, the diversification in agriculture, and the Export Processing Zone. These will be discussed in more detail below.

Investment and Savings

The higher economic growth rate of Mauritius and Costa Rica can be attributed to a steady rise in investment. As shown in Table 4.3, from 1970 to 1997, the ratio of investment to GDP increased substantially in Mauritius because of: (1) the prospects in exports, (2) return on investment, and (3) an increase

Table 4.1
Indicators of Economic Growth in Mauritius and Costa Rica (1965–2000)

	1970–1980[a]	1980–1995[b]	1996–1997[c]	2000	1965–1980	1980–1995	1990–1998[d]	1980–1992	1992–2000
Mauritius	6.8	5.7	5.2	7.5[e]	3.7	4.6	3.8	1.1	1.1
Costa Rica	5.7	3.4	2.6	3.0	3.3	0.7	2.0	2.8	1.9

Sources:a) World Bank, *World Development Report* (1985, 1993, 1994). Washington, DC: Oxford University Press.

b) UNDP, *Human Development Report*. Oxford: Oxford University Press, 1998, p. 26.

c) World Bank, *World Development Report*, 1998/99. Oxford: Oxford University Press, 1999.

d) World Bank, *World Bank Atlas*, 2000. Washington, DC: Communications Development, pp. 42—43.

e) Estimated by CIA—The World Factbook–Costa Rica, 2002.

Table 4.2

GNP Per Capita (at PPP), Inflation Rate (%), and Government Budget (%) Status
of Mauritius and Costa Rica

Applicable	Year(s)	Mauritius	Costa Rica
GNP Per Capita[a]	1998	$3,730	$2,770
PPP[b]	1997	$9,360	$6,410
PPP[c]	1998	$8,236	$5,812
GDP Implicit Deflator	1980–90	9.5	23.6
	1990–98	6.2	17.4
Unemployment Rate	1999	6.4%	
	2000		5.2%[d]
Government Budget	1980	–10.3	–7.4
	1996	–4.0	3.9

Sources:

a) World Bank, *World Bank Atlas*, 2000. Washington, DC: Communications Development, pp. 42—43.

b) GNP, measured at PPP and then converted to U.S. dollars by the purchasing power parity (PPP) exchange rate. At the PPP rate, one dollar has the same purchasing power over domestic GNP that the U.S. dollar has over U.S. GNP. (*World Development Report*, 1996 and 1998—99).

c) World Bank, *World Bank Atlas*, 2000. Washington, DC: Communications Development, pp. 42—43.

d) Estimated by CIA — The World Factbook — Mauritius & Costa Rica, 2002.

in the level of confidence in the economy. On the other hand, in the case of Costa Rica, though the ratio of investment to GDP declined in 1997, there was an increase in the gross domestic growth rate.

Similarly, domestic savings, which could be used for capital accumulation, increased by 120 percent in Mauritius and by only 44 percent in Costa Rica from 1980 to 1997. Costa Rica performed less well in capital accumulation than Mauritius because there was no official development assistance growth to support its investment. In Mauritius "two main factors seem to explain the trend in the savings rate: the distribution of income and the population's perception of the prospects of the Mauritian economy."[26]

Looking at economic efficiency—that is, the ratio of investment (derived from the contribution of the rate of domestic savings, foreign aid, and foreign private investment) and growth in GNP—we clearly notice that Mauritius is more efficient in its investment capital output ratio (ICOR) than is Costa Rica (Table 4.4). Investment capital output ratio refers to the ratio between rate of investment and growth of GNP (that is, the ratio of domestic savings, foreign aid, and foreign private investment divided by growth of GNP). Whereas the only significant factor that contributed to Mauritius' investment has been its domestic savings, Costa Rica's investment was to a large extent financed by domestic savings and foreign direct investments.

While a high rate of investment offers a partial explanation of the high rate of growth, in order to have a clear understanding of the most important factors that contributed to Mauritius' economic growth, it is necessary to analyze: (1) its diversification process, (2) the establishment of its Export Processing Zone, and (3) its income distribution.

Table 4.3
Gross Domestic Investment, Gross Domestic Savings, and Official Development Assistance (% of GNP) in Mauritius and Costa Rica

	1970a	1980b	1997c	1970	1980	1997	1991	1996
Mauritius	10	21	26	11	10	22	2	0.51.1
Costa Rica	21	27	24	14	16	23	3	-0.1

Sources:a) World Bank, World Development Report (1993), pp. 254—255.

Table 4.4
Economic Efficiency of Mauritius and Costa Rica (1970–1997)

	Average Savings Rate 1980–1997	Foreign Direct Investment (FDI) 1980–1986	Official Development Assistance (ODA) 1991–1996	Investment Capital Output Ratio (ICOR) 1970–1997
Mauritius	120.0	-10.0	-75.0	5.93
Costa Rica	44.0	152.0	-103.0	23.85

Sources: World Bank, World Development Report (1993—1999); United Nations, Human Development Report (1998).

DIVERSIFICATION IN AGRICULTURE: THE TRANSFORMATION OF MAURITIUS FROM A MONOCROP COUNTRY INTO A DIVERSE ECONOMIC SYSTEM

At the time of its independence in 1968, Mauritius was highly dependent on sugar for its economy. The sugar industry employed about 30 percent of the labor force, and consumed 95 percent of the arable land on the island. Over 93 percent of annual exports and almost 100 percent of the foreign exchange came from sugar. At that time, unemployment was over 10 percent, and young people were entering the workforce far more rapidly than the economy could provide them with jobs.[27]

Sugar became very dominant in the Mauritian economy because in 1951 Britain signed the Commonwealth Sugar Agreement (CSA), which made Mauritius the most reliable supplier of sugar among the Commonwealth countries. Thus, Mauritius had to follow the colonizer's economic policy and tie its financial stability to the marketing guarantees of the CSA. Its annual quota was increased from 470,000 tons in 1953 to 570,000 tons in 1974.[28]

However, in 1975, one year after the CSA ended, Mauritius' sugar began to be marketed under guidelines established under the Sugar Protocol. Under the Lome Convention (1975), the Africa-Caribbean-Pacific (ACP) countries and the European Economic Community (EEC) set formal quotas and price guarantees under which sugar is supposed to be exported to the European Community. Under the Sugar Protocol, and with British and French assistance, Mauritius' quota was set at 506,000 metric tons per year. This comprises 70 to 80 percent of the average annual sugar harvest in Mauritius and almost 35 percent of the total ACP allowance. Mauritian sugar receives a highly favorable guaranteed price, well above current world market rates.[29]

With favorable access conditions to EEC, under the Lome Convention and the Multifibre arrangement, the economy of Mauritius grew at over 6 percent per year from 1984 to 1991.[30] Although Mauritius had a favorable status in marketing its sugar under the Sugar Protocol, the government's main objective, since independence, became the diversification of the Mauritian economy into other sectors, so that the economy could generate economic growth and provide productive employment to the emerging labor force. In the 1970s alone, about 10,000 young people were annually completing school and joining the labor market.[31]

Though sugar has remained Mauritius' primary agricultural crop, it made great efforts, starting with the 1985 action plan, toward diversification into the tea industry. Tea grows well in the wetter, higher elevations of Mauritius and, as a labor-intensive crop, it was initially perceived as having the potential to reduce unemployment. In the years since independence, tea production has stabilized at about 8,000 tons per year. This meets local needs and provides a modest amount for export, most of which historically has gone to South Africa.[32]

But as world prices for tea fell, maintaining tea production through government subsidies was not found to be very economical. Thus, the tea industry is at present given over to domestic use and not for commercial purposes.

In its diversification efforts, Mauritius has moved toward becoming self-sufficient in the production of fruits and vegetables. Pineapples, mangoes, and cut flowers are promoted for export. Significantly assisted by foreign aid, Mauritius has expanded into the fishing industry. "The Japanese International Cooperation Agency is helping develop Trou Fanfaron, a fishing port with cold storage facilities on the north of the island, and a joint venture between Mauritius, Australia, and the United States is developing a tuna processing center."[33]

Although diversification efforts have benefited Mauritius, major constraints remain. These include limited available land (60 percent of arable land is allocated to sugar plantation, and the small planters keep nearly 90 percent of arable land under sugar cultivation), lack of sufficient rainfall in many areas, the rising rental costs for lands and storage, labor shortages, the high cost of agricultural inputs, and the environmental effect of pesticide use.

To create about 130,000 new jobs, the government had no choice except to diversify the economy. Thus, the government issued a policy paper on development for the decade 1971 to 1980 and created the Mauritius Export Processing Zone.

EXPORT PROCESSING ZONE

Setting aside land as a basic strategy for industrialization has been a common practice in the newly industrialized countries of Asia. For instance, as described by Herman Kahn:

> The industrial park strategy for economic development offers key advantages for both slow and fast growth countries such as South Korea, Taiwan, and Singapore. By simplifying bureaucratic procedures, cutting red tape, and decentralizing in an organized way many of the diverse requirements for industrialization, it greatly reduces the risk that bottlenecks will disrupt or slow down growth.[34]

Taiwan played a key role in assisting Mauritius to develop its EPZ in 1971 as a means of undertaking the Mauritian industrialization process. To entice new investments, Mauritius, like Taiwan, offered both foreign and domestic prospective investors a substantial package of fiscal, tax, infrastructure, credit, and other incentives in exchange for their investment in industries that would manufacture goods for export. For example,

> incentives included relief from income taxes for the first ten years, with a further moratorium or reduced rates promised if

profits were reinvested in the island; exemption from import taxes on equipment and raw materials; complete freedom to repatriate or transfer capital, dividends, and salaries; priority access to credit and foreign exchange; subsidized rates of water, electricity, and plant construction; and substantial public support for export promotion efforts overseas. Also implicit in the enticement was the assurance that the labor force would be competent, compliant, and inexpensive.[35]

About 50 percent of the investments of Mauritius in the EPZ mainly came from domestic and foreign sources. Given the government development priorities on the domestic zone, tax incentives led the domestic sugar corporations to divert much of their capital into EPZ investment. Means of attracting foreign investment included free repatriation of all profits, access to low-cost labor, and the absence of income taxes and import duties. In addition, in 1985, the government established the Mauritius Export Development and Investment Authority (MEDIA) to promote foreign direct investment and EPZ exports around the world (see Table 4.5).

Table 4.5

Percentage of

Private Investment Gross Domestic Fixed Investment: Foreign Direct Investment (Millions of Dollars)

	1980	1996	1997
Mauritius	64.0	64.8	73.5
Costa Rica	61.3	75.1	73.2

Sources: World Bank, *World Development Report* (1998). pp. 220—221; World Bank, *World Bank Atlas,* 2000.

In addition to financial benefits and low domestic wages, entrepreneurs from Hong Kong were enticed to Mauritius because Hong Kong was in the process of becoming part of China. Other "foreign entrepreneurs were attracted by preferential access to the US and EU markets, by the availability of literate, bilingual and relatively inexpensive labor, by economic and political stability, and a reasonably conducive business environment" (see Table 4.6).[36]

Table 4.6

Foreign Direct Investment in the EPZ (Rs Million)

	1985	1986	1987	1988	1989	1990	1991	1992	Total
China	0	0	0	20	6	13	11	3	54
France	10	4	8	13	32	58	8	23	156
Germany	1	3	1	2	50	4	0	1	61
Hong Kong	91	24	10	120	19	55	11	29	359
Taiwan	0	1	13	2	13	63	0	1	93
U.K.	2	3	6	12	29	7	24	11	95
Others	10	37	96	66	149	71	76	135	640
Total	114	73	133	236	299	270	130	203	1,458

Source: World Bank, "Mauritius: Technology Strategy for Competitiveness," p. 18.

Table 4.7

Growth of Export Processing Zone in Mauritius

Indicator	1987	1988	1990	1992	1994	1996
Firms	531	591	568	558	494	481
New	141	95	62	33	27	43
Closures	18	35	57	61	69	43
Employment	87,905	89,080	89,906	86,937	82,176	79,793
Exports (fob Rs M)	6,567	8,176	11,474	13,081	16,533	21,000
Net Exports (Rs M)	1,766	2,286	4,126	5,948	6,408	8,893
Value Added at 1982 Prices (Rs M)	1,390	1,557	1,766	1,965	2,173	2,441
Labor Productivity Index (1882 = 100)	87	91	105	117	140	160

Source: Adapted from Ministry of Economic Development and Regional Cooperation, Mauritius, *Economic and Social Indicators*, Issue 282 (November 13, 1998), p. 1.

Initially, investments in the EPZ of Mauritius were mainly in labor-intensive light industries such as the textile industry. For example, in 1976 alone, 85 of the enterprises, 17,163 workers, and 309 million rupees worth of textile products were exported from the EPZ of Mauritius. But

> Industrial workers in the early years of the EPZ were often paid 5 rupees a day or less (under $1.00). Moreover, EPZ workers were denied the right to unionize, to strike, to have paid maternity leave (most EPZ workers were women), or to benefit from health care, social welfare, or pension programs available to workers in other sectors of the economy.[37]

Though the conditions of workers in the EPZ did not improve, the domestic infrastructure, the manufacturing sector of the EPZ, was fundamentally restructured in order to attract more sophisticated set of manufacturing enterprises.

As shown in Table 4.7, in 1987 there were 531 enterprises established in the EPZ; in 1996 the number had fallen to 481. But the EPZ overtook the sugar industry and grew sevenfold in Mauritian rupee terms. Employment in and out of the EPZ is very cyclical, but the value added at constant 1982 prices and the labor productivity are very substantial. Also, there has been a shift from basic cutting and sewing operations to higher-technology textiles, informatics, and electric and electronic products. In 1997 alone, the EPZ companies accounted for over 50 percent of manufacturing's total output. For example, as shown in Table 4.8, the productivity performance of the EPZ subsector is characterized by relatively high growth of real output and labor productivity, but the capital input was more or less stable.

In Mauritius, the EPZ not only provided jobs, but also became the major exporter and earner of foreign exchange. As shown in Table 4.9, export of goods and services constituted 61 percent of the GDP in Mauritius, while it was only 46 percent in Costa Rica.

Table 4.8
Comparing Productivity Growth Trends (1983–1997)

Year	Output (%)	Labor (%)[a]	Capital (%)[b]	Multifactor (%)[c]
1983	0.4	−4.0	−1.2	−2.6
1985	6.9	0.3	3.0	1.7
1987	8.3	2.0	1.1	1.5
1989	4.6	1.4	−3.6	−1.3
1990	7.3	4.3	−2.8	0.4
1991	4.4	2.3	−4.2	−1.1
1992	6.7	4.7	−1.4	1.2
1993	4.9	3.0	−2.7	−0.4
1994	5.3	3.6	−2.5	0.1
1995	5.6	4.3	1.2	1.8
1996	6.0	4.3	0.9	1.9
1997	5.2	3.1	0.0	1.0

Source: Ministry of Economic Development, Productivity and Regional Development, *Productivity and Competitiveness Indicators 1982–97.* Central Statistical Office, 1998, pp. 35—36.

Notes:

a) Labor productivity refers to gross domestic product divided by the number of people employed.

b) Capital productivity indicates real output per unit of capital used in the production process or for the economy as a whole—gross domestic product divided by capital stock.

c) Multifactor productivity refers to output divided against both capital and labor employed. It measures the effect of changes such as technological progress, improvements in management practices and other qualitative variables.

Mauritius has also stimulated a number of backward and forward linkages, such as packaging, precious-stone cutting, electronics, printing, plastic, and paper industries. To augment these industries, catering, security, insurance, banking, construction, and transport were established in the EPZ.[38] But,

Table 4.9
Export of Goods and Services (% GDP)
in Mauritius and Costa Rica

	1980	1997	1998[a]
Mauritius	51	61	0.8
Costa Rica	26	46	-4.4

Sources: World Bank, *World Development Report* (1998—1999), pp. 214—215; a) World Bank, *World Bank Atlas*, 2000, pp. 42—43.

Table 4.10
Employment by Product Group (1997)

Product	Group Enterprises	Number of Male	Number of Female	Employment Total
Food	12	706	1,004	1,710
Flowers	45	251	296	547
Textiles, Yarn & Fabrics	34	2,869	951	3,820
Wearing Apparel	231	18,370	49,330	67,700
Leather Products & Footwear	10	283	1,053	1,336
Wood & Paper Products	29	433	169	602
Optical Goods	5	267	215	482
Electronic Watches & Clocks	3	161	298	459
Electric & Electronic Products	10	233	329	562
Jewelry & Related Articles	20	734	851	1,585
Toys & Carnival Articles	7	108	1,003	1,111
Other	72	1,025	976	2,001
Total	478	25,440	56,475	81,915

Source: Mauritius, Ministry of Economic Development & Regional Co-Operation, *Productivity and Social Indicators* (November 13, 1998), p. 3.

as shown in Table 4.10, a large number of the foreign enterprises in 1997 were concentrated in textiles and apparel.

Though the EPZ is more concentrated in producing low value added products, it can be shown that Mauritius is more diversified than Costa Rica. For instance, as shown in Table 4.11, while agriculture's share of the economy had fallen from 12 percent of the GDP in 1980 to 10 percent in 1997, industry and manufacturing grew by about 23 and 53 percent respectively. In Costa Rica, on the other hand, the share of the GDP taken up by industry and manufacturing declined by 11 percent during that same period. Of the two countries, Mauritius is the more industrialized economy. In 1997, manufacturing and industry dominated the Mauritius economy, whereas there was a decline in the services industry. However, in Costa Rica the shares of industry and manufacturing in the GDP declined by 11 percent for each between 1980 and 1997, whereas the share of services *increased* by 11 percent for the same period. Thus, Costa Rica seems to have restructured its economy around the services sector, whereas Mauritius' economy has moved toward industry and manufacturing.

Together with increased factor mobility arising from improved technology and commitments to open trade, Mauritius and Costa Rica have shown a dramatic increase in international trade. But, as shown in Table 4.11, though export push and foreign investment have contributed to a dramatic increase in economic growth of the two countries, the amount of foreign exchange that Mauritius gets from exporting manufactured goods is more than for Costa Rica. Similarly, the terms of trade of Costa Rica have declined from 1985 to 1994.

However, as pointed out by the World Bank, in order to achieve further economic growth, Mauritius needs to restructure out of the lower value-added activities for which the island is no longer competitive into higher value-added activities involving more advanced skills.[39] Concerned about its competitive status, Mauritius, like the other newly developed countries in Southeast Asia, has been attempting to develop or attract capital-intensive industries such as steel mills and petroleum refineries.[40]

To summarize, over the last two decades Mauritius has manifested a healthy economy. Mauritius' development experience can be attributed to the interplay of economic, sociopolitical, and cultural factors—for example, the availability of preferential treatment under the Lome Convention, in which Mauritius was provided a guaranteed outlet for sugar exports at a stable price that was higher than the prevailing world prices. In line with its economic diversification policy, from the late 1970s through most of the 1990s, Mauritius had been able to sustain annual GNP growth rates of between 5.2 and 6.8 percent, while its per capita income grew between 3.75 and 4.6 percent. As discussed by Subramanian and Roy, the economic growth of Mauritius between 1982 and 1990 was engineered predominantly by the growth of inputs—capital and labor— which together accounted for 90 percent of the annual aver-

Table 4.11
Sector Structure and Percent of Gross Domestic Product (GDP) in Mauritius and Costa Rica

	Agriculture		Industry		Manufacturing		Services		Terms of Trade	
	1980	1997	1980	1997	1980	1997	1980	1997	1985	1994
Mauritius	12	10	26	32	15	23	62	58	77	121
Costa Rica	18	15	27	24	19	17	55	61	111	92

Source: World Bank, *World Development Report* 1998/99. New York: Oxford University Press, pp. 212—213.

Table 4.12
Life Expectancy, Adult Literacy Rate, Infant Mortality Rate, Human Development Index

	Life Expectancy at Birth (Years)	Adult Literacy Rate (%)		Infant Mortality Rate (1,000)		Human Development Index	
	1998	1970	1995	1970	1998	1970	1995
Mauritius	71	66	84	70	19	0.52	0.83
Costa Rica	77	66	84	85	13	0.65	0.89

Source: United Nations, Human Development Index (1998).

age rate of GDP growth of 6.2 percent. In contrast, economic growth in the 1990s has been driven to a greater extent by total factor productivity (TFP) growth.[41]

Foreign direct investments have significantly contributed not only to capital formation but also to substantial transformation of the economy, and an expansion in manufactured exports. "The overall competitive edge that Mauritius has enjoyed enabled it not only to benefit from the cyclical growth in export markets but also from the general movement of delocalisation of manufacturing industries from high-cost industrial countries to lower-cost developing countries."[42]

In addition, the cultural affinities or family ties also facilitated accumulation of joint ventures in the EPZ as reflected in the prominence of Hong Kong, Taiwan, and European businessmen in Mauritius.[43] Thus, in the World Competitiveness Report of 1999, it is shown that Mauritius was not only on top of African countries but also outperformed some of the "Asian Tigers."[44]

Given the high rate of economic growth in Mauritius, how well are the benefits of economic growth distributed among the citizens?

THE SOCIAL WELFARE DISTRIBUTION SYSTEM IN MAURITIUS

As shown in Table 4.12, while achieving a high per capita growth rate, Mauritius and Costa Rica have successfully met the social needs of their citizens. Progress in reducing poverty in Mauritius and Costa Rica has been to large extent accompanied by substantial increase in life expectancy (longevity is an indicator used to measure a country's ability to provide a high quality of life to its citizens) and adult literacy (indicates how well a country prepares its people to function successfully in the economy); and a reduction in infant mortality (for children under age five years). Also in Table 4.12, the two countries

Table 4.13
Poverty Measures

	Gini Coefficient of Inequality			% Below Poverty Line	
	1980–1982	1986–1987	1991–1992	1986–1987	1991–1992
Mauritius	0.46[a]	0.40	0.38	19.5	10.6
Costa Rica		0.48[b]	0.47	NA	NA

Sources:a) World Bank, Mauritius Country Economic Memorandum: Sharpening the Competitive Edge, Country Operations Division II (April 12, 1995), Appendix B. p. 1.
b) M. Torras, Inequality, Resource Depletion, and Welfare Accounting: Application to Indonesia and Costa Rica, *World Development* (July 1999), Vol. 27, No. 7, p. 1197.

have translated their per capita income growth into improvements in the lives of their people as expressed in terms of the Human Development Index. (The HDI, developed in 1990 by the United Nations, encompasses social indicators of life expectancy, literacy, and purchasing power.)

The distribution of income (particularly the Ginico efficient and the percentage of the citizens living below the poverty line) is a good measure of whether a nation shares the benefits of its economic growth widely or concentrates the benefits in the hands of a wealthy, powerful elite.[45] As shown in Table 4.13, Mauritius appears to have a more equal income distribution than Costa Rica. In addition, the proportion of people below the poverty line in Mauritius declined by 46 percent in 1991—1992 when compared to 1986—1987.

But other data contradict these findings. In Costa Rica, 1996 data show that the poorest 20 percent of the population received only 4 percent of the national income, whereas the richest 20 percent received more than half (51.8 percent) of the national income.[46] Based on the most sensitive indicator, the Human Development Index, Costa Rica seems have to better distribution of its national income than Mauritius, although Mauritius' HDI has increased by 60 percent between 1970 and 1995 compared to 37 percent for Costa Rica.

SUMMARY

To summarize Mauritius' situation, since its independence in 1968, Mauritius has attained a highly participatory democratic system based on free elections, and all racial/ethnic/religious communities have been encouraged to flourish on an equal footing. Not only has the stable political system enticed foreign direct investors, but also Mauritius' openness to the global economy has contributed to its economic growth. The system designed for redistributing its national income has become an effective safety net. For instance, the openness ratio (the ratio of trade in goods to GDP) increased from about 70 percent to 100 percent starting the mid-1980s. "Particularly strong was the growth in manufacturing exports, originating predominantly from the export processing zone."[47]

Nonetheless, much less empirical research has been carried out to determine whether Mauritius' high-speed economic growth is sustainable from environmental and social points of view. The focus of the next chapter, then, is to explore whether Mauritius has incorporated and institutionalized its natural resources into its economic development strategies to make its growth sustainable in the long run. If not, what lessons, if at all transferable, can Mauritius learn from Costa Rica in terms of integrating its natural resources into its economic development plans?

CHAPTER 5

SUSTAINABLE ECONOMIC DEVELOPMENT IN MAURITIUS AND COSTA RICA

In order to compare the environmental strategies of Mauritius with Costa Rica, Chapter 5 is divided into two parts. The first part addresses the conceptual framework necessary to understand the environmental issues surrounding sustainable economic development. The second part compares the environmental progress of Mauritius with Costa Rica on a set of environmental indicators. In simple terms, Section 2 highlights the linkages between environmental performance and sustainable development in both Mauritius and Costa Rica.

CONCEPTUAL FRAMEWORK FOR UNDERSTANDING SUSTAINABLE DEVELOPMENT

As narrated in a previous chapter, in the First United Nations Development Decade of the 1960s, environmental issues and economic growth were seen as incompatible. During the Second Development Decade in the 1970s economic growth paradigms emphasized "redistribution with growth" and environmental issues played a peripheral role in economic development.

During the Third Development Decade in the 1980s, the United Nations established the New International Economic Order (1974) and stressed the distribution of resources and the improvement of the terms of world trade between the developed and developing countries. Following the publication of "The Limits to Growth" (1972) by the Club of Rome on the present and future predicament of humankind,[1] the world community was also made to be aware that "grow first, clean up later" environmental practices might be consuming the foundations of sustainable economic development by depleting the natural resources as a result of continued growth in population, industrial capital, and pollution. Stated differently, much of the debate in the 1970s and 1980s was whether the existing economic growth paradigms, which stressed that investment in machines, factories, and infrastructure was needed if growth in real per capita incomes were to be recorded, had raised real per capita incomes and fulfilled basic needs without giving much attention to the finite nature of natural resources. Thus, unlike the nonadaptation to environmental concerns of classical economic framework, the Third Development Decade, tried to take into account the negative externalities and the possibility of internalizing such externalities through environmental charges. Cost-benefit analysis was broadened to include the monetary value of Environmental Management Schemes (for example, ISO 14001).

In the Fourth Development Decade (the 1990s) the world community (also known as *Our Common Future* of 1987) had come to accept the premise that economic development can coexist alongside sound environmental policies. The World Conservation Union, the United Nations Environmental Program (UNEP), and the Worldwide Fund for Nature merged economics and ecology and coined the term "sustainable development." Sustainable development "is ...development that meets the needs of the present without compromising the ability of future generations to meet their own needs."[2]

Though intuitively appealing, the definition contains controversial phrases such as "meeting needs" (particularly, the essential needs of the worlds' poor), which could differ from culture to culture, and cannot be easily translated into practice. But the notion appears to be forward-looking because it includes intergenerational (entails leaving future generations with abundant resources) and intragenerational (entails distributing the environmental costs and benefits fairly among people living now), distributional equity (sharing the capacity for well-being between present and future generations), and protecting resources and the environment from degradation.[3]

1992 RIO EARTH SUMMIT

At the 1992 Earth Summit, the United Nations Conference on the Environment and Development (UNCED) introduced a program of action for sustainable development worldwide for the twenty-first century (Agenda 21). The program "stands as a comprehensive blueprint for action to be taken globally from now into the Twenty-First Century by governments, United Nations organizations, development agencies, nongovernmental organizations and independent-sector groups in every area in which human activity impacts on the environment."[4]

One of the important outcomes of the 1992 Earth Summit at Rio was the creation of the Business Council for Sustainable Development (BCSD) and the development of the Natural Step for sustainability at the institutional level by Karl-Henrik Robert of Sweden. Central to the Natural Step paradigm was the notion of "quality."

The second law of thermodynamics tells us that the world is winding down, that is, that structures of greater complexity are breaking down into structures of lesser complexity, and that these substructures are in turn breaking down in a regression that will eventually return the planet to the inorganic chemical soup whence it came. At the same time, however, matter is evolving into structures that are ever more complex and efficient and elegant. It is these attributes—the sophisticated (and interdependent) architecture of living systems—that Robert has in mind when he speaks of "quality." And it is precisely this quality that is at risk through the progressive junking of the planet.[5]

The Natural Step was heavily used by educational and business institutions to map out their environmental and strategic directions. Robert distills sustainability into four basic principles or "system conditions." These are:

System Condition #1: Substances from the Earth's crust must not systematically increase in nature. That is, the by-products of fossil fuels, metals, and other minerals must not be ejected into the air and water. In practical terms this means that we should radically decrease use of fossil fuels and mining.[6]

System Condition #2: Substances produced by society must not systematically increase in nature. In the sustainable society, nondegradable materials such as plastics and toxic chemicals must not be produced and dispersed at a faster pace than they can be broken down and integrated into the cycles of nature or be deposited into the Earth's crust.

System Condition #3: The physical basis for the productivity and diversity of nature must not be systematically deteriorated. In a sustainable society, we cannot harvest or encroach on the productive parts of nature (forestry, thickness and quality of soils, availability of fresh water, etc.) in such a way that productive capacity and diversity systematically deteriorates.

System Condition #4: There must be just and efficient use of energy and other resources. This means that in the sustainable society, basic human needs must be met with the most resource-efficient method possible, including as just a resource distribution as possible, and their satisfaction must take precedence over luxury consumption.

If organizations want to invest for their future, Robert insists that these four system conditions are nonnegotiable and have to be met adequately. In recent years, the Natural Step has been making the transition into an international movement. For instance, it has been launched in the United States, United Kingdom, Netherlands, Australia, Canada, and other countries.[7]

But, to meet the concerns of the developing countries (such as reducing poverty, illiteracy, infant morality, and also to impede industrialized countries for not using this new form of conditionality as de facto requirements for granting loans or have access to markets in the industrialized countries), and particularly to fulfill the conditions set in Agenda 21, special grants and concessionary funds were created. Under the 1994 Agreement to Restructure and Replenish the Global Environment Facility, donors agreed to provide US$2 billion in core funding over three years, a significant increase over monies allocated to the pilot phase but still well short of the additional financing estimated to be required for developing countries to implement their Rio commitments.[8]

In addition, the Commission on Sustainable Development (CSD) was set up in 1997 to follow-up on and monitor the achievements of nations that have pledged themselves to the concept of sustainable development. However, it needs be pointed out at this juncture that the final agreements of the Earth Summit implicitly assumed that there needed to be

> a process of leadership and diffusion of new technologies and techniques from the industrialized North to the South. The developed economies and their industries are expected to extend their existing policies and methods to curb pollution and reduce waste, developing clean technologies along the way. The developing world, in the course of its inevitable industrialization, will learn from this experience and come to adopt cleaner technologies and processes through 'technology transfer', accelerated by international financial aid provided on the grounds that this is essential to protect the global environment.[9]

Because many environmental problems are international and their causes or consequences cross political borders, combating these problems requires coordination among states. Thus, the World Bank promised special grants especially to the developing countries and other industrialized countries in order come up with effective sustainable development strategies.

For nearly all the international problems on the agenda today, inadequate attention to implementation at both national and international levels is a large part of the reason why international agreements have fallen short of their promise. And as the policy agenda has grown more demanding, requiring that international agreements play an even greater role in coordinating the behavior of national governments, private firms, and individuals, the importance of implementation has grown.[10]

What is being asked of developing countries by the international organizations in practicing sustainable development seems to be unachievable, so identifying some of the most basic problems facing developing countries in the planning and management of natural systems and environmental quality needs to include the following:[11]

√   inadequacies in monitoring and enforcement of existing environmental protection laws and regulations

√ extensive poverty that puts a premium on current income-producing activities to the detriment of long-term protection of natural systems

√ scarcity of financial resources in relation to current needs, which constraints the willingness to protect natural systems

√ the often-perverse distributional effects of environmental quality plans and programs, which may worsen the existing inequitable distribution of income

√ difficulty in controlling the environmental quality effects of private sector and public sector development activities, which limits the effectiveness of public programs for environmental quality management

√ inadequacies in the technical, economic, and administrative expertise available for planning and implementation of environmental management programs

√ widespread market failures, which require extensive use of shadow prices to replace market prices

√ minimal participation in environmental quality planning, either by the general public or by many affected governmental agencies, which reduces the effectiveness of implementation

√ inadequacies in environmental, economic, and social data, including difficulties in data collection and processing and lack of knowledge of past trends and baselines, which limit the quality of analysis

√ wide diversity of cultural values, which increases the difficulty of social evaluation of environmental quality effects

As discussed above, sustainable development involves the harmonization of economic, social (mainly equity within and between generations), and environmental concerns. But developing countries have limited capacity of implementing it because they have limited resources and it is not within their priorities. Given the definition and these problems, the road map for achieving sustainable development in the developing countries requires:

√   internal policies and economic incentives that constitute the basic building blocks for sustainable development (i.e., human and social development, public transparency in government, rule of laws and education, etc.)

√   policies from international lending organizations that emphasizes public involvement and transparency in decision making

√   bilateral and multilateral assistance that enhance domestic policies, not substitute for them

√   governments and private sectors that work together to ensure that the concepts of industrial ecology are made operational and used to improve the economy and the environment[12]

INDICATORS OF SUSTAINABILITY

A reliable (consistent) and valid (i.e., measures what it is designed to measure) indicator needs to: (1) describe the state of the system, (2) detect changes in it, and (3) show cause-and-effect relationships.[13]

In the area of sustainability, for example, there are three basic frameworks: (1) the topic-based framework, which measures specific topic areas such as economic growth; (2) the goal-based framework, which assesses if the outlined objectives are fulfilled; and (3) the pressure-state-response framework, which focuses on the human activities that lead to degradation and ultimately to its remedial actions. For example, pressure covers the use of resources and discharge of pollutants and waste materials. State covers the concentration of pollutants, exceeding of critical loads, and degradation of environmental quality. Indicators of societal response show individual and collective action, and reactions, intended to solve the problem.[14]

Following the criteria set by the Organization for Economic Cooperation and Development (OECD) identifying the policy relevance, analytical soundness, and measurability are very pertinent to identifying the criteria needed for selecting environmental indicators.

The Policy Relevance Environmental indicator should: (1) provide a representative picture of environmental conditions, pressures on the environment, or society's responses; (2) be simple, easy to interpret, and able to show trends over time; (3) be responsive to changes in the environment and related human activities; (4) provide a basis for international comparisons; (5) be either national in scope or applicable to regional environmental issues of national significance; and (6) have a threshold or reference value against which to compare it, so that users can assess the significance of the values associated with it.

The Analytical Soundness Environmental indicator should: (1) be theoretically well founded in technical and scientific terms; (2) be based on international standards and international consensus about its validity; and (3) lend itself to being linked to economic models.

A Measurable indicator should be: (1) readily available or made available at a reasonable cost/benefit ratio; (2) adequately documented and of known quality; and (3) updated at regular intervals in accordance with reliable procedures.[15]

As shown in Figure 5.1, the "pressure-state-response (PSR)" model is used to assess the environmental concerns of Mauritius and Costa Rica. Though the analytical model is very comprehensive, it needs to be stated here that, short of well-functioning formal institutional factors and the participation of the public at the grass roots, environmental policies cannot be effectively implemented.

Figure 5.1
Pressure–State–Response Indicators of
Major Environmental Concerns in Mauritius and Costa Rica

Indicators of Pressure:

1.   Climate change
2.   Ozone layer depletion
3.   Eutrohication
4.   Acidification
5.   Toxic contamination
6.   Urban environmental quality
7.   Biodiversity
8.   Cultural landscapes
9.   Waste

Indicators of Environmental Conditions (State):

10.   Water resources
11.   Forest resources
12.   Fish resources
13.   Soil degradation (desertification, erosion)

Indicators of Social Response:

14.   Economic response
15.   Social response

Adopted from OECD Environmental Indicators, 1998, p. 110.

Without a well-functioning, formal system of institutions to support an environmental strategy, good designs will not be translated into reality. Similarly, without public input into policy design and implementation, policies intended to achieve a more equitable society are less likely to be developed. A substantial part of the implementation of sound environmental management practices depends critically on the public at the grassroots level and on active involvement by the public.[16]

Because governments in developing countries have limited resources, they need to set priorities in implementing actions for their environmental issues. That is, they need to "determine these areas based on the severity of a problem; the ability to resolve the problem, which depends on the level of technological and human capital available; the benefits associated with resolving the problem; and the costs of implementing the necessary measures."[17]

Also, marginalized groups (such as women, the elderly, the poor, and the indigenous) usually suffer the most from environmental threat, because they rely heavily on natural resources, and they need to be consulted until joint responsibility of the problem is taken and a consensus is established how to solve the problem.[18] Broad-consensus local involvement, with accountability and transparency, may yield some of the following benefits:

1. It may result in more equitable policies and improve the likelihood that projects and programs will succeed. Local communities will support environmental programs and projects only if they reflect local beliefs, values, and ideology and use the community.

2. Effective community-government interaction gives policy makers a better and broader understanding of issues and access to new sources of local knowledge and expertise.

3. True local participation can be used as an important mechanism of resolving conflicts, because various divergent voices can be heard.[19]

THE INSTITUTIONALIZATION OF ENVIRONMENTAL POLICIES IN THE ECONOMIC DEVELOPMENT OF MAURITIUS: LESSONS FROM COSTA RICA

"We have learned from the mistakes of other countries ...by acting in good time to protect our environment, instead of trying to clear up the mess after the damage has been done."

—Ministry of Economic Development & Regional Co-operation of Mauritius, *Vision 2020: The National Long-Term Perspective Study*, Vol. 1, 1997, p. 181.

Mauritius has achieved economic growth, but because there is a link between protecting the environment and a lasting economic development, the government has realized that environmental deterioration may arrest the gains in economic growth. But, much less empirical research has been carried out to determine the environmental consequences of Mauritius' incredible growth rate. The central question of the study is then, has Mauritius been able to incorporate and institutionalize its natural resources into its economic development strategies in order to achieve sustainable growth in the long run? If not, what lessons, if at all transferable, can Mauritius learn from Costa Rica in terms of integrating its natural resources into its economic development plans? In order to compare the environmental strategies of Mauritius with Costa Rica (see Table 5.1), the data available from the United Nations Devel-

Table 5.1
Profile of Natural Resources Balance Sheet
of Mauritius and Costa Rica

	Mauritius			Costa Rica		
	1980	1995[a]	1996[b]	1980	1995	1996
1. Forest and woodland (as % of land area) 1995	—	5.9	6.0	—	24.0	24.4
2. Annual rate (%) of deforestation (1990-95)	—	0.0	—	—	3.0	—
3. Annual rate (%) of reforestation (1980-90)	—	2.0	—	—	27.0	—
4. Carbon dioxide emissions per capita (1995)	0.6	1.3	1.5	1.6	1.5	1.4
5. Pesticide consumption 1,000 people (1982-84)	—	0.89	—	—	1.15	—
6. GDP per unit of energy use $ per kg (1987)	3.7	6.6	—	4.2	3.3	—

Source:
a) United Nations Development Program Human Development Report, 1994 & 1998 (New York: Oxford University Press, 1998), 180.
b) World Bank, *World Bank Atlas: 2000*, 34—35.

opment Programs and the environmental strategies of the two countries are analyzed based on the theoretical framework presented in the first part of the chapter, and a combination of indicators used by the United Nations Development Program. (For the UNDP indicators, please refer to the Appendix at the end of this chapter.) The OECD indicators are also used.

LAND DEGRADATION IN MAURITIUS AND COSTA RICA

Land degradation—that is, deforestation, erosion, and resource depletion—not only reduces the land's actual and potential uses but also influences the climate and contributes to a loss of biodiversity (plants and animal species). For example, reduced timber supplies, flooding, and soil degradation affect economic and social activities. The destruction of mangroves threatens the existence of some fishing communities.

Four factors that may contribute to deforestation are: (1) supply-induced scarcity (such as the promotion of agricultural exports and being involved in commercially oriented agriculture); (2) demand-induced scarcity (an increase in population and poverty is the driving force for resource consumption); (3) marginalization (i.e., unequal distribution of resources, lack of secure property titles, and lack of credit and agricultural extension programs); and (4) the breakdown of traditional resource management systems.[20]

According to an expert panel appointed by the International Tropical Timber Organization (ITTO), sustainable forest management includes 'the production of a continuous flow of desired forest products and services without undue reduction of its inherent values and future productivity and without undue undesirable effects on the physical and social environment.'[21]

As shown in Table 5.1, Mauritius has a small resource base when compared with Costa Rica. About 45 percent of its arable land is used to grow sugar cane and it has also attempted to reforest only 2 percent of the land (against 27 percent in Costa Rica), which was cleared for firewood, farms, and building materials.

Because sugar plantations serve as a backbone of the economy in Mauritius, the use of pesticides (often used to maximize crop yields and for disease and weed control) can cause pollution of surface waters (through leaching and surface runoff), pollution of food, and death of wildlife on land, in streams, and in the ocean. The development of pesticide resistance and the appearance of new pest species may threaten soil fertility as well as surface and groundwater in the future. Moreover, as the price of fertilizer increases, it could lead to a shift to more land-extensive systems.[22]

Forests are very essential for soil conservation, the protection of water catchments, and the conservation of fauna and flora. In Mauritius only 30 percent of the total surface area of the island is covered by forest. The main economic use of forests is for deer ranching and the production of timber, poles, and fuel wood.[23]

Because a quarter of the population depends on wood for building materials and wood charcoal as domestic fuel, about 3 percent of the forest and woodland has been deforested from 1990 to 1995. However, "since the early seventies, emphasis has been laid on [reforestation] of degraded forests and abandoned tea lands."[24]

On the other hand, Costa Rica was once covered with forest, but most of the native forests were cleared in the eighteenth and nineteenth centuries and have gradually been replaced by fast growing exotic species like pine and eucalyptus.[25] Also, in Costa Rica, pesticide use has lead to tragic results:

> One recent example was DBCP; a pesticide used in Standard Fruit's Rio Frio banana plantations to control nematodes. After the chemical was found to cause sterility in humans, its use was

suspended in 1977 in the US. In Costa Rica, however, it was not banned until 1988. In addition to abuse of pesticides, unregistered pesticides have been found in use. Pesticide bombardment of the mining fly, which plagues the potato fields, has become so heavy that fly has developed a resistance.[26]

The five major factors that have been identified to cause deforestation in Costa Rica are as follows:

1. Though logging requires a special permit from the government, the timber industry cuts about 200,000 hectares of forest annually.

2. The expansion of banana plantations have substantially contributed to soil erosion.

3. Cattle ranchers have expanded their activities rapidly at the expense of forested area.

4. Squatting is an important cause of deforestation in Costa Rica. By clearing the land, it has been possible to get formal ownership to the land in Costa Rica.

5. The coffee-producing regions have relatively deep soil, yet the soil has lost nutritional content due to erosion-prone topography.[27]

With the development of reforestation programs in Costa Rica in 1986, it is estimated that at least 40 percent of the land is now covered with scrub forest and pasture. For example, the area under secondary forestation has nearly doubled from 229,000 to 425,000 hectares between 1984 and the early 1990s.[28] However, the conversion of forestland to pasture in areas with low-fertility soils, on steep hillsides, where heavy rainfall is common, has resulted in serious soil erosion and poor productivity. A rough estimate of soil loss in 1986 was 680 million tons per year.[29]

Considering air pollution, although the atmosphere is the ultimate environmental amenity, human activities emit pollutants in such quantities that they can build up in the atmosphere to levels that degrade the quality of the environment and human health.[30] Some examples are pieces of ash, smoke, soot, dust, urban smog, and acid rain released into the air. Generally, air pollution has three principal human-activity sources: energy use, vehicular emissions, and industrial production.

Many researchers indicate that there is an inverted U-shape of the Kuznets curve that describes a negative relationship between air pollution and GDP per capita. For instance, T. Panayotou indicates that when a certain level of per capita income is reached, economic growth quickly turns through the environmentally unfavorable stage of development to the environmentally favorable range of the Kuznets curve.[31]

In developing countries, air pollution arises when households cook with or heat their homes with biomass (wood, straw, or dung). Though the World Health Organization (WHO) guidelines indicate that suspended particulate matter (SPM) should not exceed more than seven days a year, "studies that have measured bio-mass smoke in household kitchens in poor rural areas have found suspended particulate matter levels that routinely exceed by of WHO guidelines."[32] The health impact of exposure to indoor air pollution from biomass burning contributes to acute respiratory infections that cause an estimated 4 million deaths annually among infants and children.[33]

Pollutants from transport fuels could intensify the environmental problems in less-developed countries. The World Bank notes that

> [i]n the cities of developing countries vehicles are a significant source of airborne toxic pollutants, accounting for up to 95 percent of lead. Three factors make pollution from vehicles more serious than in industrial countries. First, many vehicles are in poor condition, and lower-quality fuels are used. Second, motor vehicles are concentrated in a few large cities. ...Third, a far larger percentage of the population moves and lives in the open air and is thus more exposed to automotive pollutants. The poor are usually the most affected....Lead and other pollutants also

contaminate food in open-air restaurants, which are frequented by the poor.[34]

On the other side, the environmental problems associated with rapid industrial development in the less developed countries are:

> First, as emissions from existing activities increase, they pass the point at which they can be readily assimilated by the environment. Second, as industrial towns expand, more people are exposed to pollution. Third, within industry the structure shifts away from activities that are moderately polluting, such as textiles, wood products, and food processing, and toward others with much greater potential for causing environmental harm, such as metals, chemicals, and paper.[35]

However, the rapid increase in industrial pollution in Mauritius is explained in terms of

> release of insufficiently treated waste water from textile dyehouses, airborne particulates, illegal dumping of textiles wastes and noise pollution. Small and medium enterprises such as metal working, machine tools, printing, tanning and galvanising are among the worst offenders because of their limited resources. Sugar factories are also considered to be major sources of organic pollution in surface water bodies and to a lesser extent in the lagoons which receive these waters.[36]

Currently, the atmosphere (which is supposed to consist mainly of 78 percent nitrogen, 21 percent oxygen, and 0.9 percent argon, and the remaining 0.1 percent includes trace of other gases) is generating global warming due to an excessive emission of carbon dioxide.

For example, as shown in Table 5.1, the atmospheric concentration of carbon dioxide emission in Mauritius due to combustion of fossil hydrocarbon fuels (coal, oil, gas, biomass burning) has continuously risen when compared to carbon dioxide emission in Costa Rica. If no remedial action (such as understanding the process and rate of change; establishing the emitters, developing of a control strategy, deciding how to fund and enforce control, and monitoring mechanisms),[37] is undertaken, Mauritius will be facing global warming in the near future.

WATER RESOURCES, USES AND POLLUTION

In Mauritius, the source of water is the rainy season, which is mainly from December to April. During the 1950s, Mauritius resorted to a massive program of groundwater prospecting to be used for irrigation purposes in the drier parts of the island. But it was the industrialization of the 1980s that led to further and intensive exploration for groundwater. The four aquifers (known as the Curepipe, Northern, Southern, and Eastern aquifers) are polluted by poor sanitation (sewage, waste water, and refuse disposal) and by poor agricultural practices. Currently, the water losses in the supply system are on the order of 55 percent. Managing efficiently the island's water resources and determining the level of investment needed for a water supply up to 2010 should be of high concern.[38]

ENERGY INTENSITY

Energy efficiency, the percentage of energy consumed per unit of output, is generally regarded as an indicator of the impact an economy has on the energy. Costa Rica and Mauritius are oil dependent. For example, in 1990, 82 percent of the total oil requirements for Mauritius were imported, and fuel consumption has increased more than threefold from 1973 to 1992. As shown in Table 5.1, Mauritius' energy intensity is higher than that of Costa Rica. That is, over the years, energy intensity in Costa Rica has declined but energy intensity in Mauritius has increased. Possible explanations might be because Costa Rica is using relatively more efficient technologies than Mauritius in its industrialization process, or it might be because Costa Rica's stage of development is to a large extent based on services and has been replacing the energy consuming industries, or both.

To summarize, the backbone of the Mauritius economy is based on sugar plantations, textiles, and tourism. Sugar plantations are dependent on inputs such as herbicides and insecticides, and cause pollution of surface water and food products. The textile and clothing industries contribute to about 50 percent of merchandise exports, but because there is little control of land use or waste disposal (almost 82 percent of the population remains unconnected to sewerage networks and mostly use soakage pits), industrial sewage flows directly into surrounding lagoons. For example, most of the expulsion from dye works is deposited mainly into the rivers and the sea, with little or no treatment of waste.[39]

The tourism industry has developed in coastal zones that are fragile and has led to considerable pressure on the ecosystems. "Incipient signs of environmental degradation, including deterioration in the coral reefs, contamination of groundwater, and reduced water quality in the bays, have become evident."[40] In addition, the increasing number of vehicles on the road that do not use unleaded gasoline has resulted in congestion. Thus, the natural resources of Mauritius have become severely depleted through deforestation, land clearing, agriculture, and rural and urban infrastructure development.

Recognizing that environmental restoration must redress the damage done to the environment by its rapid economic growth, Mauritius has been engaged in country-driven sustainable development strategies. For example, the Environmental Investment Programme (EIP), which was developed in 1988, focused mainly on setting the appropriate legal and institutional frameworks for environmental management and upon curative measures such as reforestation, restoring natural habitats, construction of gabion and retaining walls to further prevent beach and soil erosion. In 1995, the Environmental Impact Protection Act (EIPA) required all firms to obtain an Environmental Impact Assessment license before any activity is undertaken.

Realizing that the EIPA Committee has not been effective in achieving the objectives of the EPA and was considered by various ministries as being an impediment to development, a comprehensive strategic plan, known as the National Environmental Action Plan (NEAP), was developed. It was a strategy for the environment and the economy and was designed for the period of 1998 to 2005 under the leadership of the Ministry of Environmental and Urban and Rural Development.

On the other hand, in Costa Rica, because the agricultural sector contributes to about 20 percent of the GDP, generates about 70 percent of its foreign exchange, and is heavily dependent on ecotourism, it is attempting to curtail the deterioration of its ecosystem. For example, in 1942, agricultural extension service projects were undertaken to conserve soil and water components. However, realizing that the sustained increase of agricultural productivity could be achieved only through the application of modern techniques of soil and water management, the government promulgated the Law of Natural Resource Conservation in 1953. In its National Development Plan from 1986 to 1990, Costa Rica emphasized the management of sustainable natural resources. For example, among the actions included in the plan were the creation of Servicio Nacional de Calidad y Salud Animal (SENACSA); the preparation of new soil conservation laws aimed at carrying out, modifying, and improving the 1953 Natural Resource Law; and passage of numerous other laws aimed at discouraging degradation of the resource stock and promoting conservation.[41]

In 1997, Costa Rica launched a detailed National Environmental Plan (NEP), which was inspired by the 1992 Earth Summit in Rio de Janeiro. In the Convention on Biological Diversity, Costa Rica and the other 957 participants analyzed the weaknesses of their existing environmental plans and, for Costa Rica at least, NEP was the result. Specifically, "the process of formulating the Strategy was ...seen as an opportunity to analyze the country's advances in relation to the fulfillment of the Convention, and to update the existing information on the country's biodiversity, to make it available for decision-making."[42] The questions that need to be asked are:

1. What are the environmental national action plans and implementation strategies that Mauritius is pursuing?
2. What lessons, if any, can Mauritius learn from Costa Rica to make its economy sustainable?

The National Environmental Plans of Mauritius and Costa Rica

Both Costa Rica and Mauritius have formulated various strategies to sustain their ecosystems. Theoretically stated, the strategic management process consists of three stages: strategy formulation, strategy implementation, and strategy evaluation.[43] Strategy formulation includes: (1) developing the mission of the organization; (2) establishing long-term objectives; (3) generating alternative strategies to pursue those objectives; (4) implementing strategies to devise policies, motivate employees, and allocate resources so that the formulated strategies can be executed; (5) monitoring to make adjustments according to feedback; and (6) measuring in order to assess whether the strategies formulated to achieve the mission statements of the organization are working or not.

The Mission Statement

Mauritius and Costa Rica have developed their environmental mission statements in order to guide them as a focal point in planning activities. For example, outlining the reasons for the current state of the environment (i.e., ecological vulnerability, inadequate land and water management, inadequate land use planning, poor coastal planning, lack of data and information, inadequate capacity to deal with environmental concerns and implementation programs, inadequate involvement of major stakeholders in natural resources management, and inadequate integration of conservation principles and approaches in national planning and development programs), as set up by the Ministry of Environmental and Urban and Rural Development, the mission statement of the Republic of Mauritius is as follows:

> The mission of the Ministry of Environment and Urban and Rural Development is to ensure the protection and management of the environmental assets of Mauritius so that their capacity to sustain the society and its development remains unimpaired and to foster harmony between quality of life, environmental protection and sustainable development for the present and future generations.[44]

The strategic framework of Costa Rica, on the other hand, establishes the orientation that should be given to the issues of conservation, sustainable use, and the distribution of associated costs and benefits. Also, before the mission statement Costa Rica identified a series of environmental weaknesses. Some of the most conspicuous weaknesses of existing environmental policies include the following twelve items:

1. Research has focused on specific taxonomic groups, in particular locations, and those responsible for biodiversity management do not receive the results of the research that is carried out.

2. Recent advances in the development of an institutional framework and regulations have not been accompanied by a program to develop and train the human resources involved with biodiversity management in the governmental and private sectors.

3. Efforts in both formal and informal education sectors have focused on teaching the importance of conserving

resources and creating opportunities for sustainable use; however, efforts have not reached the entire population, in terms of the use and acquisition of the benefits derived from biodiversity. Moreover, most of the actions undertaken to date still do not incorporate a gender perspective or contribute to the preservation of traditional knowledge.

4. The different sectors of society have not been effectively involved in the sustainable management of biodiversity.

5. The information on the country's biodiversity is not yet systematized nor is it available in formats that are suited to the needs of the different social actors, such as educators, conservationists, local governments, farmers, and the like.

6. There is insufficient institutional capacity at the level of the Conservation Areas for the follow-up of environmental impact evaluations and the application of existing regulations and guidelines.

7. Efforts to consolidate the country's protected areas are incomplete, and do not yet include samples of all the ecosystems, which are necessary to achieve ecological representation.

8. Efforts undertaken for the ex situ conservation of wildlife and domesticated species are inadequate. There is insufficient coordination between these projects and Ministerio del Ambiente y Energía (MINAE), and also a lack of necessary funding.

9. The issues of conservation and sustainable use have not been properly integrated into the national, regional, and local decision-making processes.

10. Payment programs for environmental services are not always based on technically defined priorities and they tend to focus exclusively on forests, which reflects only a fraction of the contribution to the national economy.

11. Production and conservation activities involving marine and coastal resources are not undertaken in a planned manner and ignore the close interrelation between terrestrial and marine resources.

12. Existing financial and human resources are insufficient to guarantee an integrated approach to conservation and the promotion of sustainable use, both from the public sector and the private sector.[45]

Then Costa Rica created a mission statement to specifically answer what the country wants to become in the future. The Costa Rican mission statement reads as follows:

> The country's biodiversity is protected, known, and used in a sustainable manner on the part of the Costa Rican society, in such a way as to improve people's quality of life. To this end, the costs and benefits derived from biodiversity conservation and use are integrated and shared equitably.[46]

To ensure unanimity of purpose within the Ministry of Environment and Energy and other sectors, the Costa Rican state, through the Ministry of the Environment and Energy, will coordinate the efforts of the different social and economic sectors to achieve the national objectives related to conservation and sustainable use of biodiversity, promoting joint actions and strategic alliances at the local, regional, national and international level.[47]

The conceptual framework needed in writing the mission statement of an organization needs to include: the institution's customers; its products or services; the kind of technology it uses; its concerns for survival and public image; its guiding philosophy; its employees empowerment; and social equity. Given these indicators, how does Mauritius compare with Costa Rica (see Table 5.2)?

The tourism industry in Costa Rica has grown dramatically. With 500,000 to 1,000,0000 tourists visiting yearly, tourism is the second foreign exchange earner next to bananas.

Table 5.2
The Environmental Mission Statements of Mauritius and Costa Rica—A Comparison

Indicator	Mauritius	Costa Rica
Architects	Government officials and consultants	Government officials, NGOs, local committees, international org. consultants
Customers	Present & Future	Improve the quality of life Present & Future generations
Product or service	Management of the environmental assets	Conservation & sustainable use of biodiversity
Technology	———	———
Concern for Survival	Ensure protection and management of environmental assets use	Conservation of sustainable use
Philosophy	Harmony between quality of life, environmental protection, and sustainable development	Improve people's quality of life
Employee	———	Responsibility assumed by each actor
Social Equity	———	Participation by each and every Costa Rican. Conserve and use the country's biodiversity in a just and equitable manner

Thus with the participation of all its citizens, to develop its ecotourism industry, Costa Rica has developed a better comprehensive view of its environmental mission than Mauritius. Also based on its mission statement, Costa Rica seems to be more effective than Mauritius in indicating its commitment to social equity.

Finally, Costa Rica promotes a sense of shared expectations in the conservation and sustained survival of its resources and motivates the use of resources by its citizens and generations of employees.

LONG-TERM OBJECTIVES

Clearly established objectives are very vital to success and identify what specifically is to be done, provide direction, establish priorities, reduce uncertainty, identify who is responsible, help in evaluation, and aid in the allocation of resources. Thus, in order to be an important measure of managerial performance, the long-term objectives of an organization need to be acceptable, measurable, realistic, flexible, understandable, challenging, achievable, congruent with the mission statement, and have a time frame for completion.[48]

In formulating its national environmental plans, while Mauritius did not attempt to outline its long-term objectives, Costa Rica on the other hand states that its general objective is to "conserve and use the country's biodiversity in a just and equitable manner."[49]

As shown in Table 5.3, an analysis of Costa Rica's long-term objectives indicates that they seem to be understandable, challengeable, and congruent with the mission statement, but they are short on a realistic, measurable, and achievable time frame.

Table 5.3

An Analysis of the Long-Term Objectives of Mauritius and Costa Rica

Criterion	Mauritius	Costa Rica
Measurable	——	No
Realistic	——	No
Understandable	——	Yes
Challenging	——	Yes
Achievable	——	Partially
Congruent with Mission	——	Yes
Time Horizon	——	No

ENVIRONMENTAL STRATEGIES OF MAURITIUS AND COSTA RICA

After briefly stating the nature and magnitude of environmental problems in Mauritius and Costa Rica, both countries outline their vision and mission statements for the future. But Costa Rica seems to be clear in stating its long-term objectives in order to achieve sustainable development. Given their institutional and resource constraints, both Mauritius and Costa Rica have discussed in general the strategic process of minimizing the environmental impacts of their economic trends. Stated differently, the two countries have designed environmental strategies to tackle their environmental problems and eventually achieve sustainable development. Then, the two vital questions that need to answered are:

1. Have the two countries generated specific courses of action that could help them to achieve their mission and objectives?
2. Have they spelled out the supporting policies in order to carry out the stated strategies?

NATIONAL ENVIRONMENTAL STRATEGIES OF MAURITIUS

To incorporate the lessons learned from the experiences during implementation of the first Environmental Action Plan (NEAP I), Mauritius initiated in 1988 a step toward the protection of the environment, which was translated into action by the formulation of 32 projects under the umbrella of the Environment Investment Program (EIP I). The second National Environmental Strategies (NES) were carried out, which contained many recommendations from Agenda 21 of the Rio Conference and the National Environmental Action Plan (NEAP II), plus the Environment Investment Program II (EIP

II), and the Review of Legal and Institutional Framework for Environmental Management in Mauritius. With the assistance of the Environmental Resources Management of United Kingdom, the government of Mauritius, and nongovernmental agencies, academics and private individuals initiated the following strategic thrusts for dealing with environmental problems, including: protection of water resources, prevention of industrial pollution, treatment of domestic sewage system, management and proper disposal of solid waste, management of agroindustrial practices, enhancement of biological diversity, improvement of transportation systems, protection and management of the coastal and marine ecosystems, handling of forecasted climatic changes, and creation of public awareness and participation among stakeholders.[50]

To protect water resources, standards for treated effluents for discharge into the ocean and standards for treated effluents for use in irrigation were prepared as per regulations made under the EPA in 1991. Also, four laboratories, which will eventually be able to carry out the chemical analysis necessary to enforce standards and monitor effects on water quality, were to be established. To avoid overexploitation of the groundwater sources, an increased supply of surface water, by the distilling and rehabilitation of existing dams, was suggested. Furthermore, the control of leakages and the use of recycled water for irrigation were highly encouraged.

To prevent industrial pollution, measures such as effluent taxes, user charges, and the "polluter-pays-principle" were applied to steer economic behavior into environmentally desirable directions. Also, large and small enterprises were encouraged to assess the impact of new technologies and generally invest in clean technologies, as well as to adopt production techniques that are not harmful to the environment.

To address the issue of sewage treatment and disposal, a National Sewerage Master Plan (NSMP) was prepared in 1994 and regions that needed an extension of sewerage networks were identified. To manage waste, the government has approved the construction of two incinerators and pilot composting plants, given that almost 50 percent of domestic waste is of organic origin. Particular attention was given to:

1. Provide waste storage receptacles to households, industries, and commercial enterprises.
2. Introduce a uniform pricing policy for collection and disposal of waste for different economic sectors.
3. Recycle and reuse waste.
4. Dispose of sludge from the sewage treatment plants.
5. Establish the concepts of customer care and continuous service based on availability, quality, responsiveness, and efficiency.
6. Develop cost-effective tariffs.
7. Avoid the formulation of cartels among waste management contracts.[51]

The strategies suggested for agriculture and agroindustrial practices were the education of farmers in the use of organic fertilizers, and the use of chemical fertilizers and pesticides to minimize the risk of contamination of food through residues. In addition, the possibility of providing incentives to small establishments to invest in the treatment and disposal of wastes was suggested.

It was suggested that better land use planning and the establishment of protected areas for endemic flora and fauna are concerns that should be addressed. Though too vague, the suggestions hoped to further biological diversity.

To address the problem of transportation and pollution due to traffic congestion, the following strategies were suggested:

1. Improve air pollution by moving to catalytic converters and cleaner forms of fuel.

2.	Establish, monitor, and enforce standards on air quality and noise levels.
3.	Provide incentives to the private sector to invest in parking facilities outside the town centers, thereby limiting parking in these areas.
4.	Introduce toll tax and green tax on fuel.
5.	Improve the public transport system so as to reduce the use of private cars.
6.	Develop bus and cycle lanes, car-free zones, and pedestrian alleys.
7.	Explore the ways and means of disposing vehicle carcasses.[52]

With the increase in tourism and the need for Mauritians to have access to inexpensive coastal leisure facilities, the pressure on the coastal belt will keep increasing. Thus, to minimize the use of the coastal belt, the following strategies were suggested:

1.	Prepare and implement Integrated Coastal Zone Management plans that will preserve and protect the productivity and biological diversity of coastal ecosystem.
2.	Phase out the use of coral sand for construction purposes and increase awareness on the use of substitutes, such as rocks and basalt-sand.
3.	Adopt corrective measures to limit beach erosion.
4.	Upgrade and open access to other beaches to relieve pressure on popular beaches.
5.	Develop inland tourism to relieve pressure on beaches.
6.	Remove silt in lagoons where necessary and adopt corrective measures to limit soil erosion.
7.	Control and monitor commercial, industrial, leisure, sport, and fishing activities.
8.	Restrict the number of hotels and recreation centers having beach frontage.[53]

Because of its vulnerability to climate changes and rising sea levels, Mauritius, under the United Nations Framework Convention on Climate Changes, has prepared a National Climate Action Plan and outlined various long-term and short-term strategies for coping the potential effects of climate change. Realizing that the effectiveness of achieving environmental management strategies depends on creating awareness and communication among stakeholders, the Mauritian government has initiated the following strategies:

1. Provide the appropriate legislation and adequate facilities in the form of equipment and trained staff for monitoring and enforcement.
2. Enhance environmental awareness within governmental agencies and improve intersectored communication among the various departments.
3. Improve and strengthen the mechanism for communication, information collection, and information dissemination among the public officers, the scientific community, the NGOs, and the public at large.
4. Get feedback and improve existing information from independent scientific groups.
5. Strengthen environmental education in school curriculums.
6. Increase public awareness of the health and economic impact of environmental degradation and generate public discussions about possible solutions.

National Environmental Strategies of Costa Rica

As a result of the planning work undertaken in the Conservation Areas and in consultations with experts in specific fields, 13 strategic issues were identified to carry out the objectives of Costa Rica's environmental problems. For each, as shown below, strategic issues, policies, strategies, and priority activities were identified.[54]

1. Strengthen the mechanisms required for prevention and mitigation of the adverse impact of productive activities on biodiversity and the integration of different social actors.

   Policy:

   √ Adapt and enhance the capacity of institutions and communities in the prevention and mitigation of the impact of production activities.

   Strategies:

   √ Internalize the concept of environmental impact evaluation within the state apparatus, as part of the environmental responsibility of different sectors.
   √ Update guidelines for the correct application of environmental impact evaluations and monitoring.
   √ Strengthen capacity at national and regional level to process, resolve, and follow up on environmental impact evaluations.
   √ Strengthen actions of protection and control undertaken by Sistema Nacional de Areas de Conservacion (SINAC) with the support of other organizations, both at terrestrial and marine levels.
   √ Establish systems to assess environmental damage.
   √ Involve civil society in the process of environmental impact studies in the Conservation Areas.

   Priority activities:

   √ Estimate and classify the impact of production activities.

√ Review and modify legislation on environmental impact.

√ Training on environmental impact.

2. Strengthen national and regional planning, as well as land use processes.

Policy:

√ Promote coordination and planning activities to optimize land use, incorporating conservation and development goals.

Strategies:

√ Incorporate elements of conservation and sustainable development into regional planning processes.

√ Incorporate measures to prevent and mitigate the impact of natural disasters into the different regional development plans.

√ Promote efficient and effective implementation of regulations and guidelines.

Priority activities:

√ Make available and systematize geographic information to facilitate decision making on environmental matters.

√ Clarify institutional competences in the area of land use.

√ Incorporate the variable of biodiversity into programs for the prevention and mitigation of natural disasters derived from human activities.

3. Establish the necessary cross-institutional and cross-sectored coordination for the integrated management of

biodiversity as a strategic element of the country's development.

Policies:

√ Strengthen the capacity of local communities to participate in and benefit from biodiversity and sustainable use projects.

√ Establish bodies and mechanisms to facilitate coordination.

Strategies:

√ Develop capacity for joint work between the state and civil society in the area of sustainable management of biodiversity.

√ Establish formal structures.

√ Develop CONAGEBIO's (Comisión Nacional para la Gestión de la Biodiversidad) capacity to project its work at the regional level.

Priority activities:

√ Develop the management capacity of the national Commission for Biodiversity Management.

√ Establish and consolidate organizations at national and local levels to facilitate coordination for integrated management of biodiversity.

4. Strengthen research activities required for the generation of knowledge on sustainable use and conservation of the country's biodiversity.

Policies:

√ Strengthen national capacity to generate and apply knowledge on sustainable use.

√ Promote and support biodiversity inventories and their application in the sustainable management of biodiversity.

√ Promote research and studies aimed at determining the status of species and ecosystems of particular interest for conservation.

√ Promote research that contributes to the sustainable use of resources.

√ Promote traditional knowledge through research.

Strategies:

√ Establish a national agenda for research on wildlife and domesticated biodiversity.

√ Promote inventories on biodiversity to support sustainable use activities with an economic impact.

√ Promote biodiversity inventories to generate information on wildlife biodiversity.

√ Develop national capacity to generate knowledge required for the conservation and management of biodiversity.

√ Integrate national efforts in the study and management of the genetic base of domesticated and potential agricultural, forest, and livestock species.

√ Promote research aimed at incorporating environmentally friendly technologies that are also socially and economically viable.

√ Promote research to monitor the impact of agrochemical on public health and ecosystems.

√ Promote the recovery and preservation of knowledge concerning the traditional and potential uses of wildlife biodiversity.

Priority activities:

√ Prepare an inventory of the country's species.

√   Promote demonstration projects on integrated and sustainable management of biodiversity.

√   Strengthen research and generate information on conservation and sustainable use.

√   Strengthen the capacity of the SINAC to control, supervise, and follow up on research.

5. Establish the necessary formal and informal mechanisms to provide the public and private sectors with information required for conservation and sustainable production based on the elements of biodiversity.

Policies:

√   Develop a national information network on biodiversity to support decision making on conservation and sustainable use. This network would be permanent and would generate, administer, provide access to, and exchange information for public and private users. The state would act as regulator, promoter, and generator of funds and would encourage the participation of other factors.

√   Facilitate the distribution of information to users.

Strategies:

√   Establish an organizational platform.

√   Guide the systematization and processing of information directed at users.

√   Popularize the information on biodiversity and facilitate access for different users.

√   Integrate research results to environmental education and extension activities.

Priority activities:

√   Establish a National Information Network on Biodiversity.

√   Strengthen SINAC's capacity to manage information on biodiversity.

6.   Strengthen public awareness of biodiversity issues.

Policies:

√   Integrate environmental education into formal education programs.

√   Develop informal education programs on the sustainable use of the elements of biodiversity.

Strategies:

√   Reinforce issues and concepts relating to biodiversity in school curricula.

√   Implement training and information activities with sectors involved in production, and with communities, on the application of sustainable production practices.

√   Integrate efforts by different institutions and organizations, as well as prioritize target groups.

√   Strengthen the participation of SINAC and conservation organizations in local shows, exhibits, and other community activities for education and extension purposes.

√   Establish mechanisms to preserve and value traditional knowledge.

Priority activities:

√   Training in sustainable use of biodiversity directed at the mass media.

√   Training in sustainable use of biodiversity directed at community leaders.

√   Establish a National Bioliteracy Program.

7. Consolidate national efforts directed at in situ conservation.

Policies:

√   Consolidate the existing protected wildlife areas.
√   Develop management strategies for protected wildlife areas based on conservation and sustainable use objectives.
√   Strengthen civil society's participation and joint responsibility in conservation projects.

Strategies:

√   Strengthen technical capacity to ensure the effective management of biodiversity in protected wildlife areas.
√   Develop financial opportunities for management of protected wildlife areas.
√   Implement proposals on land use for conservation purposes (GRUAS Project).
√   Strengthen planning initiatives in protected wildlife areas in order to identify opportunities to complement protection efforts or generate economic benefits for their management and for local communities.
√   Establish active management programs for the conservation of species that require this approach.
√   Promote the creation and development of private wildlife areas.
√   Promote conservation of genetic resources of interest to agricultural and forestry sectors.
√   Strengthen capacity to control the entry and impact of exotic species.

Priority activities:

√   Make a financial consolidation of the protected wild-life areas.

√   Identify habitats of particular interest for conservation outside the protected wildlife areas and define technical criteria for the establishment of biological corridors to facilitate research and production activities.

√   Provide training in monitoring and active managing of species of particular interest and in conservation of biological reserves and farms.

√   Provide technical analysis of the management categories in existing protected wildlife areas and their adaptation to comply with conservation and sustainable use objectives.

8.   Strengthen national capacity to carry out ex situ conservation activities with species of particular interest.

Policy:

√   Develop national capacity to carry out ex situ conservation activities as a complement to the management of protected wildlife areas and as an instrument to strengthen public awareness and research.

Strategies:

√   Strengthen MINAE's capacity to advise and supervise ex situ facilities.

√   Strengthen the participation of the academic and private sectors in ex situ conservation activities.

Priority activities:

√   Establish policies, legislation, and strategies for ex
     situ conservation.
√   Provide training in ex situ conservation techniques.
√   Carry out feasibility studies and subsequent devel-
     opment of a national center for research, training,
     and transfer of technology in ex situ conservation,
     with outreach in the Central American region.

9. Establish the necessary mechanisms to facilitate access
    to genetic resources of biodiversity and for the fair and
    equitable benefit-sharing derived from these.

Policy:

√   Establish a technical, regulatory, and organizational
     framework to guarantee fair and equitable access to
     the elements of biodiversity.

Strategies:

√   Protect the intellectual and industrial property rights
     of the products of biodiversity.
√   Guarantee equality and gender equity in access to
     and control of biodiversity resources and eradicate
     discriminatory social practices.
√   Establish formal bodies to coordinate access to ge-
     netic resources.

Priority activities:

√   Harmonize national and international legislation on
     access and transfer of technology and on intellec-
     tual property rights.
√   Train decision makers, media workers, judges, re-
     searchers, and the peasant and indigenous commu-

nities on access, transfer of technology, and intellectual property rights.

√ Establish a participatory process to determine the scope and requirements of intellectual property rights of communities.

10. Develop national capacity for the preservation of social, economic, and environmental risks arising from the management of modified living organisms that result from biodiversity.

Policy:

√ Establish a technical, regulatory, and organizational framework to guarantee the safe transfer, manipulation, and release of modified living organisms resulting from biotechnology.

Strategy:

√ Develop institutional capacity and the necessary regulations to guarantee environmental security.

Priority Activity:

√ Develop national capacity in the area of biosecurity.

11. Strengthen actions to internalize the costs of environmental services and incentives for the sustainable use of biodiversity.

Policies:

√ Consolidate the national program for payment of environmental services.

√ Develop innovative mechanisms to promote conservation activities and sustainable use.

Strategies:

√ Define criteria for the assignation of quota as payment for environmental services.

√ Strengthen actions directed at developing projects for joint implementation.

√ Establish a verification and follow-up system in the areas included under the different modalities of payment for environmental services.

√ Expand the range of environmental services subject to financial compensation.

√ Develop new mechanisms to internalize the costs of providing environmental services.

√ Diversify conservation and sustainable use incentives.

Priority activities:

√ Promulgate a legal framework specifically on the subject environmental services.

√ Develop valuation and administration mechanisms for the charging and payment of environmental services.

√ Promote and consolidate projects that generate financial resources for the payment of environmental services.

√ Zone priority areas for payment of environmental services according to their biological importance and other benefits to the country.

√ Promote and strengthen incentives for research, development, and marketing of products of biodiversity.

12. Define a national strategy for the development and protection of marine and coastal resources.

Policies:

√ Develop technical and institutional instruments for the effective management of marine and coastal resources.

√ Revise, improve, and apply a legal framework that integrates marine and coastal resources.

√ Incorporate marine and coastal resources into the everyday life of the national population.

Strategies:

√ Identify critical coastal zones for the formulation of protection strategies or the rational (sustainable) use of marine-coastal resources (integrated management plans for marine and coastal areas).

√ Strengthen institutions and organizations for the effective management of marine and coastal populations and resources, facilitating their use of society.

√ Define the requirements for revising the legal framework on the integrated management of marine and coastal resources.

√ Establish extension and education programs on marine and coastal resources (medium- and long-term) at the institutional level.

Priority activities:

√ Design and implement a training program on the management of marine and coastal biodiversity.

√ Develop a National Program for the Integrated Management of Marine and Coastal Resources.

√ Overhaul the national legal framework to regulate the use, development, and protection of marine and coastal ecosystems and resources.

13. Strengthen national capacity for the sustainable management of biodiversity in both the public and private sectors.

Policies:

√ Strengthen the capacity of institutions and civil society to promote conservation and sustainable use.
√ Promote organic and conservationist agriculture.
√ Incorporate concepts of technical and financial sustainability into biodiversity management.
√ Promote exchange of experiences in sustainable biodiversity management at regional level in Central America.

Strategies:

√ Identify and address the training needs of institutions and organizations involved in biodiversity management.
√ Promote specific activities aimed at developing organizational and decision-making capacity for sustainable production.
√ Strengthen knowledge of the existing guidelines and regulations among those responsible for guaranteeing their application, and among users of biodiversity.
√ Consolidate the proposed institutional framework for the management of biodiversity.
√ Strengthen training activities and marketing of products of organic and conservationist agriculture.
√ Strengthen actions to promote the application sustainable practices in forestry activities.
√ Develop innovative financial mechanisms.
√ Strengthen capacity to incorporate biodiversity conservation into regional development.

Priority activities:

√   Establish a training program directed at the different social actors involved in conservation and the sustainable use of biodiversity.

√   Strengthen technical capacity in the public and private sectors, in terms of environmentally friendly technologies.

√   Strengthen funding programs for sustainable production activities based on biodiversity use.

EVALUATION OF THE MAURITIAN AND COSTA RICAN ENVIRONMENTAL STRATEGIES

From a review of the environmental action plans of both Mauritius and Costa Rica, it is possible to say that both countries have transcended from an environmental protection paradigm, which stresses that environmental protection can be achieved only at the expense of economic growth (win-lose situation). Instead, they have moved to the win-win paradigm (which argues that there should be closer interaction between the environment and economic growth), and to a more balanced approach (which recognizes that the relationship between environmental and economic interests should be neither purely competitive nor cooperative). As discussed by Andrew Hoffman:

> [T]he reality of environmentalism in the business context is becoming more complex than regulatory compliance or social responsibility reveal. We now live in an age when environmental concerns originate from a broader system of pressures than merely government and activist forces. Insurance companies, investors, local communities, labor unions, international regimes, the media, financial institutions, consumers, and suppliers all apply pressure on corporations to handle environmental affairs. Through so complex a web of constituents, environmentalism becomes transformed from something external to the market

environment to something central to the core objectives of the firm. As such, corporations must trigger a more complex set of organizational and strategic responses than merely the management of these external pressures.[55]

However, Costa Rica's strategic policy seems be more comprehensive than that of Mauritius. For example, not only does Costa Rica formulate strategies to carry out its long-term objectives, but also it proposes various supporting policies and priority activities to achieve sustainable development.

In addition, as shown in Table 5.4, Mauritius undertakes its environmental problems by using mainly "command and control" regulations, such as environmental tax, government regulations, fines, charges, sanctions, and jails terms for non-compliance. On the other hand, Costa Rica's environmental management strategy is to a large extent based on "market-based instruments" such as consumer advocacy, polluter-pays, incentive programs, and recycling of waste. That is, according to the market-based system, a country tries to decentralize "decision-making to a degree that the polluter or resource user has a maximum amount of flexibility to select the production or consumption option that minimizes the social cost of achieving a particular level of environmental quality."[56]

The Lessons That Mauritius Can Learn from Costa Rica

In the last three decades, Mauritius has achieved dramatic economic growth. National policy assumed that the general welfare of citizens could automatically improve with the expansion of the economy. In other words, the environment was commonly regarded as something to be dealt with after economic development. However, with the linear increase of GDP and production, there was a significant increase in environmental crises such as pesticide residues, soil erosion, loss of biodiversity, solid waste, and water and soil erosion. The over-

Table 5.4

Instruments Used by Mauritius and Costa Rica to Reduce Environmental Degradation

Activities/Policies	Mauritius	Costa Rica
Regulations & Guidelines	In Place	In Place
Credit subsidies	—	In Place
Incentives	Proposed	In Place
Effluent tax	In Place	In Place
Polluter-pays	In Place	In Place
Green tax on fuel	Proposed	In Place
Tax/Tariff relief	In place	In Place
Zoning of priority areas	—	In Place
Waste fees and levies	Proposed	In Place
Forestry taxation	—	In Place
Use of organic products	—	In Place
Recycling and reuse	Being Introduced	In Place
Resource taxes	—	In Place
Inventory of country's species	—	In Place
Public awareness on environmental education	Being Introduced	In Place
Promote research on friendly technologies	—	In Place
Environmental education through school curricula	In Place	In Place
Environmental education through nonformal systems	Proposed	In Place
Health impacts of environmental degradation	—	In Place
Joint venture between the state and civil society on sustainable planning & management	Being Introduced	In Place
Participation of public, academic, private, NGOs, & industry in conservatio	Proposed	In Place
Implement training and information to community	—	In Place
Preserve traditional knowledge on environment	—	In Place
Develop funding programs for sustainable production	—	Proposed
Guarantee equality & gender equity	—	Proposed

use of agricultural chemicals and the misuse of water can have serious effects on the environment and ecosystems.

The growth of the tourism industry in Mauritius, which is concentrated primarily on fragile coastal zones, is likely to degrade the environment. The coast is transformed into a chaotic assortment of hotels and resorts. Tourism is an industry strongly dependent on the aesthetics and health of the environment. In the long run, the consequential environmental damage, brought about by an unregulated tourism industry, will harm the industry's own interests and eventually cause a decline in the industry. Having endured decades of environmental degradation, Mauritius can no longer continue on this route of economic development without a serious regard of the environment. The very welfare of Mauritius' residents and its marine and terrestrial ecosystems are threatened.

Thus, given the constraints of limited national resources, the political climate in Mauritius has become ripe for comprehensive environmental regulations. It is the first African country to set the vision and adopt a national environmental plan with the assistance of international agencies. Certainly, the national environmental plan of Mauritius was successful in assessing critical issues affecting the quality of the environment. However, the implementation of the environmental programs has been hampered by lack of funding, weak enforcement capacity, and lack of a technical and scientific base for setting standards and measuring compliance.

Compared with Costa Rica, however, Mauritius has a long way to go in terms of strategically designing its environmental policy, and then to finding ways and means for achieving them. Given the fact that Costa Rica is environmentally sensitive, the most valuable lessons that Mauritius can learn from Costa Rica may include: (1) making environmental protection a budgetary priority; (2) designing the development and the implementation of resource planning, with a focus on coastal zones;

(3) controlling soil erosion; (4) managing toxic wastes; (5) reducing waste; and (6) improving urban air quality.

In addition to the establishment and maintenance of scientific data on the environment, to solve these problems, Mauritius could follow a multitude of approaches. These include:

1. Formulate a comprehensive, environmentally sensitive strategic plan to release its efforts.
2. Coordinate of the governmental institutions in their activities, as well as the credibility of their enforcement efforts.
3. Manage the environment need not be directed merely through regulations, but should also include economic incentives and various market-based instruments.
4. Design environmental education and making a blanket campaign for public awareness of environmental concerns.
5. Encourage social activists and grassroots political entrepreneurs to invest in environmental awareness programs.

Appendix:
Selected Indicators:
UN Commission on Sustainable Development

1. Income inequality
2. Population growth rate
3. Difference between male and female school enrollment rates
4. Per capita consumption of fossil fuels for transportation
5. The ratio of the average house price to average income
6. Living space (floor area) per person
7. Environmentally adjusted net domestic product
8. Energy consumption
9. The intensity of materials use

10. Percentage of pollution with adequate excreta disposal facilities
11. Share of renewable energy resources consumed
12. Annual withdrawals of ground and surface water
13. The ratio of debt service to export earnings
14. Amount of new funding for sustainable development
15. The maximum sustained yield for fisheries
16. Changes in land use
17. Percent of arable land that is irrigated
18. Energy use in agriculture
19. Percentage of forest area that is protected
20. Emissions of greenhouse gases
21. Waste recycling and reuse
22. Access to information
23. The representation of major groups on national councils for sustainable development

Source: Alex Farrell and Maureen Hart, "What Does Sustainability Really Mean? The Search for Useful Indicators," *Environment*, Vol. 40, No. 9 (November 1998), 9.

CHAPTER 6

ECONOMIC DEVELOPMENT BY INVITATION:
Can NEPAD Rejuvenate Africa's Economy in the Twenty-first Century?

As discussed before, it was due to a mismatch between transplanted Western institutions and indigenous social systems that the various economic development models that were attempted in Africa within the last 50 years have been less than successful. Moreover, the SAPs of the 1980s had negative impact on the low-income people of Africa. They heavily concentrated on price distortions and demanded that African governments need to cut down on their budget deficits. That is, the Washington Consensus model insisted that African countries had to reduce their budgets on education, health, and other social services.

As a result of Africa's diminishing role in the world economic system, recently a number of African heads of state have established the New Partnership for Africa's Development to jump-start development in Africa.[1] In short, NEPAD is a comprehensive, integrated, strategic framework for the socioeconomic development of Africa in the twenty-first century, initiated primarily under the leadership of South Africa, Nigeria, Algeria, Senegal, and Egypt.

NEPAD has undergone several changes of name. Originally, it was known as Africa's Renaissance under South African President Thabo Mbeki. Then, the Omega Plan under President Abdoulaye Wade of Senegal merged with the Millennium for African Recovery Program (MAP) to form the New African Initiative (NAI). In 2001, the Organization of African Unity in Lusaka, Zambia, endorsed the NAI. Finally, the document was introduced by calling it the New Partnership for Africa's Development.

NEPAD is designed to be the "African solution to African problems," or Africa's answer to globalization—that is, an alternative development strategy for achieving sustainable development in the twenty-first century. To tackle major impediments to the economic growth and political stability in Africa, NEPAD forged a partnership with donors from the G8 countries.

> In essence, NEPAD calls for $64 billion a year in debt relief, aid and, most importantly, direct investment in Africa to help the continent catch up with the rest of the world. It aims to increase the economic growth rate to 7 percent for the next 15 years and to reduce by half the number of Africans living in extreme poverty by 2015. What makes NEPAD different from previous schemes is that, in exchange, African leaders must commit themselves to a hard road of democratic reforms, open government and a corruption-free business environment. Signatories must also accept limited terms of office for elected leaders ...and adopt an independent judiciary. Compliance will be monitored through the African Union, an inter-African body to be established in July [2002].[2]

The sentiment behind NEPAD is that: (1) it is a visionary and dynamic initiative; (2) it is African-led, developed, managed, and owned; (3) it brings the concept of a new partnership; (4) Africa is undertaking certain commitments and obligations on its own in order to extricate the continent from: (a) the malaise of underdevelopment, (b) increasing exclusion in the area of globalization (due to structural impediments and resource outflows and unfavorable terms of trade), and (c) revitalize its economic system; and (5) it puts Africa's development firmly on the global agenda and generates a new confidence in Africa, that it is not a doomed continent.

In addition, NEPAD assumes that Africa's rejuvenation cannot be achieved outside of the process of globalization. But as stated by Zo Randriamaro,

> according to the NEPAD's initiators, what Africa needs is simply more globalization; they do not mention the need for a meaningful change in power relations between Africa and the North, or a significant transfer of resources for financing Africa's development through a fairer redistribution of wealth at the global level.[3]

There is a deep feeling by a number of Africans that instead of being based on equal partnership, NEPAD is largely imposed on some African heads of states and the emerging hegemonic class by the ideologies of the neoliberal view, championed by the World Bank, World Trade Organization, and International Monetary Fund. The local hegemonic elites

> have been inexorably drawn into process, with the leading capitalist groups in the Third World having transnationalized by integrating into global circuits of accumulation through a variety of mechanisms, ranging from subcontracting for global corporations [to] the purchase of foreign equity shares, mergers with corporations from other countries, joint ventures and increasing foreign direct investment (FDI) abroad of their own capital.[4]

Thus, Africa's integration into the global economy may benefit only the upper classes in Africa.

Jimi O. Adesina has gone one step further to claim that NEPAD is a form of neocolonialism with the consent of African leaders. NEPAD's primary audience does not seem to be African citizens but northern donors and institutions. NEPAD is neither new in its policy prescriptions nor is it Africa-driven. Rather, he argues that it is donor-focused and is rooted in the neoliberal macroeconomic discourse of the post-Washington Consensus model rather than among the people the initiative is supposed to serve.[5] Adesina argues that the macroeconomic orientation suggested in NEPAD is a call to persist on the same path that Africa has been on for the past two decades. While NEPAD claims that it is not asking for more aid, it asks for more Official Development Assistance (ODA) as an important component of its financing. Moreover, Adesina argues that "it is paradoxical that at the time NEPAD seeks to re-make African states developmental[ly], it recommends a framework that weakens the capacity of the state to deliver. Yet the structure of many of these economies is fundamentally different from those at the heart of a neoliberal regime."[6]

If not controlled at its initial stage, these critiques of NEPAD argue that NEPAD may contribute to Africa's perpetual and diminishing role in the world economic system rather than revitalizing it. The fact that NEPAD encourages privatization of social services is very likely to endanger the rights of those who cannot afford user fees for basic services. Though NEPAD includes scattered references to Africa's natural resources, it blames Africa's environmental destruction on the poor rather than incorporating it in the historical processes on slavery, colonialism, and imperialism that has impoverished the continent and left it woefully underdeveloped.

It is imperative that women play a major role in Africa's informal sector. But NEPAD fails to address the empowerment of women in the global economy that it envisages to pursue in twenty-first century. Interesting enough, though

NEPAD advocates for partnership on equal footing with the donors, it

> shies away from calling for the kinds of initiatives that would truly benefit Africa, such as: (1) fundamentally reforming global trade and investment regimes and (2) ensuring effective participation, transparency and fairness in the governance of multilateral institutions. ...While African leaders justly challenge Northern donors to reform ODA delivery mechanisms and to meet the UN target of 0.7% of their GNP, the G8 has already indicated that NEPAD will be used to target aid only to [a] short-list of "winners" in Africa. Such a triage is likely to result in even further reduction in aid to those (marginalized) countries most disadvantaged by the global economy.[7]

If NEPAD is to gain greater public support, discussions need not be limited only to government officials but the downtrodden masses need to be engaged to transform the continent. Finally, because HIV-AIDS, tuberculosis, malaria, and other diseases are the consequences and causes of the growing crisis of poverty, therefore NEPAD should have designed a long-term public health programs for addressing these issues because

> [t]he HIV/Aids epidemic has the capacity to neutralize the lofty aims of African leaders enshrined in the envisaged partnership for development. With 28 million Africans living with HIV/AIDS and more than 20 million already dead, the Number One development emergency in Africa deserves priority attention in NEPAD.[8]

Realizing that there are pros and cons concerning NEPAD, here are the main questions examined in this chapter: (1) Are the economic assumptions of NEPAD valid? (2) Given the economic assumptions, can NEPAD reengineer Africa's development in the twenty-first century? and (3) Can the foreign direct investment strategies of NEPAD be implemented?

The Economic Goals of NEPAD

Before we analyze the economic goals of NEPAD, we need to use an analytical framework known by the acronym SWOT (strengths, weaknesses, opportunities, and threats). In Table 6.1, a SWOT analysis consists of a candid compilation and appraisal of Africa's *internal* strengths and weaknesses and its *external* opportunities and threats during the twentieth century.

Now, let us review if the economic goals developed by NEPAD attempted to exploit Africa's strengths and environmental opportunities, neutralize its external threats, and eradicate poverty in order to achieve sustainable growth, sustainable development, and active participation in the world economy and political system. As set by NEPAD, the cardinal economic goals envisaged for NEPAD include:

1. Achieve and sustain an average gross domestic product growth rate of above 7 percent per annum for the next 15 years

2. Ensure that the continent achieves the agreed International Development Goals (IDGs), which include:
    *   reducing the proportion of people living in extreme poverty by half between 1990 and 2015
    *   enrolling all children of school age in primary schools by 2015
    *   making progress toward gender equality and empowering women by eliminating gender disparities in the enrollment in primary and secondary education by 2015
    *   reducing infant and child mortality ratios by two-thirds between 1990 and 2015
    *   reducing maternal mortality ratios by three-quarters between 1990 and 2015

Table 6.1
SWOT Analysis of Africa in the Twentieth Century

A: Internal Analysis

Strengths	Weaknesses
• Rich complex of minerals, oil and gas deposits • Varieties of flora and fauna • Unspoiled natural habitat (rain forest) • Minimal emissions and effluents • Paleontological and archaeological sites (cradle of humankind) • Open uninhabited spaces • Rich cultures and creative community • Cheap labor and raw materials • Richness of agriculture	• Weak domestic market • Lack of highly skilled labor • Weak states • Lack of long-term policies • Implementation of programs • Price distortions • Lack of advanced information and communications technology • Lack of capital • Unfavorable terms of trade • Poor purchasing power • Lack of conflict prevention and management • Poor health services (HIV/AIDS, malaria) • Class and gender inequity • Poor infrastructure • Nonparticipatory governance • Undemocratically elected leaders • Lack of transparent legal and regulatory framework • Inadequacy in research and development • Political instability • Heavy external debt • Persistent balance of payments deficits

B: External Analysis

Opportunities	Threats
• Become the architects of their own sustained, uplifting growth • Regain their self-confidence • Integration of national systems of production • Value chain in manufacturing and service sector • Ready to acquire modern knowledge and skills • Natural and diversified work force to be harnessed	• Competition with the Newly Industrializing Countries (NICs) • Dependence on external agencies and markets • Internal upheavals and border conflicts • Bilateral and multilateral aid • May be based on insurmountable conditionality • Heavy subsides on primary products by US and European countries

- providing access for all who need reproductive health services by 2015
- implementing national strategies for sustainable development by 2015, so as to reverse the loss of environmental resources by that date
- restoring and maintaining macroeconomic stability, especially by developing appropriate standards and targets for fiscal and monetary policies, and introducing appropriate institutional framework to achieve these standards
- instituting legal and regulatory frameworks for financial markets and auditing of private companies and the public sector
- revitalizing and extend the provision of educational, technical training, and health services, with high priority given to tackling HIV/AIDS, malaria, and other communicable disease
- promoting the role of women in social and economic development by reinforcing their capacity in the domains of education and training
- developing of women's revenue-generating activities through facilitating access to credit
- assuring women's participation in the political and economic life of African countries
- promoting the development of infrastructure: agriculture and its diversification into agroindustries and manufacturing to serve both domestic and export markets[9]

To achieve sustainable development in the twenty-first century, the contents of the NEPAD document were conceptualized and structured with the following grandiose strategic goals: (1) the Peace, Security, and Political Governance Initiative, (2) the Economic and Corporate Governance Initiative, and (3) sub-regional and regional approaches to development.

To achieve sustainable development the following sectors are given high priorities: bridging the infrastructure gap, human resources development (reversing the brain drain), agriculture, the environment, culture, and science and technology.

To implement sustainable development the following resources are anticipated to be mobilized: (1) capital flows (increasing domestic resources, debt relief, ODA reforms, and private capital flows); and (2) market access (through diversification of production, mining, manufacturing, tourism, services, promoting the private sector, promoting African exports, and removal of nontariff barriers). Finally, in order to make Africa determine its own destiny, NEPAD is calling on the industrialized countries and other multilateral organizations to complement its effort to achieve: (1) economic growth and development and increased employment; (2) reduction in poverty and inequality; (3) diversification of productive activities, enhanced international competitiveness, and increased exports; and (4) increased African integration.[10]

THE ECONOMIC ASSUMPTIONS OF NEPAD

Recognizing the historical and colonial roots of Africa's underdevelopment, NEPAD's aim includes the noble goal of making Africans the architects of their own sustained development in the twenty-first century rather than being left as benevolent guardians of western institutions.[11] As Africa's "Marshall Plan," NEPAD developed short- and long-terms plans for Africa's development agenda in the twenty-first century. However, as shown in Table 6.1, NEPAD's document does not seem to be independently conceived by Africans. Indeed, there seems to be a synergy or linkage between NEPAD and the report prepared by the World Bank (cosigned by the Africa Development Bank, UN Economic Commission for Africa, Global Coalition for Africa, and African Economic

Research Consortium), entitled *Can Africa Claim the 21ˢᵗ Century?*

For example, without locating Africa within the global economy and undertaking a careful estimation of the global economy in the future, both NEPAD and the World Bank group estimate that Africa's economy would need to grow at the rate of 7 percent per year, with a 2 percent to 3 percent African savings rate, in order to meet its development goals for 2015. This estimation is based on the assumption of political openings, continuing post-Cold War realities, and the mushrooming of globalization, new technology, and foreign direct investments. But due to corruption, payments of past debts, transfer pricing by transnational organizations, underpricing of exports, and the like, Africa's external expenditure is always very low and its saving rate can be estimated to be negative instead of 2 to 3 percent.

The World Bank group's attempts have been very scanty (i.e., based on very few countries), but NEPAD should have used contingent statements such as high, medium, and low scenarios to forecast Africa's economy in the twenty-first century, in order to be used by development practitioners in Africa in mapping out various strategies and monitoring Africa's development path for the future (see Table 6.2). In short, instead of cursory statements, the economic projections should have been based on past history and included ranges of different possibilities and their interactions. In addition, mapping out potential surprises would have helped to anticipate important factors that would have far-reaching consequences if unexpected conditions did occur. For example:

> As the NEPAD was being finalized, we witnessed a very major shift in US foreign policy with the establishment of the international coalition against terrorism. As such, the discourse has changed. African states are being categorized into "failed" or "failing" states which could accommodate terrorists, as opposed to governments which can demonstrate control. ...In other

Table 6.2

Similarities (=) Between NEPAD and the World Bank Report for Africa's Development in the Twenty-first Century

NEPAD's Goal \ World Bank's Goal	Economic growth Resolving Conflict	Improving Governance & Inequality	Addressing Poverty	Investing in People Barriers	Lowering Infra-structure & Information Development	Spurring Agri-cultural & Rural Regional Integration	Diversifying Exports & Pursuing Global Partnership	Reducing Aid & Strength-ening
Condition for Sustainable Growth:								
1) Peace & Security		=						
2) Democracy & Political Governance		=						
3) Economic & Corporate Governance	=							
4) Sub-regional & Regional Development	=							
Sectoral Priorities:								
1) Bridging the Infrastructure Gap	=				=			
2) Human Resources & Reversing the Brain Drain				=				
3) Agriculture						=		
4) Environment Intiative								
5) Culture								
6) Science & Technology Platform							=	
Mobilizing Resources:								
1) Capital Flows							=	
2) Market Access							=	=
3) New Global Partnership								=

217

words, the NEPAD could just be the new policy platform to fight international terrorism from Africa as opposed to tackling the other issues that are critical for women and the poor.[12]

What is surprising is that, although the twenty-first century is slated to be the century of development, NEPAD and the World Bank group did not fully address how export strategy based on primary products would bring about long-term economic growth in Africa without damaging the environment. In line with the development paradigm for the decade, the environmental consequences of export strategy based on primary products, rather than naming the "environmental initiatives," should have been explored in detail if Africa is expected to achieve sustainable economic development in the twenty-first century. Finally, it is worth noting that, "conventionally measured, Africa has the world's second highest inequality (0.45 Gini coefficient) after Latin America (0.493 Gini coefficient),"[13] but the NEPAD document does not adequately address this issue now, nor does it address how it could be minimized in the future.

Moreover, because most African economies currently depend on very few primary exports (which are vulnerable to world market fluctuations, since primary products are heavily subsidized by the industrial countries), and because diversification into manufactured exports and African countries' demands for greater market access in the advanced countries have hardly worked in the past, it is puzzling to note that NEPAD feels that a plea to the industrialized countries to open their markets to African products in the twenty-first century *could* work. Given the anticipated economic slowdown in the industrialized countries, can the industrialized countries afford to sacrifice their economies so that Africa could reverse the "resource outflows," "unfavorable terms of trade," and rejuvenate in the twenty-first century?

Africa is heavily dependent on aid or Official Development Assistance. Although aid is relatively marginal in its developmental impact, recently ODA transfers to Africa have declined (for example, in 1999, sub-Saharan Africa received 31.2 as compared to 37.2 in 1990). Given this situation, and the fact that aid is entangled with various conditions involving social policies, it is quite alarming that NEPAD would place emphasis on foreign sources of capital as a means of achieving the forecasted economic growth in Africa in the twenty-first century. Moreover, though NEPAD claims to be based on a new partnership,

> the patterns of power distribution prevalent in most African countries provide ample support to the dependency relations of their countries. The industrialized countries and their transnational corporations do their best (through aid and now as a number of foreign technical experts are displacing Africans) to exercise all sorts of pressures and temptations to keep this balance of power undistributed.[14]

Foreign Direct Investment Flows to Africa

NEPAD anticipates the flow of private capital through foreign direct investment would enhance the continent's economy while achieving an estimated 7 percent annual growth rate. This is needed to meet the goal of reducing the proportion of Africans living in poverty by half by the year 2015. NEPAD also anticipates that FDI will fill an annual resource gap of 12 percent of its GDP, as well as create an increase in domestic savings, an improvement in the public revenue collection systems, a reduction in external debt, and an increase in complementary Official Development Assistance.[15] Nonetheless, NEPAD offers no sense of cohesion by mentioning that FDI has been declining because of the perception of Africa as a "high risk continent, especially with regard to regulatory framework and property rights."

In addition, a review of the literature on political risk assessment indicates that investment in a number of developing countries is declining because of: (1) lack of symmetry between corporate objectives and the developmental goals of the host countries, (2) the operational setup of the subsidiary (ownership, structure, employment policies, infrastructures, labor, degree of integration, the existence of Free Trade Zones, business leaders' attitudes, degree of competition, domestic demand, taxes, transfers, and the like) and the lack of adequate and transparent regulatory policies, and (3) the national and external environments of the host countries, which are not conducive to foreign direct investment.[16]

Though very challenging, NEPAD goes into considerable detail (paragraphs 71 to 92) to spell out the preconditions for foreign direct investments. These include:

1.   sustaining long-term peace as one of the primary conditions to attract FDIs;

2.   efforts made by Africans to find a lasting solutions to existing conflicts;

3.   respecting the global standards of democracy, whose core components include: political pluralism, principles of democracy, transparency, accountability, integrity, respect for human rights, promotion of the rule of law, and promotion of Economic Governance Initiatives;

4.   commitments by participating countries to create or consolidate the basic processes and practices of governing using the appropriate diagnostic and assessment tools, in compliance with the shared goals of good governance;

5.   strengthening of national, subregional, and continental structures that support good governance;

6.   monitoring by the leadership of NEPAD periodically and assessing the progress made;

7.   state capacity-building as a critical aspect of creating conditions for development; and

8.   promoting a set of concrete and time-bound programs for economic and corporate governance practices and

creating a task force from the ministers of finance and Central Banks to review them.[17]

About 75 percent of foreign direct investment flows within the developed countries. Now, can Africa assume that the remaining 25 percent of the FDI will be invested in all developing countries, and can be diverted to flow into Africa? And can it minimize operational, ownership, and financial risk? This is wishful thinking. Even if the above conditions of the economic and political initiatives are put in place, the document knowingly or unknowingly seems to undermine the very innovative strategies of Asian, East European, and Latin American countries to enter to a competitive bid with Africa in order to attract foreign direct investments. As stated by Yosh Tandon:

> It is sad to see how little mainstream economists that have drafted the NEPAD documents have learnt from history, or from the experiences of other countries in the third world. There is even a degree of innocent belief that FDIs will really come to true, that conditions of peace and security will be maintained in Africa …that the investors will finally acknowledge that Africa has been the "origin of mankind" and has nurtured the world for thousands of years with its rich resources and now it is "payback" time.[18]

The envisaged foreign investments are a pipe dream and cannot materialize. This is because, in order to entice foreign investors, "African governments are going to be dragged into [a] downward spiral of offering to the owners of capital competitive terms, including tax incentives or tax holidays, free land, borrowing in local currency, and so on. Indeed, such competition may take place not only between states but also between provinces within the same state."[19]

CONCLUSION

Because the aim of the New Partnership for Africa's Development is to make the African continent on a self-reliant path for the twenty-first century, all Africans would feel that the sentiment behind the NEPAD is a noble mission. However, a careful evaluation of the development strategy outlined in the NEPAD document seems to be contradictory. The first section of the document locates the underdevelopment of Africa on colonialism, imperialism, and structural impediments imposed on Africa by the World Bank, International Monetary Fund, World Trade Organization, and other nongovernmental institutions. The second part of the document, on the other hand, was written as an afterthought to satisfy the forged partnership (i.e., prospective Western donors) without paying attention to the diagnostic analysis on the first part of the document.

For example, contrary to its radical views in the first part of the document by neglecting social services (such as food, adequate housing, basic education, and other essential infrastructures), it recommends neoliberal orthodoxy as the most viable strategies to solve poverty and underdevelopment of Africa.[20] Thus, NEPAD, being incoherent in its analysis, cannot be used to revitalize Africa's economy. In other words, it is an inappropriate strategy for Africa's development.

Anyone who designs a strategy that would be used to develop the African economies must ensure that it would generate an economy that protects the poor. The strategy, to a large extent, must be based on agriculture and tailored to a people-centered model of development. It must also have catching-up and forging-ahead policies built into the model.

The NEPAD strategy assumes that the problem of underdevelopment is the result of a malaise endemic to Africa, and it is its problem to solve. It is assumed that Africa would develop by following the footpaths of the Anglo-Saxon development experience system and under the neoliberal, Washington Consensus ideology. Contrary to Africa's social values, these ethnocentric models place heavy emphasis on free markets, deregulation, privatization, and the limited role the state has to play in the development process.

The only way Africa can reclaim its development in the twenty-first century is if its development process is rooted in African systems of thought and is people-centered, rather than based on western capitalist models transplanted by apostles of external agencies. Because agriculture is the backbone of Africa's economy, we conclude that cooperative agrarian development strategies, rooted in local culture, would not only achieve growth with equity but also could collectively empower the African people to fully participate in the design and management of long-lasting development paradigms in harmony with the objective conditions of Africa. We would like the agrarian sector to become the leading sector in the developing process.

There is a need for African social reformers to try to design viable agrarian strategies of development to solve some of the mounting economic problems facing the African economies, in an era of rapid globalization. This need is necessitated by the fact that all previous models have failed to transform the African economies on a path of sustained rising per capita incomes.

NEPAD does not present an economic model for development, which is based on economic theory. Development models and strategies have been taken out of the university classrooms and handed over to international agencies including the IMF and the World Bank. NEPAD presents a strategy to obtain funds or loans from industrialized countries (the G8) to finance African development efforts by imposing a fixed set of contemporary Anglo-American institutions on Africa.

Chapter 7 is based on developing a strategy to transform the agrarian economies of Africa. We believe that such an agrarian strategy of development will take us away from a strategy that is being forced on Africa. This strategy has been implemented since the colonial period in different forms, with different names, and it still has not solved Africa's problems. This strategy is industrialization by invitation (IBI), which has been programmed and instituted in Africa without the African policy makers knowing that this strategy has been forced on them from the outside. In addition, the Structural Adjustment Participatory Review International Network (SAPRIN) in Argentina, Ecuador, Mexico, Central America, Ghana, and the Philippines initiated research projects to assess the economic and social effects of neoliberal policies. These policies include financial-sector liberalization, trade liberalization, privatization, and public-sector reform—imposed by the World Bank and the IMF. These research projects indicate that "the effects of adjustment policies, particularly on the poor, are so profound and pervasive that no amount of targeted social investments can begin to address the social crises that they have engendered."[21]

We hold a view that the African Leadership Forum organized under the leadership of President Olusegun Obasanjo was not originated through African ideas, but rather through Western ideas for Africa. We hold the view that NEPAD comes out of Western policies for Africa as well as institutions that have been set up for Africa as "think tanks" for developing African policies. We believe that adopting an agrarian strategy of development avoids that IBI strategy. This is one of the reasons why NEPAD, which is in fact an IBI strategy in disguise, should be avoided. It may be argued, further, that NEPAD comes out of disjointed ideas in wishful thinking rather than from ideas developed in economic theory. This is part of the reason why NEPAD should not be implemented.

In our judgment, African societies are agrarian societies. As a result, they deserve to be transformed from economic policies developed for agrarian economies. We believe that the agrarian strategy of development we present in Chapter 7 would bring about a faster growth rate in the region with redistributive justice.

CHAPTER 7

A HISTORICAL PERSPECTIVE OF AFRICA'S FORTY YEAR EMPTY HARVEST

During the last 40 years, development economists and international development agencies have courted African policy makers with a number of divergent theoretical views about how agricultural development can bring about economic growth. It is believed that the economic stagnation that Africa faced in the 1950s and 1960s was due, in part, to structural imbalances in the traditional and neotraditional institutions.[1] Generally, development economics in that period was influenced by W. Arthur Lewis, who equated it with the structural transformation of the economy. That is, by discovering ways to transfer resources, especially labor, from indigenous, noncapitalist sectors dominated by subsistence farming to capitalist, industrial sectors. This structural transformation was presumed to be the engine of growth.

The distinguishing characteristics of the capitalist sector were its use of reproducible capital, its hiring of labor, and its sale of output for profit. …the transfer of labor from the subsistence inputs sector (where the marginal productivity of a laborer approached zero as a limiting case and peasant farmers were often regarded as tradition-bound and unresponsive to market incentives) to the capitalist sector facilitated capitalist expansion through reinvestment of profits.[2]

In other words, agriculture was viewed as a backward sector with slim prospects of becoming the motor of development. It was generally assumed that industry could be developed in isolation from agriculture and that rapid industrialization would enable new nations in Africa to leapfrog over the agrarian stage and catch up with industrial nations by the year 2000.[3]

In addition, A. O. Hirschman argued that investment in industry would generally lead to more linkage and more broadly based economic growth than would investment in agriculture.[4] That is, according to the Hirschmanian argument, gains in farm production lead to increases in farmers' cash incomes. The growth in farm incomes would contribute to expenditures for agricultural inputs and households would tend to buy consumer goods, thereby stimulating domestic industrial production. In short, the rationale for this model was based on the assumption that industrial development can stimulate agricultural development by expanding the demand for farm products and supplying the industrial inputs needed to improve agricultural productivity.

Similarly, the "diffusion model of agricultural development" assumed that Third World farmers could increase production by more effective dissemination of technical knowledge (for example, better husbandry practices) and allocating existing resources more efficiently from Western advanced countries. Based on this assumption, it was suggested that Third World countries need to be introduced to Western assistance in planning local development projects, such as cottage industries.

Nevertheless, one of the limitations of the diffusion model is that it failed to take into consideration that the productivity of rural land depends not only on modern inputs, but also on the type of landownership. For example, small farms operated by sharecroppers and tenant farmers with the land owned by absentee landlords are likely to be less productive than farmlands owned and operated by the farmers who have security of tenure. Agrarian reform therefore needs to be considered as a precondition for agricultural productivity. As stated by A. P. Thirlwall, "There is impressive evidence that where a change in the tenure system has permitted the producers themselves to reap the rewards of new techniques, peasant farmers have been ready to break with custom and tradition."[5]

On the other hand, contrary to Lewis' and Hirschman's model of development, that the agricultural sector is bound with surplus labor that could be transferred at no cost to the industrial sector and that regarded the peasant farmers to be unresponsive to market incentives—the "grass-roots" development economics of the 1960s persuasively argued that most of the world's poor people earn their living from agriculture. So if we knew the economics of agriculture, we would know much of the economics of being poor and identify the preferences and scarcity constraints that determine the choices that poor farm people make. Based on this assumption, it was hypothesized that peasants in traditional agricultural systems are rational and efficient with allocation of resources, and respond to price changes but are kept poor because of limited access to education and technology. Given these extrapolations, Theodore Schultz has the following recommendations: (1) increase the capacity of public- and private-sector research institutions to produce new technical knowledge, (2) increase the capacity of the industrial sector to develop, produce, and market new technical inputs, and (3) increase the capacity of farmers to acquire new knowledge and use new inputs effectively.[6]

In the 1970s, the World Bank switched from an economic growth paradigm to a broader development paradigm by creating what was called the basic human needs strategy. By focusing on distributive rather on growth objectives, the World Bank initiated Integrated Rural Development (IRD) to directly attack Africa's rural poverty. However noble, the underlying limitation of the basic human needs paradigm was the absence of any strategy for achieving short- and medium-term growth. It generally regarded agriculture as a passive supplier of food and capital to other sectors of the economy.[7]

Concurrent with the basic human needs strategy, the basic development strategy designed for Africa from 1970 to 1979 was for regional integration of industry and national self-sufficiency in food production. However, because the post-1973 energy crisis contributed to foreign exchange shortages and a massive budget crisis, the World Bank initiated structural adjustment programs in 1980 to 1984 to correct the distorted price incentives in favor of producers. Thus, it suggested a sharp depreciation of domestic currencies and severe fiscal austerity packages as part of bailout programs, in order to reduce government outlays and to curtail social programs.

But because the World Bank's SAPs for Africa were highly contested by the Economic Commission for Africa, the Africa Development Bank, and a number of African scholars, this led to the emergence of:

1. Supply Shifters in Agriculture (1973 to 1989): This was similar to the Asian Green Revolution and was designed to focus on public investment in research, extension, infrastructure, and market liberation to boost food production in Africa.

2. Regional Integration II (1973 to 1989): This stressed that food self-sufficiency needed to be under regional protec-

tion arrangements, along with the continuation of the 1973 to 1989 policies.

3. Structural Adjustment II (1985 to ?): This called for macroeconomic adjustment with some programs in order to mitigate the impact on poverty and emphasized the potential for labor-intensive growth in rural areas in order to solve rural poverty.

4. Sustainable Development (1990 to ?): This is the most current agricultural development in Africa, which generally emphasizes the belief that rapid population growth, agricultural income stagnation, and environmental degradation constitute a nexus of problems for Africa and could be resolved in an integrated manner through agricultural research, human capital formation, and sustainable investment policies.[8]

According to the Consulting Group on International Agricultural Research (CGIAR), some of the major factors that contribute to food crises in Africa are:

1. African leaders neglected agriculture and focused instead on industrialization as the expressway to property.

2. Except in a few countries, there was an absence of political power for farmers. Instead, the various regimes focused on giving food subsidies to their constituents mainly living in the urban areas.

3. The prolonged delay in the food production crisis was caused by the ready availability of "food aid subscriptions" from the advanced countries during the Cold War period. Food aid generally acted as a plague across the continent because it took the pressure off African governments to rearrange development priories in favor of agriculture.[9]

Agrarian-dominated African nations experienced some false starts, such as:

√ They caught up through an industrial spurt (industrial fundamentalism) and mechanizing state farms in isolation from the agrarian stage of development (for example, Ghana, Nigeria, and Senegal in the 1960s).

√ They relied on command systems versus market systems as a vehicle for economic growth (for example, Ghana in the 1970s; Guinea in the 1960s and 1970s, Tanzania in 1960 to 1980, and Ethiopia in the 1980s).

√ They pursued agrarian capitalism versus state-led agricultural (communal farming) and production schemes (Kenya and Zimbabwe in the 1970s and 1980s).

√ They underwent the false dichotomy of producing cash crops for export rather than food crops, which were generally taxed through the colonial-style marketing boards (for example, Kenya in the 1970s and 1980s).

Drawing valuable insights from some of these false starts, CGIAR recommends the following agricultural strategies for Africa's long-run development:

√ Promote national and regional consultative processes for agricultural research and development.

√ Set up an African Capacity Building Initiative for Sustainable Food Security as a major inter-CGIAR initiative.

√ Set up a task force to develop a special, focused program for African food security.

√ Launch a well-planned Lab to Land program.

√ Develop research programs in urban and suburban agriculture.

√ Emphasize modern ecological farming methods.

√ Set priorities on staple and relevant food crops.

√ Promote partnerships between strategic National Agricultural Research (NAR) facilities based in Africa and strong NAR facilities in various parts of the world.[10]

To summarize, since independence, a number of African countries have gone through various agricultural development paradigms. As we showed in Chapter 2, agriculture was seen as peripheral to the task of industrialization since the post-World War II era, as with the industrialization by invitation strategy that was tried in Ghana and contributed to the systematic structural neglect of the food-producing sector—and ultimately to the impoverishment of most of the people in that country. This is because the Lewis development paradigms were mainly designed for Puerto Rico and the Caribbean, and thus had little or no relevance to Ghana—a traditional African country with quite different culture norms and institutions.

So there have been basic structural imbalances such as the relative compartmentalization of modern sectors and activities from traditional sectors and activities. Thus, we assert that these basic structural imbalance problems that face Africa today emanate from "the dual nature of the present evolution of African societies," that is, the indigenous traditional institutions interacting with extraneous modern institutions and cultures, mostly Western and alien. This has disrupted the subsistence economy, the farm and nonfarm sectors, and has impoverished the traditional sector. It should be clear that modern development and foreign economic intrusion into the surviving "indigenous" Third World economies disrupted or ruined the traditional or indigenous sector. In other words, according to the dependency theory, during the pre- and postcolonial stage Africa's economy was shaped to a large extent to fulfill the needs of global capitalism. For example, there was

> a pronounced tendency to favour export agriculture over the production of food crops for domestic consumption. Dependency gives rise to a pronounced dichotomy between the export sector and the food-producing sector. For export production is often carried on in large plantation-sized farms which are highly

favoured in terms of agricultural inputs (high-yield seeds, pesticides, agricultural-extension services, advanced irrigation technologies, etc) whereas food crops for local consumption are grown on peasant farms which are badly deprived of needed agricultural supports.[11]

We think that these models have bypassed the central need, that is, strategies for agrarian transformation, and have focused instead on industrialization. Because the decision-making process and models for development that have been designed for Africa are carbon copies of the West or the East without any modification to suit the African continent, we need to correct this approach. As stated by Dudley Seers:

> The major inadequacies of conventional economics for those dealing with the typical case are that analysis focuses on the wrong factors, and the models do not fit at all closely the way in which non-industrial economies operate. ...In brief, institutions are taken as given, whereas the question is precisely what institutions to change and how.[12]

Africa is an agrarian-dominated continent where more than 80 percent of the population depends on agriculture and rural off-farm activities. However, it is in Africa where the level of malnourishment has significantly increased in the recent years. Though many innovations in agriculture have been introduced, Africa has not benefited from the new agricultural technology. For example, as enumerated by Jaques Diouf, a survey of the main agricultural commodities shows that generally yields in Africa are extremely low, but have increased notably in other continents. For example,

> [t]he major crops in Africa are: in the Sahlian zone, millet and sorghum which represent 40 percent and 18 percent of world production, and in the tropical zone, yam, plantain, and cassava which represent 95 percent, 70 percent, and 44 percent of world production. Neither rice nor wheat, which spearheaded the Green Revolution, are of importance to Africa. The continent's output for each is only 2 percent of world production. Besides, the available rice technology was mainly developed for irrigated land,

which does not suit African conditions where upland, deep-flooded, and mangrove swamp rice are prevalent.[13]

Thus agricultural growth is likely to significantly reduce the cycle of poverty, hunger, and famine, if policy makers concentrate on mobilizing the hidden creativity of Africa's farm families to rediscover their agrarian heritage and achieve sustained, broad-based agricultural growth. It is imperative, therefore, that we weave our development strategy around the traditional sector because agriculture needs to be the engine of broad-based economic development in Africa. In the following case study, the Abibirim development strategy is used because it recognizes the unique historical background of the different African societies and uses the historical, structural, institutional, and economic analysis approach to problem solving. The Abibirim strategy sees a dynamic role reserved for the traditional economy if economic development is to take place at all in the "indigenous traditional African economies."[14] As summarized by Kofi, the philosophy behind the Abibirim strategy is based on the following premises:

1. We cannot formulate adequate economic development theory for the indigenous African economies without a careful analysis of the role we have played and continue to play in the development of western capitalism on the global stage, and also peripherally in the socialist development.

2. For a viable economic development, we must change our internal structures and external relations. Internally, our sociocultural milieu prevents our societies from utilizing effectively the surplus we generate to spur development. Externally, the dependent role we play in the capitalist new world order inhibits our growth.

3. The African countries should examine critically the western capitalist economic theories, because they were de-

veloped for a different social order, and modify them, if
need be, before using them.

4.   Traditional African countries should critically study and
examine the socialist models and adapt and use the more
relevant aspects.

5.   African states must work closely together to create and
enforce development strategies and learn from each other.
African unity will only make sense if a common ground
is established for a development policy.[15]

The Abibirim strategy then calls for a different strategy
to absorb the displaced traditional and neotraditional people,
so they contribute effectively to growth. To do this, we would
like to follow the special United Nations approach in asking
consultants to develop and write a policy paper. The United
Nations would normally provide the consultant with terms of
reference (TOR) and the consultant is required to develop and
write the policy paper along the lines suggested by the TOR.
This case study follows the United Nations format. However,
in this case, the TOR was designed for the Adangme traditional chiefs. Also included in the case study are the discussions we had with Dr. Ako Adjei, a veteran politician of the
nationalist era of Ghana's political history.

Case Study: Getting Agriculture Moving Again: People-Centered Approach to Development in the Songor Lagoon Region of Ghana

Previous models, especially models based on neoclassical paradigms, have failed because they do not recognize the agrarian
base of African economies and instead try to implement capitalist models of development. In order to bring this point home,
we want to introduce the transformation of a sector of the
Ghana economy—the Songor Lagoon. This is a resource in

the form of a lagoon that literally creates vast amounts of salt without any human intervention. To cultivate this resource, previous governments have used a capitalist strategy to transform the sector. The agrarian people have fought this strategy and would like to implement a strategy that is more humane to them. We propose that this resource could be cultivated under an agrarian strategy of transformation, which would provide equitable incomes to the agrarian people.

TERMS OF REFERENCE: A BACKDROP

The Songor Lagoon and its allied resources—salt, rivulets, fish, lands—have not been utilized optimally for economic development to enhance the welfare of the traditional inhabitants of the area, during the colonial and postcolonial periods. The African economies have been facing deepened economic crises since the collapse of commodity prices as a result of recession in the industrialized countries in 1980 and 1981. The Ghanaian economy was too fragile to overcome the external jolt brought about by the weak demand for its commodities. The economic crises have forced individuals and communities to engage in unwholesome competition for resources in the areas that are held under communal or individual ownership.

The chiefs in the Adangme areas have decided to come together to discuss and devise policies on how best to utilize resources in the area to the benefit of the inhabitants in the area. To do this, the chiefs would like an economist to provide guidelines to enable them to discuss some issues in order to arrive at optimal policies to utilize the resources in the area to the benefit of the inhabitants in the region with distribution justice.

Two terms of reference are presented below. The first TOR was stated in a challenge to Dr. Kofi (one of the authors of the book), by Dr. Ako Adjei, who was kind enough to grant

an interview a few months before his death. Dr. Victor Akrofi
Kumoji was 'present at the interview as well. However, Dr.
Kumoji gave the second TOR via telephone.

Dr. Ako Adjei's Terms of Reference

Design the basic outlines of a development strategy that uti-
lizes the Songor Lagoon resources to ensure economic growth
accompanied by equitable distribution of income to the traditional people of the Adangme region, especially the old women.

Dr. Victor Akrofi Kumoji's Terms of Reference

The consultant is required to comment on the following questions:

(1.) Explain why, in the colonial period, the Songor Lagoon resources were underutilized and why these resources
could not be used optimally so that the industries so generated
could become the "growth poles" or the "leading sectors" for
economic development in the Adangme area.

(2.) Explain why the Appenteng Songor Lagoon Development Strategy (ASLDS), proposed by the Provisional National Defense Council (PNDC), the National Democratic Congress (NDC), and the People's National Party (PNP), and other
state and/or private capitalist models were unworkable and
exploitative given the structure of the traditional economy in
the region.

(3.) Demonstrate that the New Patriotic Party (NPP)
strategy is similar to the ASLDS, PNDC, and NDC models.
The NPP model is also an exploitative model given the structure of the traditional economy of the Adangme region and
would result in unequal distribution of income to the people
in the region.

(4.) Provide an alternative development strategy that
could be used to organize the Songor Lagoon resources for
production and trade so that the allied industries so developed

would become the "growth poles" or "leading sectors" for economic development of the Adangme areas. This alternative strategy should ensure rising incomes to the agrarian or traditional people with distributive justice.

Analysis of Dr. Ako Adjei's Terms of Reference

Dr. Ako Adjei's TOR asks for a development model dedicated to enhance the welfare of the traditional people. Thus the appropriate development strategy should be based on a "people centered" approach with a "human face."

In a tribute to Dr. Ako Adjei, Dr. Kofi has presented analyses of his terms of reference under the heading *Ako Adjei's Unfinished Work Defined and Identified.* These analyses set the tone for the second TOR (that of Dr. Victor A. Kumoji), and are presented next.

Ako Adjei's Unfinished Work Defined and Identified (as Presented by Dr. Kofi)

In one of my conversations with Dr. Ako Adjei in 2001, he asked of my mother's trade. I told him that she was a bread baker. He told us that his father was a farmer and his mother was a merchant. Then he told me that the old people at Ada are grieving for me to come and help them. He wanted to know when we are going to improve the lot of the traditional people in the agrarian sector. He asked me what I was going to do about the Songor Lagoon problem. He said that the traditional people, the old women, are waiting for an economist to come and develop a strategy to produce salt under a system that would ensure growth and equitable distribution of income to the people of Ada. I assured him that I would take on his challenge.

Dr. Ako Adjei lived in "two worlds." He never forgot the traditional sector. As a member of the Nkrumah government, Ako Adjei and other nationalists could not develop an agrarian strategy of development, as they would have wished. This, perhaps, is because academicians were held in high esteem in the 1950s and Lewis' capitalist models were imposed on the Nkrumah regime by the colonial power structure. Lewis not only developed an industrialization policy for the Caribbean, but also for the Gold Coast (Ghana). In the Lewis model it was assumed that the capitalists would invest in Ghana after the regime had built the necessary infrastructure. Though the regime spent all the hard currency it had on building the necessary infrastructure, the capitalists hardly invested in Ghana and the whole episode resulted an economic disaster. For example, with no capitalist investment, in the agrarian sectors the ensuing economic difficulties brought about political difficulties and the Nkrumah regime was finally overthrown, in part because the soldiers said they did not have new uniforms. These are debatable issues; all we know for fact is that once the economy collapsed, political chaos ensued.

When the house began to fall down during the Nkrumah regime, several people tried to help. For example, according to C.L.R. James "Africa (and other countries as well, but Africa in particular) will go crashing from precipice to precipice unless the plans for economic development are part of a deep philosophical concept of what the mass of the African people need. This is where Nkrumah failed."[16] What, then, are the solutions to Africa's development problems? What is to be done? James argues that the answer lies in organizing a cooperative movement—"the only task that remains to be done is to organize the population in co-operative societies," because it would be the "simplest, easiest and most intelligible to the peasantry."[17]

Our own work seems to be in the direction explained by James. For example, Professor Desta, in his book *Environmentally Sustainable Economic Development*, faults capitalist development for degrading and depleting the environment as opposed to agrarian development, which is friendly to the environment.[18] Professor Kofi, on the other hand, has suggested in numerous publications over the past three decades that a cooperative movement based on African traditions will go a long way to solve Africa's development problems. He has characterized this movement as the "Abibirim strategy of development" or simply the Abibirim strategy.[19] This is the only way available to African societies to raise the productive forces of the peasantry or the traditional sector. Any other way would destroy the traditional sector and it would be a brutal transformation exercise.

It is important to realize that even in a country like South Africa, where there is a higher degree of industrialization than any other African country, there are still large pockets of agrarian sectors that are bigger than the capitalist sectors in terms of population; hence there is need for a people-centered approach.

It is also important to recall that the debate over agrarian transformation, vis-à-vis capitalist transformation, was a subject of heated debate in Russia in the 1880s and 1890s. The agrarian social reformists (Narodniki Movement) were pitted against Lenin and the Marxists. Lenin's group won the debate but they were not necessarily right, as is proven by the ultimate demise of Marxism in Russia. The agrarian sector was replaced by a collectivization policy, which failed to smoothly transform the agricultural sector into an industrialized sector. In the case of Ghana, where the transformation to industrialization was never achieved, Lewis' model did not support change but instead veiled their models in pleas for foreign investment.

Dr. Ako Adjei did not forget his agrarian roots. His philosophy was that of a people-centered approach to development. This, according to him, would help alleviate poverty in the rural sectors. He has been and will be an inspiration for the coming generation. He will be an inspiration for Africans to develop a strategy to transform the traditional sector, humanely. He has contributed immeasurably to the emancipation of Ghana and Africa from colonial rule.

Toward an Analysis of Dr. Victor Akrofi Kumoji's Terms of Reference

Dr. Ako Adjei has challenged the chiefs of the Adangme region. He is asking the chiefs to serve their constituency and their people. The chiefs should develop a people-centered development strategy. In this way, the chiefs would serve the interests of the traditional people, according to what their culture demands.

It would be useful if the chiefs would discuss the philosophical implications of Dr. Ako Adjei's beliefs. It should be pointed out that when he came to live in Accra, Ako Adjei learned how to speak Adangme before he learned how to speak Ga. The people in his father's village, Adjeikrom, were all Adangmes. Thus Ako Adjei was schooled in Adangme culture when he was growing up. This is why his analyses of a development strategy had a "humane Adangme cultural flavor."

The point we are making here is that the chiefs should dig deep into Adangme culture to design a strategy based on the philosophy of Dr. Ako Adjei. This is the philosophy of Adangme culture that is in turn based on the indigenous culture of Adangme theocracy.

Second Terms of Reference

With the above backdrop, we turn to the second terms of reference. We argue that all the colonial and post-colonial development strategies designed for transforming the Songor Lagoon resources have been based on grafting an exploitative capitalist model onto an agrarian economy with institutions based on the Adangme theocracy. This is a perverse capitalist development of the worst type.

In the first sections of the second terms of reference, we demonstrate that *all* the past development strategies, including the most recent NPP strategy, could be characterized as "perverse" capitalist developments. In such a strategy, there is no room for distributive justice. What we have is a cruel exploitation of the traditional people. However, in doing so, we also exploit the modern sector. What is not known and understood is that a development of the traditional sector is a prerequisite for a viable development of the modem sector.

Analyses of the Second Terms of Reference (Kumoji's TOR)

Analyses presented here are taken, in part, from Dr. Kofi's manuscript entitled: "National Democratic Congress (NDC) Problem and New Patriotic Party (NPP) Nightmare Accumulation of Capital and the Saga of Ada Songor Lagoon."[20]

Analysis of TOR (i)

Explain why during the colonial period, the Songor Lagoon resources were underutilized, and why these resources could not have been used in a more optimal manner, so that the industries so generated could become the "growth poles" or the "leading sectors" for economic development in the Adangme area.

The colonial regime was not interested in the resources that the Adangme region could supply. These imperial powers were interested in minerals and tropical produce—palm oil, rubber, cocoa, coffee, kola nuts, and the like. These resources were not available in the Adangme region. As a result, the area was ignored by successive colonial administrations. In this region, the economic activity that did take place during this time was due to indigenous initiatives.

Cheap river transport systems, an indigenous salt industry, and a traditional fishing and fish-curing industry underpinned economic activities in the Adangme region, during the early stages of colonialism in the Gold Coast. These natural or indigenous industries, in turn, generated other linkage-related economic activities such as canoe building.

Economic activities in the Ada region expanded steadily from about the 1820s. It accelerated during the last quarter of the nineteenth century, due to high demand for palm oil and rubber. These commodities were transported to Ada Foah on the Volta River and then shipped to Europe. The golden age of economic development in the Ada region reached its peak in 1901.

The main reason why the Adangme economy collapsed after 1901 is that the colonial administration built roads, railways, and a port facility at Secondi-Takoradi. These competed with the industries of the indigenous Adangme economy. The aims of the colonial government were to increase the value and volume of exports between England and the Gold Coast. The Adangme economy felt the negative impact of these activities. The Ada Foah port lost its business to the Takoradi port because it was less risky and cheaper to transport goods through Takoradi to Europe than through Ada Foah. Thus, economic activities in the Adangme region declined because of the development of motorized transportation and railway lines provided stiff competition to river transportation.

Any major development projects that have been undertaken during the colonial and post-colonial eras have had a direct negative impact on the Adangme economy:

(1.) The Adangme people lost a good chance when it was decided to build a new port at Tema rather than at Ada. The Adangme area would have revived river transport, as well as the economic activities, which were lost when the Gold Coast economy switched from river transport to motorized and railway transport systems.

(2.) The fishing industry in Adangme areas declined when the Tema Harbor became a fishing port with the use of modern fishing boats and equipment.

(3.) The Adangme area was negatively impacted when the Akosombo Dam was built. The ecology in the area was negatively impacted. Some streams dried up. Shrimp and crab have lost their breeding grounds and are in short supply.

(4.) The Adangme people lost a great deal of income when portions of the Songor Lagoon were leased to Leon Appenteng (Panbros Salt Company, an investor to manufacture salt on capitalist lines). The traditional system for producing salt was based on a "people centered" approach to development. This approach ensured that the inhabitants in the region received some income. The new production system, based on laissez-faire ideology, does not ensure that the traditional people would receive some income.

The Adangme chiefs should find a way to reverse the impoverishment of the Adangme people, which has been taking place since 1901. The Songor Lagoon provides the Adangme people with a resource that could be utilized optimally to become a "growth pole." This could, in turn, stimulate other economic activities to bring about viable economic growth for the people of the region. This is the challenge facing the Adangme chiefs.

Analysis of TOR (ii)

Explain why the ASLDS, the state models (PNDC, NDC, and NPP), and the private capitalist models were unworkable and exploitative given the structure of the traditional economy in the region.

All of these models are based on private or state enterprise (capitalist) modes of production. The traditional method of using the Songor resources for production, consumption, and trade was different from the ASLD, NDC, and NPP models.

The question that needs a clear and unequivocal answer is this: Which model would best serve the welfare of the Adangme people? We would like to hypothesize that the traditional system of organizing for production and trade is the superior model. We would like to suggest that the chiefs should use this system as a starting point to building a new development model for the region.

On Capitalist Models Versus Cooperative Models

Why do we think the ASLDS, PNDC, NDC, and NPP models are oppressive? We think that capitalist developments are considered oppressive in a case whereby a mode of production is superimposed on another mode of production to exploit or take advantage of a social class. In our case, Mr. Appenteng uses the British capitalist institutions, and takes advantage of the Ada social classes who are the rightful owners of the Songor resources.

The point discussed above may be made clear by comparing the mode of production in feudal France (at the time of the physiocrats) and the capitalist mode of production in England (see Table 7.1). The analyses may be extended to the case of the traditional Adangme mode of production (theocracy) and the modern mode of production in Ghana (capitalism).

A careful analysis of Table 7.1 gives an idea of the probable nature of exploitation and distributive justice involved in the different modes of production. We can infer possible causes of conflicts. For example, Schumpeter speaks glowingly about the fact that, in feudal Europe, everybody was employed. However, he could not say capitalism provided employment for all workers.

Table 7.1
Analyses of Models of Production and Distribution: European Mode of Production (England and France)

Feudalism [At the time of Quesnay (physiocrats in 1700s)]		Capitalism	
Social Classes	Rewards	Social Classes	Rewards
Landlords (Aristocrats)	Rent of land	Landlords	Rent of land
Artisans	As negotiated between artisan and his lord	Capitalists	Profits
Peasants (farmers)	Surplus after paying rent	Workers	Wages

A qualitative analysis of Table 7.2 seems to indicate that the Adangme traditional mode of production receives a high mark in distributive justice. You may note that the lowest class combines the roles of producer and owner. These common people have the right to claim a portion of the Songor Lagoon to collect salt. A worker in the capitalist system has lost the means of production and so is open to exploitations such as being paid only low wages.

An argument used against peasants as producers in the agrarian sector is that they use poor and archaic production methods, and therefore their marginal product is low and the quality of what they produce is poor. We would argue that this is where the government should step in to provide the necessary education to raise the level of skill. For example, in the 1920s, the Ghanaian government decided to raise the quality of cocoa beans being produced in farms. Three grades were identified representing low, high, and excellent quality. The peasants were able to produce better quality grades by drying the cocoa properly. The ministry of agriculture decided to abol-

Table 7.2
Africa Systems of Modes of Production
(Precolonial and Postcolonial)

Adangme Traditional Mode of Production (Pre-colonial and Postcolonial)		Capitalist Mode of Production			
		Appenteng and NPP		PNDC and NDC (State Capitalism)	
Social Classes	Rewards	Social Classes	Rewards	Social Classes	Rewards
Private	A third of taxes	Chief and Priests	Rent	Chief and Priests	Rent
Tax collections	A third of taxes	Capitalist (Appenteng)	Profits	Government	Profits
Tekperwiawe	A third of taxes	Workers	Wages	Workers	Wages
Common people combine role as producers and owners	Surplus after tax payments				

ish Grade 3 (low) quality cocoa because the cocoa produced on the farms was better.

We argue that it would be possible to build a modern version of the traditional mode or precapitalist mode of production to ensure distributive justice. It was a mistake to impose the Appenteng model of production and distribution on the Adangme people. This has brought about a brutal transition from the traditional to the capitalist mode of production.

The Adangme chiefs should demand that the government refrain from imposing a particular model of production on the agrarian or traditional economy of the Ada area. If the chiefs allow the NPP government to do this, they would condemn the traditional people to brutal exploitation by the capitalist class. Unfortunately, the NPP government does not seem likely to give in.

The NPP government wants to implement the same Appenteng-type model for developing the salt industry. The

NPP's development strategy for Ghana is based on an unadulterated capitalist model of development. They do not realize that by doing this, they would be imposing an oppressive mode of production. This, we have argued and hypothesized, could lead to exploitation of the traditional people.

The Hon. Dr. Kwaku Afriyie, minister for Land Forestry and Mines, inaugurated the Songor Salt Project Interim Management Committee (TMC) at the ministry in Accra on April 6, 2001. The IMC members were carefully selected to reflect certain core skills such as legal, security, engineering, administration, and accounting. According to Hon. Dr. Kwaku Afriyie, the interim committee would be required to manage the affairs of the Songor Lagoon Project on a daily basis. They are expected to maintain the integrity of the existing salt producing facility until an investor(s) is found to take over.

It was wrong of the minister to decide on a model for development without consultation of the Ada chiefs. They should demand that he open the door for us to examine other models. The model he has chosen is prone to violent conflict between social classes.

The NPP government would like to choose an entrepreneur to run the Songor Salt Project until an investor is found. Does this rule out a cooperative strategy of development? Even if the cooperative model is designed and implemented along capitalist lines?

The minister said that the Vesting Law of 1992 would be repealed "to make it possible to return the lands confiscated by government to the people of Ada. *It must be clarified, however, that the return of confiscated lands gives only surface rights to the people and not the mineral rights, which remain with the government. Government being the owner of all minerals in the country, including salt, will be responsible for the issuance of mining licenses to prospective applicants for salt mining at Ada Songor Lagoon area*" (emphasis ours).[21]

It may be pointed out from the outset that the minister has made a grievous mistake by treating salt from Songor Lagoon as a mineral that is mined. Songor Lagoon salt is not mined. It is a renewable resource, which is scooped from the surface. The minister is making the same mistake that was made by the PNDC policy makers including Mr. Tsatsu Tsikata. This assumption by Dr. Kwaku Afriyie and Mr. Tsatsu Tsikata makes it easier for the PNDC and NPP governments to confiscate the Songor Lagoon from the people of Ada and hand it over to the Ghanaian government. This will not sit well with the Ada people, especially the youth and Tekperbiawe clan who are the allodial owners of the lagoon.

The Adangme chiefs should demand that all renewable resources in Ghana, including all the forests and all the timber, should be confiscated by the government and then the government should find an investor to exploit the resource. If this would not sit well with the Ashanti, Fanti, and northern chiefs, then the government should stop imposing its will on the Adangme people.

The Adangme people should develop their own model to organize the Songor resources for production based on the Adangme theocratic philosophy and culture. The role that the NPP government should play is to enable the Adangme chiefs to meet, discuss issues, and draw up their own strategy to develop their region.

The NPP strategy is faulty and will not work because it is prone to political conflicts and violence. The NPP model, like the ASLD, PNDC, and NDC models, is an exploitive model. It will sanction entrepreneurs from other regions in Ghana who will, with access to bank loans and political power, gain control over a resource that should be held in trust for the entire Adangme tribe and which should be exploited for the benefit of all Ghanaians and especially to the benefit of the Adangme people.

Analysis of TOR (iii)

Demonstrate that the NPP strategy is similar to the ASLDS, PNDC and NDC models. The NPP model is also an exploitative model given the structure of the traditional economy of the Adangme region and would result in unequal distribution of income to the people in the region.

The NPP strategy is similar to the ASLDS, PNDC, and NDC models because they are all based on the capitalist mode of production as it has evolved in England and other parts of Europe. The model recognizes an entrepreneur who finds or gains access to capital and organizes for production by hiring labor. The income generated from the production and sale of the output is distributed among the claimants. In the case of the PNDC and NDC models, the state played an important role in organizing for production, however the model is the same as the private enterprise model.

It has been argued that in cases where a precapitalist sector interacts with an advanced capitalist sector, incomes are distributed to favor the capitalist sector. Capitalism develops on the tomb of precapitalist sectors, and unless the government takes steps to level the playing field, the precapitalist sector will face brutal exploitation.

We have demonstrated that the Adangme region has been underdeveloped through negative impacts on its economy, as a result of development projects implemented in other regions of the Ghanaian economy. The records show that underdevelopment in the Adangme region is due to the negative impacts that resulted from colonial and postcolonial projects in several sectors of the Ghanaian economy. It is therefore justified for the government to set aside resources to develop the Adangme region as compensation for the negative impacts the Adangme region has suffered.

ANALYSIS OF TOR (IV)

Provide an alternative development strategy that could be used in organizing the Songor Lagoon resources for production and trade. The developing industries would become the "growth poles" or "leading sectors" for economic development of the Adangme areas. This alternative strategy would ensure rising incomes to the agrarian or traditional people with distributive justice.

Ako Adjei's terms of reference presented the elements of an alternative strategy of development for the Adangme region. Kofi has articulated in several articles that some of the major problems facing the African economies could be solved if the resources in the traditional sectors, including labor, could be organized under a cooperative system of production.[22]

To resuscitate economic activity in the Adangme area, therefore, we need to design an alternative development strategy. The alternative strategy is a combination of the Finnish cooperation model and the Cuban Alternative Model for agricultural production. In the pages that follow, we will explain why the Finnish and Cuban models are superior to the NPP model and, as a result, the Ada people would be advised to draw lessons from both the Finnish Pellervo Movement and the Cuban Alternative Model to solve the problem of impoverishment in the Adangme area.

THE FINNISH PELLERVO MOVEMENT: ECONOMIC COLLABORATION THROUGH COOPERATION

It is argued that transformation in Finland was undertaken, to a large extent, through the efforts of a cooperative organization called the Pellervo Movement.[23] To find a name for the cooperative movement, the Finnish people dug into their past and derived a name from *Kalevala* epos, a Finnish mythology where gods destroy forests to create fields for planting. The word for field in the Finnish language is pelto. Thus, the Finnish cooperative movement was called the Pellervo Movement.

The movement was most active from 1900 to the beginning of the World War II. By this time, the Pellervo Movement had achieved its aim and had fulfilled the necessary preconditions for industrialization.

The Pellervo Movement still exists, but has fallen on hard times. This current situation must not be used to downplay the important role it had in transforming the rural sector in Finland from 1899 to 1939. It may be hypothesized that Finland is the only country in Northern Europe that transformed its rural economy mainly by the use of a cooperative organization through a movement. In Germany, Denmark, Sweden, and Norway, among others, cooperatives played a big role in the agrarian transformation process. However, it may be argued that the Finnish model was unique because:

1. The movement was relatively stronger because the society faced an external threat and the movement became an agent to modernize the economy as quickly as possible to face the challenge.
2. It was used as a tool for development of the entire society.
3. The activities of the movement are said to approximate a unique type of institutional model for economic development.

FINLAND'S ECONOMIC DEVELOPMENT PROBLEMS

Finland has always been a country of small farmers. Full-blown feudalism did not take hold in Finland as it did in Western and Eastern Europe. As a result, the peasants trained and exercised their personal freedom and individualism. This condition was formalized in 1789, the same year as the French revolution, when Finnish peasants received unlimited rights to their hereditary lands. The problem that Finland faced was to raise productivity in the agricultural sector given the following conditions: (1) there was surplus land, (2) the population was spread out on a large land base, and (3) contact with the outside world was limited.

Under these conditions, the answer lay in developing an institutional model of agrarian reform. As a result, they had to develop a relatively closed economy, by using their internal markets. In 1809, the population of Finland was 1 million. In 1880, 75 percent of the population received their livelihood from agricultural activities.

Taxes collected from the agricultural sector were used for administration and other services. In 1867 and 1868 there was famine in Finland and over 100,000 people died. This forced the authorities to attempt to modernize agricultural output intensively and extensively. The Pellervo Movement came in at the right time. Between 1890 and 1910, the cultivated area doubled. Between 1920 and 1930, over 60,000 hectares were brought into cultivation. Agricultural productivity improved and by the end of 1930 Finland was 90 percent self-sufficient in food grains.

In part, the Finnish Pellervo Movement developed as a political reaction against the Russian threat to colonize and absorb Finland as "paternalistic form." Thus, the Pellervo Movement fits the class model of challenge and response developed by Gerschenkron who, in turn, borrowed the analytical tool of the model from the British historian Arnold Toynbee.[24] Professor Toynbee had argued that history teaches us that societies develop when they are challenged. The challenge is a necessary condition but not a sufficient one. The sufficient condition is for the country to mount a successful development response. In this case, Finland was challenged by Russia. Russia wanted to absorb Finland, Finland responded by implementing a successful agrarian development strategy, to create an operational groundwork for industrialization.

Gerschenkron argued that when Britain began to industrialize, it challenged the other European powers: France, Germany, and Russia. According to Gerschenkron, France responded by challenging its banking institutions and by relaxing the credit laws so as to provide cheap loans to emerging capitalist industrialists. France used this strategy to initiate and develop the industrial sectors and catch up with Britain. Germany used the same method by discriminately giving cheap credits to German industrial concerns. Russia, on the other hand, failed to mount a proper capitalist response. Japan mounted a viable response when the Meiji reformation was put in place. The rallying cry of the response strategy was to develop Eastern morals and Western technology in order to catch up with the West.

In the case of Finland, the challenge came in the form of a manifesto proclaimed by Czar Nicholas II in February of 1899. By this manifesto, a great deal of Finnish legislative power was given to Russia, but the Finns protested by collecting over half a million signatures against the intentions of the manifesto. The Finns also protested in another form. They put into operation the Pellervo Movement, in order to develop a strong economy as fast as possible. This movement can be considered as an optimal model for economic development of Finland for many reasons:

1. It was a self-reliant strategy of development.
2. It was a self-help model that sought to raise the skills and techniques of production of unskilled peasants in the rural sector.
3. By setting up consumer and producer co-operatives, the model sought to develop the economy via the use and expansion of internal markets.

Thus, it can be shown that the Pellervo Movement succeeded in transforming the rural sectors of Finland, because the productivity of labor increased, real incomes increased, internal markets expanded, purchasing power increased, poverty was reduced, the rate of unemployment was reduced, and the overall welfare of the population increased.

Can we draw any lessons for Africa from the Finnish model? What role can a cooperative movement play to help resolve some aspects of the African economic crises? We will use the Pellervo Movement, as examined above, as a backdrop. From this, we will draw lessons to help us develop a viable model for the Adangme region, using the Songor Lagoon salt industry as the leading sector.

LESSONS FROM THE PELLERVO MOVEMENT: IDEOLOGY

Ghanaians are at a loss when confronted with a third way to capitalism or socialism as a system of production. The complex relationship between cooperation, competition, and capitalism needs to be analyzed carefully, especially by countries that are late to industrialize and have little or no capital. The issue is finding a third way to industrialize without being dominated by the advanced nations under capitalist systems of production.

The Pellervo Movement wanted to build a society based on free will and moral evolution of people, a society based on economic collaboration between citizens in a nation-state. The Pellervo Society believed that economics dictated politics and not vice versa. The movement believed that education of the individual was a precondition to social progress.

The Pellervo Movement understood that capitalism based on selfishness creates misery and poverty for the losers. Socialism evolved to solve some of the problems created by capitalism. Socialism, however, engendered the doom of true individualism. The Pellervo Society found a third way, which was a peaceful endeavor of the peasants and those suffering from the consequences of the untrimmed competition of capitalism. Thus, the Pellervo Movement did wonders for the underprivileged of Finland. A poor agrarian economy, Finland underwent rapid transformation, industrialization, and urbanization in less than a century. The "growth pole" industry of the movement was Valio, the diary cooperative.

LESSONS FROM THE PELLERVO MOVEMENT: VALIO

The agricultural sector played a leading role in changing the economic focus from the tar industry to the butter industry. There is a rural community in western Finland called Kuortane. The political and economic conditions there made it an ideal setting for the development of a cooperative organization. In the nineteenth century, economic activity was based on field clearing for timber. When the demand for these commodities dried up, new cash crops had to be found. Rye had been the main cash crop in the nineteenth century, but the price of rye fell as a result of cheap imports of grain from America and Russia. The grain import duties were repealed in Finland because of the famines of 1860s. Because of these and other factors, Finland's small farmers could not compete in the international grain market. As a result, Finnish freeholders turned to dairy farming.

Dairy farming became a lucrative business because butter prices were rising at the time. The invention of the refrigerator, the ease of transportation due to steamships, and the opening of ports to winter traffic made it possible for producers to supply the market. As the demand curve shifted to the right, the supply curve followed by shifting to the right also. Dairy technology had been revolutionized in the 1880s by the separator, and it became lucrative for wealthy farmers to enter the dairy business. This was followed by freeholders and storekeepers, who set up dairy companies and bought milk from the farmers. The industry expanded and production had to be operated on a larger scale.

Freeholders were forced to operate the dairy farms on joint-stock company basis, in order to attract more capital. The joint-stock companies were converted into cooperatives. Many of the founders of the dairy business had been raised in Pietist homes and they were deeply religious people. The church underlined their personal faith. The religion created a bond between people of different socioeconomic groups. These were some of the ingredients that made it possible for the Pellervo Movement to succeed.

In 1901, the Finnish government passed the first Cooperative Society Act. Before the act was passed, the Pellervo Society had urged farmers to organize and engage in joint buying and selling cooperatives. One of the industries that became the most important growth pole for modernization was Valio, the dairy cooperatives. The government strictly controlled the dairy industry. State loans were provided to jumpstart the cooperatives. The cooperatives made sure that the dairy products were of high quality and enjoyed high prices. The cooperatives ensured that livestock were raised under proper hygienic conditions.

Valio cooperatives fit the Finnish conditions very well, as the farms were spread out in vast areas of Finland. The milk was collected to central places where the cooperative factories took over production of milk, butter, and cheese. At first, milk was conveyed by horse drawn cart. Next, it was drawn by truck or tractor. In modern times, since the 1960s, milk tankers have transported the farm milk. It may be argued that the Finnish conditions were naturally suited for a cooperative movement.

YOMO-LIBI COOPERATIVE MOVEMENT: ALTERNATIVE STRATEGY TO THE NPP AND NDC SONGOR LAGOON SALT PROJECT

We argue that the analyses presented above indicate that a cooperative movement of the Finnish type could be used to develop the impoverished Adangme region. Our alternative development strategy could regenerate economic activity in the Adangme area with minimal conflicts arising from its operations.

To find a name for our Songor Lagoon salt project, we would like to draw an analogy from the Finnish case. The purpose of our project is to use the Songor resource to resuscitate economic development in the Adangme region, and Ghana in general. Like Finland, we dug into our past and found the Adali legend of Yomo and Korle. The Yomo's deity was Libi (salt). In the legend, Yomo (the old lady) appeared to Korle (the Terkpebiawe hunter), who had found the Okor forest. Yomo then instructed Korle on how to worship her deity. It was under this condition that Korle and his people were allowed to settle in the Okor forest. Therefore, we will call this strategy for development the Yomo-Libi Cooperative Movement (YLCM).

We may surmise that the Songor Lagoon is sacred to the Adangme nation, and because the Adali do not sell, rent, or lease their deities, we would argue that no part of the Songor Lagoon should be sold, rented, or leased to the government, to then be divided among prospective investors. The sensible thing to do is to go back to the precapitalist, common-ownership model of the lagoon. This is what we suggest as a "third way" of administering the lagoon resource. The NPP strategy is impractical because it will invite violence and conflicts between stakeholders.

The NPP government may use this and other documents to establish a cooperative model of development for Adangme area. We would like to examine and comment on the four pillars of our institutional model: Ownership, Production, Distribution, and the Role of Government.

Ownership

The NPP government would like to know who the true owners of the Songor resource are. We have explained that this is a difficult issue. The process of ownership was legislated by a theocratic government, and it is difficult to identify the owners under the precapitalist mode of production. Under the theocratic rules, the land belongs to those who were the first to find it and settle on it. While it is Korle and his Tekperhiawe clan who have been recognized as the allodial owners of the lagoon, it may be argued that the older clans of the Adali are also owners. During the precapitalist era, all Adali had the right to go and scoop salt from the lagoon and pay a token fee. Thus, common ownership of the lagoon was accepted. See Table 7.2 for analysis of income distribution to the factors of production.

We have argued that there was relatively more peace and tranquility concerning ownership rights under theocratic government than under secular (capitalist) government. We would hypothesize that there would be more violence and conflicts over ownership rights under capitalism than under a Yomo-Libi cooperative arrangement. The empirical evidence shows that under the Star Chemical and Task Force ownership arrangements there was violence and conflicts. Under a Yomo-Libi cooperative arrangement, ownership rights over the lagoon would be understood in the theocratic sense.

Production

The NPP has assumed without proper cost/benefit analysis that the capitalist intensive method for developing the Ada Songor Lagoon is the way to go. We beg to disagree. We would hypothesize that the traditional way of mining salt was more price efficient than the capital-intensive strategy. Besides, the traditional way would employ more labor and income distribution, and thus would be more egalitarian.

The Ghanaian government is morally bound to repair the damage to the Adali economy by the Tema harbor and the Akosombo dam. To do this, the government may build the necessary modern infrastructure, which would bring more saltwater and Volta water into the lagoon. We have explained that during the pre-Akosombo days the lagoon produced more salt and more fish than in the post-Akosombo era.

We have explained that the modem method for producing salt would destroy the Adali culture and way of life. The Songor Lagoon lands would be leased to investors. The traditional people would be forced off the land and massive unemployment would result. The ecology in the area would be destroyed. The production capacity of the lagoon has been estimated at 1.2 million metric tons a year. The demand for salt in West Africa has been estimated to be 870,000 metric tons a year. We would like to argue that a Yomo-Libi cooperative could be set up to produce enough salt to meet West African demand. We should note that the Pellervo diary cooperative was able to modernize milk processing and deliver butter and milk products to service the European markets. This success story could be reproduced by the proposed Yomo-Libi cooperative. This movement would keep traditional farmers on the land, and democracy and equality would not be destroyed.

The NPP strategy would be a disaster. The fruits of international capital accumulation would be unevenly distributed. Most of the salt profits would go to the pockets of international investors.

Distribution

Table 7.1 shows the claimants of the income that is generated under different models of production. A qualitative analysis of Table 7.1 may reveal the levels of unequal distribution or equitable distribution of incomes. In the precapitalist period, incomes were low, however, these incomes were distributed equitably. The shares of income collected by the Okor priests and chiefs were very small indeed. During the capitalist period, royalty incomes going to the Adangme traditional mode remained small. However, the profits earned by the capitalist class were relatively large. A substantial share of these profits went to the capitalist class, the investors, who are disproportionately from Europe and America. Thus under capitalist mode of mining salt, a qualitative analysis of income distribution in Ghana mainly favored the foreign investors.

In week ending August 26, 2001, the <u>Statesman</u> (newspaper) reports that mining areas are unhappy. Andrzej Lukowski reports that

> representatives from mining communities from eight of Ghana's ten communities have expressed their dissatisfaction regarding the country's major surface mining operations and government's attitude towards them. J. A. Osei, a senior mining representative head[ed] the attack, condemning the callous attitude of the companies towards the Ghanaian environment and the people living in it. Osei, for example, described the extent that the mining companies have gone to in order to acquire more land to mine. He told some of the intimidating tactics used to remove locals from their homes when the land has been chosen for exploitation, including using private and state troops to assault, falsely imprison, and even torture individuals. One company, G.A.G., was singled out as having been responsible for the demolition of a church, a mosque, a nursery and forty-five other buildings in their ruthless desire to remove communities. ...The government was equally attacked as having provided much too favourable conditions to foreign mining corporations since 1983.

The Star Chemical Company and other salt-mining companies also exhibited this type of behavior. In the case of the Adangme traditional area, the people reacted violently to the attacks by the mining companies. A proper cost/benefit analysis of these mining and salt-mining projects may reveal that the social costs of these projects may outweigh the private costs. In this case, the nation and its people would be short-changed. It is clear that the government must play an active role to find solutions to the problems explained above before the nation can benefit from mining and salt-mining projects. We believe that a cooperative strategy based on the Pellervo model would go a long way to solve some of the problems raised above.

The government has an important role to play. The NPP strategy calls for a capital-intensive system to mine salt under a capitalist mode of production, investors would be found to organize for production and trade. Our model of social transformation calls for a third way. We have studied the Finnish model for transforming an agrarian society to a modem industrialized country. As we have indicated, the Pellervo strategy would yield much better results than the NPP strategy.

POLICY RECOMMENDATIONS AND CONCLUSIONS

Economic development in the Adangme region reached its peak or golden age in 1901. Since then, the economic activity in the area has been in decline. The area is now one of the poorest regions in Ghana. We recommend that economic activity in the area be regenerated by stimulating the Yomo-Libi Cooperative Movement, through a cooperative development strategy.

The YLCM takes a people-centered approach to economic development. The movement seeks to raise the productive forces of the traditional or agrarian people in the Adangme economy, and to strengthen the capabilities of the citizenry to undertake cooperative development activities. This is the only way whereby the welfare of the traditional people could be enhanced and the empowerment of marginalized groups could be fostered.

The movement seeks to organize the population into co-operative societies and prepare the traditional people for production and development. It is believed that the design of a cooperative movement for development would be the simplest, easiest, and most intelligible to the peasantry or traditional people.

A special role is reserved for the chiefs to play. The chiefs would become the leaders of the movement, organizing cooperatives, and informing the government that, like the salt of Songor Lagoon, the Ada people are a renewable resource, and thus, should not be mined. The members of the movement would design policies and the Ghanaian government, on the other hand, would play a facilitating role.

In addition, to develop the agricultural sector in Africa, particularly the Adangme region, we recommend that Africa emulate the low-input, sustainable agricultural model practiced in Cuba.[5] This model relies on traditional and new methods of agriculture but seeks to promote the ecological sustainability of agricultural production by replacing the dependence on heavy machinery and chemical inputs. Given Africa's level of development, it can modify and use the following low input agricultural development models from Cuba: (1) soil fertility management, (2) management of plant diseases, insect pests, and weeds, and (3) effective labor mobilization.

To control soil erosion, loss of fertility, and other forms of soil degradation, like Cuba, African countries need to evaluate, map, and reclassify the continent's soil. For example, in addition to crop rotation, the soil fertility of farming land could be maintained by using organic manures derived from poultry and livestock. Because plowing the soil with tractors leads to soil erosion, an ox-drawn multiplow, made locally, could be used to slice the soil surface and cut weed roots. Intercropping can be used to take maximum advantage of the land. As is done in other parts of Africa, African farmers need to be encouraged to concentrate on alley cropping, crop rotations including legumes, and improved fallow techniques utilizing nitrogen-fixing trees. These techniques can be supplemented with locally available rock phosphate in some locations.[26]

As practiced in Cuba, the second alternative model of agriculture that could be used in Africa should include the management of plant diseases, insect pests, and weeds. As discussed by Media Benjamin and Peter Rosset, to the Cuban farmer, using integrated pest management means going back to traditional methods of biological controls that have been improved through biotechnology. For example, pest and disease monitoring systems have been established at local research centers to be used in small plots where the most important crops are grown. When resistance is detected in a pest, the pesticide in question is retired immediately and replaced by other control methods. These plots also serve as indicators for the breakout of diseases and new pests in the crops. This system prevents crops loss and cuts down on cost of concentrating pesticide use.[27]

Africa should not depend heavily on imported agrochemicals, which are mainly toxic substances, to effectively manage weeds. Like the Cuban farmers, Africans should focus research on: (1) monitoring techniques which predict weed pressures and community composition a year in advance, (2) predictive models of system rotation based on monitoring, (3) very selective use of herbicides in combination with the above monitoring, and (4) tillage methods and the designation of new farm implementations.[28]

Finally, as is done in Cuba, African countries can mobilize their high school and college seniors to temporarily give their services to the rural farm areas. For example, students would be required to perform an internship of one semester in the farmlands, thereby transferring their knowledge and skill to farmers. This would help the farmers to make better decisions by providing information, such as prices of farm products, new research products, or other new human capital. Thus, it would also stimulate desirable agricultural development. The government needs to provide temporary housing, food services, and limited allowances to those involved in national extension internship service programs in order to ensure its success.

In short, assuming no unpredictable external shocks (such as natural disasters, change in rainfall, or disease), we argue that substantial growth in Africa's agricultural system, and more particularly in the Adangme region, is possible and sustainable. There needs to be improvements in the production possibilities, like land, input supply, infrastructure, and biological and agronomic technology. The government needs to provide incentives to individual farmers and firms for building infrastructure and research. The YLCM needs to inspire and establish cooperatives, trading networks, and rotating credit associations, but a high-level pro-agriculture political commitment needs to be "translated into policy support to agricultural institutions that will, together, prove necessary for accelerating Africa's agricultural growth."[29]

We hope that our efforts will open up discussion of a YLCM-style agricultural development policy in the Adangme region. The YLCM can become a fundamental thrust around which policy makers can strategize in waging the battle against Africa's underdevelopment.

CHAPTER 8

EDUCATIONAL AND SUSTAINABLE ECONOMIC DEVELOPMENT IN AFRICA

As discussed in Chapter 7, agriculture accounts for a large percentage of the labor force of the African continent. Agriculture also constitutes a large percentage of exports and the GDP. It was shown that over the past 50 years some of the agricultural policy experiments attempted in Africa were either poorly designed or not properly implemented. Given the legacy of pervasive and severe poverty in rural Africa, we have suggested that Africa needs to reconcile its traditional way of farming with modern methods of agricultural systems. In short, we reject modern agricultural methods that increase the costs of energy-based inputs and cause poor ecological diversity, soil erosion, and water pollution. We have proposed an African-based sustainable agricultural policy, called the Yomo-Libi Cooperative Movement, in which agricultural practices meet the human need for food in the long term by mitigating environmental problems. The ability of the YLCM to effect positive economic change for the rural agrarian people of Africa depends on a relatively equitable land allocation, the opening up of capital improvements in the infrastructure (such as water, roads, irrigation, drainage facilities, agricultural extension, improved seeds, credit, and access to markets) and massive investment in environmental education.

To drive sustainable agrarian development, the formal educational programs in African schools need to readily blend the curriculum with environmentally sound management of natural resources, so that the school graduates can be aware, sensitive, and concerned for the environment and have the motivation to be active at all levels in solving environmental issues. In short, the central theme of this chapter is that in addition to mastering the three R's (that is, reading, writing, and arithmetic), the curriculum in African schools needs to prepare students to be involved in a hands-on approach to solving environmental problems. Thus, educational institutions can have an important contribution to make for the sustainable economic vitality of their communities. This chapter explores the status of environmental education in four regions of Africa. The sample of countries analyzed in this chapter include Kenya from the Eastern part; South Africa from the Southern region of Africa; Ghana from the Western part; and Egypt from the Northern region of Africa.[1]

THE CURRICULUM IN AFRICAN EDUCATION

The curriculum in every country's education system guides what each individual student ultimately learns. Curriculums around the world tend to be well rounded, involving criteria that include mathematics, reading, writing, science, history, visual arts, religion, and environmental studies. It is vital that a teacher stresses each of these criteria in the classroom. Students need to know about all these areas in order to apply the experience to their personal development, academic development, and the development of their country in the long run. Learning at the primary level is what makes children want to continue learning and dream of being someone very important to society someday. Without a strong curriculum to encourage continuous learning, students are likely to drop out of school after the primary age and will miss out on further education opportunities. Furthermore, it is primary education that teaches individuals how to behave in society and what society expects from them. For example, each student learns about the natural resources that one would use everyday in society and how to protect those resources so that one will have them for a long time in the future. Without these natural resources, an economy cannot flourish and keep up with other economies. In short, the curriculum taught in primary school is going to affect the students for the rest of their lives. It can either help them help their country or add to the problem of having uneducated individuals that use up the country's natural resources.

Therefore, teaching environment-related information to children is a key subject that every country should cover within their curriculum. The environmental material that is taught to the students should give them a general knowledge of their ecosystem and how to preserve and protect it. Students need to have an understanding of living things and how they survive in their natural habitat, including the survival needs of human beings and the earth's biosphere. Without this knowledge base, students will not know the importance of natural resources and the effect they have on the economy. Citizens of a country cannot truly appreciate everything their environment has to offer them without thinking about the natural resources available to them, such as trees, water, marine life, and the like. Without these things, economies would be unable to flourish. It is of great importance that students recognize the need to preserve these natural resources in order to help their country's economy function and develop in the long term. How can African schools integrate environmental studies into their course material? We will review several possibilities in the following sections.

THE STATUS OF ENVIRONMENT STUDIES IN THE KENYAN SCHOOL CURRICULUM

The private and public schools in Kenya follow the "8-4-4 Standard One Curriculum," meaning eight years in primary school, four years in secondary school, and four years at the tertiary or university level. This curriculum was created in 1985 in order to teach students a wide variety of subject matter and to produce well-versed graduates.

The Ministry of Education created the curriculum for the Kenyan schools with the best of intentions. However, the curriculum is not exactly portrayed in the fullness or the manner in which it was intended. The curriculum in Kenya can almost be seen as unproductive and negative. The learning environment seems to be so negative that it creates obstacles that block future success in school for the students.[2] Even though the majority of the subject matter covered in the primary school level does cater to the needs of students, the curriculum hardly covers environmentally sensitive issues.

In addition, the main idea encompassed in the 8-4-4 Standard One Curriculum is "to build self-reliant, patriotic, responsible individuals with critical thinking skills to serve the nation."[3] Students in the Kenyan formal education system are taught skills in vocational and academic subject areas. Teachers in Kenya are expected to encourage students to be independent and to think on their own in order to further their education. However, the teachers seem to be inadequately prepared and seem to use ineffective implementation in their teaching methods, which leave the students feeling lost in the material. Classroom size also has a negative effect on the curriculum in Kenya. There seems to be a lot of desks jam-packed into small rooms, which creates a lousy working environment with a lot of noise. All of these things place obstacles in the way of a child's learning experience in the Kenyan formal education system.

There are 13 subject areas that are covered by the 8-4-4 Standard One Curriculum; they are English language, Kiswahili, science, GHC (geography, history, and civics) combined, geography, history, civics, physical education, religious education, mathematics, music, mother tongue, and arts and crafts.[4] All of these subjects help to make the student a well-rounded individual, but the Kenyan education system fails to adequately relate the subject matter to the living environment. In other words, the system seems lacking in subject areas dedicated to teaching students about the land they live in and the natural resources they are constantly utilizing. If the Kenyan teachers are neither portraying the subject matter correctly nor in a manner where the students feel comfortable, they are more likely to drop out after the primary education level. The students need to be treated fairly, taught properly, encouraged to do well in society, and encouraged to become leaders. In a country that is struggling with economic development, it is extremely important that emphasis be placed on the teaching about natural resources and how to protect them from being depleted. Without environmental education, it is highly probable that the citizens of Kenya will deplete their resources and implicitly contribute to the underdevelopment of their country.

For example, there is a significant shortage of fertilizer within the Kenyan economy, worrying farmers who have intentions of planting crops in March. The lack of fertilizer will affect some food production, such as cereal, and it will decrease the farmers' annual earnings. In addition to this, Kenya has a lack of water and land, which is currently damaging their economy and the future of its citizens.

Another significant issue in the Kenyan environment is forestry. Some of their forests are being taken over by citizens who are making homes in the forest. This is slowly destroying the forests and the natural resources that Kenyan residents need to survive now and into the future. "The ongoing destruction of the Mau catchment area [Kenya] is threatening the survival of over three million people."[5] Without the use of this land and the forestry it has to offer, citizens will be losing a large amount of natural resources. Citizens rely on this forest for its land, trees, water, fresh air, and animal life in order to survive. This is a trend that cannot continue if Kenyan residents want to be able to survive in their own country. With the population increasing, this problem may not disappear overnight, but teaching prevention of problems like these in the schools will increase the likelihood that it won't happen again.

THE STATUS OF THE ENVIRONMENT IN THE SOUTH AFRICAN SCHOOL CURRICULUM

In South Africa, there has been a major change to the formal education curriculum within the past ten years. They adopted the new "Curriculum 2005," which is intended to be an outcome-based approach to learning the material. "The curriculum aims to reduce the emphasis on factual information and encourages teachers to spend more time helping learners to develop concepts, skills and values, and attitudes."[6] It is assumed that the skills, which students learn in the formal education system, will be useful to them for the rest of their lives. They can use their skills to become leaders in South Africa and help the development of their country.

There are eight major subjects covered by Curriculum 2005: language, mathematics, natural sciences, human sciences, technology, economics, life orientation, and arts and culture. Language is seen as a vital subject to the South African Department of Education because it is the key to lifelong learning. Without the ability to communicate and read, a child's lifelong learning process is already handicapped. Mathematics is seen as a significant cultural achievement in South Africa and students are taught numeric, spatial, temporal, symbolic, and communicative concepts, as well as other conceptual tools.[7] The natural sciences area seems to be extremely broad. It covers subject matter from manufactured to natural resources and their necessity to society. The human sciences portion of Curriculum 2005 is intended to create responsible citizens out of the South African students by teaching them to make proper decisions and judgments. The technology area of the curriculum teaches students to be inventors throughout their lifetimes.

The teachers are expected to encourage students to formulate new ideas and pursue them with their peers as well as teaching them about the technology in South Africa and its development. The students are taught art and culture in order to give them an idea of the spiritual and visual arts in the human society that gives South Africa its culture. The economic subject area is the portion of the curriculum that teaches the students about sustainable growth and the need for economic development in South Africa's future. The last portion of Curriculum 2005 is life orientation. This area tends to tie together all the other areas of the curriculum by encouraging students to use all the tools they have learned. The life orientation curriculum encourages students to lead meaningful, fulfilling lives and to make a difference in their society.

South Africa's Curriculum 2005 seems to have the right idea about educating students. They go over the economic status and development of the country as well as the environmental issues in South Africa. However, if these topics are not discussed in depth in a manner that the students can grasp, they will be ineffective and will not aid in developing South Africa.

In the mid-2000s, the South African economy is having a hard time with growth because of its agricultural sector, which is down -0.8 percent from 2001. The agricultural sector is "contracting 5.9 percent, as farmers planted less grain crops because of lower prices and a worsening drought."[8] Recently, an action plan has been put into place to aid farmers in year-round irrigation of their crops. "Kwazulu-Natal Agriculture and Environmental Affairs MEC Dumisani Makhaye have launched a water irrigation scheme for the community of amaDungeni in Highflats [South Africa]. ...it will be used to develop the amaDungeni irrigation scheme that will help farmers irrigate their fields all season."[9] It is hoped that this will allow farmers to increase the amount of crops that they grow each year, providing more food for the South African society.

South Africa continues to grow in population, yet its natural resources are plummeting. This is a trend that can change only with an awareness of environmental issues that affect the economy. This information is best conveyed in the schools where the students pay attention to the teachers and respect what they have to say. Yet, without a special curriculum dedicated to environmental studies, this negative trend is likely to continue.

THE STATUS THE ENVIRONMENT IN THE GHANAIAN SCHOOL CURRICULUM

Education in Ghana is a segment of the economy that is continuously raising attention. Formal education has had a rich historical background that has been recorded back as far as the mercantile era. During this time it is said that European merchants and missionaries set up the first educational institutions.[10] In 1957, Ghana gained independence and has since gone through many reformations of its educational system. By the late 1980s the education system was brought closer to the American educational standard of that time.

Today Ghana's educational system a is large and increasingly decentralized structure. There are three education levels found in Ghana. The first level, the pretertiary, is controlled by the Ghana Education Service (GES). The GES is responsible for implementing procedures that the Ministry of Education has formulated. The Ministry of Education also formulates procedures for the tertiary and nonFormal education systems. The tertiary level acts on the requirements from the National Council for Tertiary Education (NCTE) and the NonFormal Education Division (NFED) controls the nonFormal level of education.[11]

At the primary level, pupils learn: English language, Ghanaian language and culture, Mathematics, Environmental studies, Integrated science, Religious and moral education, Physical education, and "music and dance" taught as physical activities.[12] For the first three years, teaching may be entirely in English or may integrate local languages. All textbooks are in English.

The junior secondary school curriculum comprises: English language, Ghanaian language and culture, mathematics, social studies, general science, agricultural science, prevocational skills, pretechnical skills, religious and moral education, and French, which is optional. Other subjects (e.g. life skills, music and dance, physical education) are taught but they are examined internally only.

In senior secondary schools, the curriculum consists of six core subjects: English, integrated science, mathematics, social studies, physical education, and religious and moral education. The secondary school students also choose electives from a number of different programs, including visual arts, agriculture, business, general arts, and general science, both technical and vocational. This allows the student to pick a subject or field that they are interested in. These electives will go on to help them with their future as they grow up and start families of their own.

In order for students graduate from the primary level, they must pass an external exam. They are also graded internally, but 70 percent of their score is based on the external exams, which take place at the end of the school year.[13]

It is worth noting that in Ghanaian primary schools, environmental studies courses are offered, though we do not know how they are taught. However, we do know Ghana is experiencing many of the same problems that face many African countries today. The battle for water needs to be emphasized in all sectors of the Ghana educational system. Trucks are currently providing water for Ghanaian residents, but this system has created a horrible situation for all citizens throughout the country. Water delivery is not only costly, but it also creates difficulties for farmers and families alike. The lack of a modern, consistent water supply may be contributing to the decline in agriculture in Ghana, which is lower by 3.2 percent from 2001.[14] The agricultural sector of an economy is important to keep a country alive and running. Agriculture gives the citizens of Ghana food, as well as economic opportunities, to sustain their lives.

The scarcity of water has also created a cry for political help. Many countries have talked about stepping in and offering money and services so that the citizens of Ghana can have fresh water whenever they need it. Without water, Ghana is feeling a negative effect on the economy. Because individuals are forced to buy water, food prices have consequently shot up.[15] As a result, citizens are faced with the tough decision of how much water to buy. This decision is even harder when there is no way to know when the water truck will come through the city again. In fact, for the past five years, *taps in the capital city of Accra have been completely dry.*

This issue is also raising a lot of awareness because without water, other natural resources cannot be effectively utilized in Ghana. For instance, without water, the country will be unable to irrigate crops and bathe their children. This is a serious issue that must be addressed sometime soon. Not only has this become an environmental issue; it has also raised a lot of political questions as well. Throughout towns there are now posters being hung that state, "No Water, No Vote."[16] Locals have decided that unless politicians decide to help this un-healthy situation, they will protest by not voting.

Water is not a resource to play around with. Citizens in Ghana soon are going to get fed up with paying high costs for their water. The minimum wage in Ghana is currently one dol-lar. Civilians are then forced to pay six to ten cents for a four-gallon bucket of water. This cost is unacceptable when water is such a necessary resource. Citizens are forced to wash more than one child with one bucket of water, or choose to bathe in the ocean. This not only creates a health issue for civilians, but soon other resources will be affected. Thus, schools need to be innovative enough to educate the students about the water shortage in the country and devise methods of desalin-ization.

THE STATUS OF THE ENVIRONMENT IN THE EGYPTIAN SCHOOL CURRICULUM

The religious battle in Egypt has always had a handle on what the educational system has looked like. Historically, schools and educational institutions were founded in churches and mosques throughout the country. These institutions were used to teach young boys religious instruction, as well as basic lit-eracy and arithmetic skills.[17] By 1986, about 84 percent of the primary-school-age population was enrolled in school. How-ever, there was less than 30 percent enrollment in intermedi-ate and secondary school, and about 16 percent of all Egyp-tian children were receiving no education at all.[18] The Egyp-tian educational ladder system consists of three levels: (1) pri-mary education (ages 6 to 12), (2) intermediate education (ages 12 to 15), and (3) secondary education (15 to 18), the latter of which students can choose a general (college preparatory) or technical track.[19]

Primary education in Egypt is similar to that found in a number of countries worldwide. The curriculum taught to students at this age encourages basic literacy and mathematical skills. Along with these skills, there is basic instruction in language, science, and religion. Graduation from the primary to intermediate level is based on a standardized written exam. This process allows the administration to control the academic aptitude of the students who are moving on to the next level of their education.

The secondary level of education in Egypt is used as preparatory time, when students prepare for their future. For a number of students, this time is used to prepare for colleges or universities. Currently, there are 14 universities found throughout the country. For other students who are not planning on attending a university, these years are to prepare for technical or vocation training. Last, there are a number of students who use their secondary educational experience to prepare them join the workforce directly.

Egypt has an ideal environment because of its physical location. But the Egyptians do not seem to have taken advantage of its resources. The major way they have abused their resources is through rapid population growth, which has depleted resources and created an uneven balance of resources per person. The largest contingent factor for resources in Africa has always been the fight over control of water.

One way that Egypt has tried to avoid this confrontation is as the main controller of the Nile River; therefore they are able to have more access to using the resources that the Nile River brings. Water from the Nile River is essential for Egypt; this river alone gives them a good supply of fresh water, as well as energy through the use of dams.[20] The Nile River is raising a lot of political issues in other countries in Africa. As time goes on, many countries feel that it is unfair for Egypt to control the river and its resources. Talk of who is allowed to use the river has begun, but there is fear of what will happen when other countries begin to use the river water as well. There is fear that if the Nile River is used even more for water and energy, the effect will be terrible. When Egypt constructed the Aswan High Dam, there was a dramatic change in the flow of the river. The effect was felt both upstream and downstream, as water flow was affected, vegetation was killed, and the fishing industry was wiped away. If the Nile River experiences an increase in resource usage, it is feared that the few resources left in the river will also deplete as they have in the past.

Another resource that is depleting at a fast rate is the coral reef off the coast of Egypt. This has occurred through the improper anchoring of boats. As these reefs get damaged, Egypt continues to lose resources that the country needs to survive. The habitats of many animals are being taken away through improper use of the coast, as well as pollution. The rapid increase in population has increased pollution in Egypt.[21] Another reason why the reefs are being damaged is because of improper disposal of solid wastes.

The curriculum in Egyptian schools involves a wide variety of subjects that lead a student to a good education, but in order to achieve sustainable economic development, Egyptian schools need to redesign their schools to incorporate environmental issues.

Summary and Conclusion

As shown in Table 8.1, the four African countries analyzed from the four regions of Africa do not seem to have systematically incorporated environmental education into their curriculum or into the outside life experiences of the school-aged children.

What is more, the different subjects identified in the curricula are not specifically stated in terms of student learning

Table 8.1
The Experiential Environmental Education
in Four African Countries

Subjects	Kenya	South Africa	Ghana	Egypt
Natural sciences	Yes	Yes	Yes	Yes
Integrated Agricultural Science	No	Yes	Yes	No
Environmental Studies	No	Yes	Yes	No
Practical Environmental Education	No	No	No	No

outcomes. Even though students, particularly in South Africa and Ghana, are made aware of the consequences of what abusing resources will do to their environment, the students are not assigned to local communities to apply what they studied in the class rooms in order to deter environmental degradation.

In order for Africa to ascertain environmentally sustainable economic development, the educational system needs to reintroduce environmental challenges. Experiential environmental education can be offered starting at the primary level, through relevant activities, so that students can manifest behavioral changes in their local ecology. Making students take care of their environment should be Africa's main focus for the future. Thus, through comprehensive environmental education, Africa must soon make environmental changes. Otherwise, with the current rate of environmental deterioration, Africa is likely to be negatively affected in all sectors of the economy.

Thus, we recommend first and foremost that Africa should attempt to increase enrollment at the primary level. More students attending primary school means there are more who are likely to continue on to higher levels of education. The more educated students there are in a country, the better off an economy will be. Educated students add to the knowledge base of a country, on subjects such as how to efficiently use their natural resources. Concomitant with a significant change in enrollment in Africa's primary education, the schools need to redesign and introduce a thorough environmental unit in their required curriculum and expand their offerings to areas that prepare students for careers that are germane to the needs of the region. Wherever it exists, environmental education needs to be redesigned in such a way that students can perform hands-on environmental service to their communities by combining their community work with academic science courses. Thus, the environmental challenges that African regions face can provide unique opportunities for students to apply their ecoliteracy skills in the form of community service. As stated by Rosemaria Russo, "The knowledge about how to implement a particular community restoration project could empower the students and therefore help them realize that they can make a difference in environmental protection and planning."[22]

In addition to this, Africa's government should implement a program to give formal and informal ecoliteracy education to their citizens on the consequences of abusing natural resources. Experiential environmental education can help students to benefit by studying collaboratively on local environmental issues.

Furthermore, by teaching environmental concerns to the underprivileged (that is, those individuals who could not get access to a formal education), Africans can be given ecological knowledge so that they can use their resources in a more sustainable manner. Whichever way Africa decides to handle this problem, it must be done soon. If resources continue to diminish at the current rate, and the economy continues to decrease, the continent will be in a severely dangerous predicament. Africa still has a chance to make positive changes for the future, but its educational institutions need to be redesigned to produce an interdisciplinary, practical, environmental education in order to become engines of change for Africa's self-renewal process.

CHAPTER 9

THE AFRICAN ENVIRONMENT AND MULTINATIONAL ENTERPRISES

Contrary to "Afropessimism" and investor perception of Africa as a "high risk" continent, NEPAD asserts that if multinational enterprises could be enticed to invest further in the continent, Africa could achieve an annual growth rate of about 7 percent reduce by half of the proportion of Africans living in poverty by the year 2015 and achieve a sustainable long-term strategy.[1]

The NEPAD argument is based on two assumptions: that multinational enterprises will introduce capital, technology, and other know-how skills into African countries; and that the home government of the multinational could be used a source of economic support. Based on this perspective, it is generally assumed that an increase of multinational enterprises in African countries is likely to increase competition, improve efficiency, create jobs, and increase government revenues through taxation. On the other hand, some argue that multinational businesses in Africa attempt to dominate the economy by enhancing their economic power; driving domestic firms into bankruptcy; never investing in research and development facilities in Africa; avoiding taxes; introducing inappropriate products; imposing excessive environmental costs; and leaving the continent barren after depleting its natural resources.[2]

This chapter explores the status of multinational enterprises in Africa. First we discuss why multinational enterprises are expected to invest more in Africa, given that the continent receives less than 3 percent of the global direct investments.[3] Then we assess the prospects for multinational enterprises and the contributions they can make for Africa's environmentally sustainable economic development.

MULTINATIONAL ENTERPRISES IN AFRICA

Multinational corporations (MNCs) or multinational enterprises (MNEs), either owned privately, publicly, or in combination, are economic organizations engaged in producing goods or marketing services in more than one country. Typically, an MNC will have a headquarters in its country of origin and expand overseas by building or acquiring affiliates or subsidiaries in other countries. In short, a company manages subsidiaries in a number of countries outside its home base through foreign direct investment (FDI) controls. Table 9.1 shows FDI inflow to Africa from 1991 to 2002.

Before investing in a country or region, MNEs generally take several factors into account. First, they determine if the host country welcomes foreign investors and accords them the necessary incentives. Then, they assess the political and economic stability of the host country. In addition, MNEs generally evaluate the country's stand on intellectual property rights and the competitive advantage they will get from the country's factors of production. Based on this, we can assume that the

Table 9.1

FDI Inflows, by Host Region and Economy, 1991-2002 (millions of dollars)

Host region/economy (annual average)	1991-1996	1997	1998	1999	2000	2001	2002
1	2	3	4	5	6	7	8
World	254,326	481,911	686,028	1,079,083	1,392,957	823,825	651,188
Developed economies	154,641	269,654	472,265	824,642	1,120,528	589,379	460,334
Western Europe	91,030	139,274	263,025	496,205	709,877	400,813	384,391
European Union	87,584	127,888	249,934	475,542	683,893	389,432	374,380
Other Western Europe	3,446	11,386	13,091	20,662	25,984	11,381	10,011
North America	53 406	114 925	197 243	308 118	380 764	172 787	50 625
Other developed economies	10,205	15,455	11,997	20,319	29,887	15,778	25,319
Developing economies	91,502	193,224	191,284	229,295	246,057	209,431	162,145
Latin America and the Caribbean	27,069	73,275	82,040	108,255	95,358	83,725	56,019
South America	14,982	48,228	52,424	70,346	57,248	39,693	25,836
Other Latin America and the Caribbean	12,087	25,047	29,616	37,910	38,110	44,032	30,183
Asia and the Pacific	59,826	109,282	100,316	108,809	142,209	106,937	95,129
Asia	59,411	109,092	99,983	108,529	142,091	106,778	94,989
West Asia	2,228	5,918	6,893	754	1,523	5,211	2,341
Central Asia	1,035	3,107	2,997	2,462	1,871	3,963	4,035
South, East and South-East Asia	56,147	100,067	90,093	105,313	138,698	97,604	88,613
The Pacific	416	190	333	280	118	159	140
Central and Eastern Europe	8,183	19,033	22,479	25,145	26,373	25,015	28,709
Africa	4,606	10,667	8,928	12,231	8,489	18,769	10,998
North Africa	1,615	2,716	2,882	3,569	3,125	5,474	3,546

Table 9.1 (cont.)

1	2	3	4	5	6	7	8
Algeria	63	260	501	507	438	1,196	1,065
Egypt	714	887	1,076	1,065	1,235	510	647
Libyan Arab Jamahiriya	-12	-82	-150	-118	-142	-101	-96
Morocco	406	1,188	417	1,376	423	2,808	428
Sudan	18	98	371	371	392	574	681
Tunisia	425	365	668	368	779	486	821
Other Africa	**2,992**	**7,951**	**6,046**	**8,663**	**5,364**	**13,295**	**7,452**
Angola	346	412	1,114	2,471	879	2,146	1,312
Benin	41	26	35	61	60	44	41
Botswana	-28	100	90	37	54	26	37
Burkina Faso	9	13	10	13	23	9	8
Burundi	1	-	2	-	12	-	-
Cameroon	9	45	50	40	31	67	86
Cape Verde	10	12	9	53	34	9	14
Central African Republic	-1	-	-	3	1	5	4
Chad	20	44	21	27	115	-	901
Comoros	-	-	3	-	1	-	1
Congo	86	79	33	521	166	77	247
Congo, Democratic Republic of	3	-44	61	11	23	1a	32
Côte d'Ivoire	158	450	416	381	235	44	223
Djibouti	2	2	3	4	3	3	4
Equatorial Guinea	66	53	291	252	108	945	323
Eritrea	37	41	149	83	28	1	21
Ethiopia	10	288	261	70	135	20	75

Table 9.1 (cont.)

1	2	3	4	5	6	7	8
Gabon	-243	-587	-200	-625	-43	169	123
Gambia	12	21	24	49	44	35	43
Ghana	105	82	56	267	115	89	50
Guinea	14	17	18	63	10	2	30
Guinea-Bissau	2	11	4	9	1	1	1
Kenya	13	40	42	42	127	50	50
Lesotho	21	32	27	33	31	28	24
Liberia	-28	214	190	256	-431	-20	-65
Madagascar	13	14	16	58	70	93	8
Malawi	-4	-1	-3	46	-33	-20	-
Mali	29	74	36	51	83	122	102
Mauritania	7	1	-	1	9	-6	12
Mauritius	21	55	12	49	277	32	28
Mozambique	39	64	235	382	139	255	406
Namibia	112	84	77	111	153	275	181
Niger	16	25	9	-	9	23	8
Nigeria	1,264	1,539	1,051	1,005	930	1,104	1,281
Rwanda	3	3	7	2	8	4	3
São Tomé and Principe	-	-	-	1	2	6	2
Senegal	20	176	71	136	63	32	93
Seychelles	24	54	55	60	56	59	63
Sierra Leone	1	10	-10	6	5	3	5
Somalia	1	1	-	-1	-	-	-
South Africa	450	3,817	561	1,502	888	6,789	754

Table 9.1 (cont.)

1	2	3	4	5	6	7	8
Swaziland	62	-15	152	100	39	78	107
Togo	11	23	42	70	42	63	75
Uganda	65	175	210	222	254	229	275
United Republic of Tanzania	63	158	172	517	463	327	240
Zambia	108	207	198	163	122	72	197
Zimbabwe	50	135	444	59	23	4	26

Source: United Nations Conference on Trade and Development, "World Investment Report 2003 FDI Policies for Development: National and International Perspectives."

MNEs that have invested in Africa probably engaged in evaluating and analyzing the competitive advantages versus the risks of doing business in Africa. For example, in spite of political instability, expropriation, external debt, overregulation, weak infrastructure, and the negative image issues that have engulfed Africa, many foreign investors have developed a perception that investing in Africa is worth the risk premium.[4] Among other things, multinational firms have been investing in Africa to gain the following competitive global strategies:

1. *Abundant natural capital:* Natural capital refers to all renewable and non-renewable natural resources, as well as the flow of ecological services derived and derivable from nature. They include the full array of minerals in the ground; the forests; the stocks of groundwater and surface water; the quality of the air; and the assimilative capacity of the atmosphere, which includes the ozone layer and its capacity to regulate ultraviolet radiation. They also include the various biogeochemical cycles that regulate hydrological and nutrient flows, and provide the very life support systems on which we all depend.[5] Africa is endowed with natural resources such as oil, gas, minerals, and other raw materials. In fact, before the precolonial period, natural resources played a crucial role in a attracting foreign investors to Africa. As discussed by Steven Hymer, Hudson's Bay Company, The Royal African Company, and The East India Company, to name the major English merchant firms, organized long-distance trade with Africa and other continents that have truly launched the process that has matured into what is currently known as "globalization."[6] As specifically articulated by Cecil Rhodes, the man after whom the colony of Rhodesia was named, "we must find new lands from which we can easily obtain raw materials and at the same time exploit the cheap slave labour that is available."[7] During

the precolonial and colonial periods, the missionaries, explorers, and colonialists who penetrated Africa destroyed the traditional economies and developed a trade in ivory, spices, slaves, and other agricultural products in exchange for Bibles, alcohol, and manufactured products. Through the barefaced exploitation of Africa's natural resources by metropolitan European powers, Europe was able to smoothly canvas the path to industrialization. Thus, colonialism not only hampered but also fettered the development of Africa.

2. *Huge market:* Africa comprises 53 nations with roughly 800 million people, with a sub-Saharan population of approximately 500 million people. Therefore, it is definitely a large market for multinational enterprises to invest in and market their products. Of course, the demographic dynamism of African markets are influenced by population growth and age. Demographic expansion drives the demand for basic goods and services. The increase of population in Africa makes it easier to render sales forecasting. The age structure helps MNEs to tailor their product for child-oriented and consumer goods that are in demand, and which they have a competitive edge over domestic firms either to sell products in the local market or to export to other foreign markets.

3. *Cheap labor costs:* In Africa, and especially in the sub-Saharan region, there is an abundance of human resource capital and low-cost labor, which could attract MNCs who seek a lower cost of producing consumer goods, such as textiles and shoes, to compete in the global market.

4. *Investment liberalization:* The policy framework with respect to FDI has also improved throughout much of Africa. First, most countries in the region have concluded bilateral treaties[8] and have signed multilateral agreements with international organizations. Restrictions on external account transactions have been largely eliminated and many

countries have shifted to market-based exchange rates. Simplification and reduction of tariffs has proceeded steadily. Such participation is an important signal that a favorable policy environment is being created and that practices are being raised to the level of international standards and contribute to creating international recognition. The binding nature of a bilateral or international treaty contributes to securing a favorable climate for FDI. Second, the harmonization of investment laws and incentives has been intensifying during the last couple of years. For example, countries in eastern and southern Africa that adhere to the Cross Border Initiative (CBI)[9] have adopted a common Road Map for Investment Facilitation. By this initiative CBI countries have agreed to simplify and codify all regulatory provisions into a single published document that would be widely available. They also agreed to establish one-stop centers that will process all applications within 45 to 60 days and grant automatic approval in the absence of objections at the end of that period.[10] Similarly, countries in various regional associations—the Central African Economic Community and Monetary Union, the West African Economic and Monetary Union (UEMOA), and the Southern African Development Community (SADC)—have either signed or are finalizing similar investment protocols. These documents are meant to set up the following: (1) common and general rules for the promotion of both local and foreign investment, (2) transparent and nondiscriminatory procedures for entry and operation of investments, (3) a common fiscal regime, and (4) the harmonization of fiscal incentives.

However, the granting of investment incentives is variable in Africa, with some countries still operating on a discretionary, case-by-case basis that gives rise to delays and non-transparent procedures. Many countries grant tax holidays for five to ten years. However, tax holidays are biased against long-term investments and equity financing, and they are very costly to governments. Only a few countries, like Ghana, have moved to a system of abolishing tax holidays in favor of low general tax rates. But many countries grant depreciation allowances on a straight-line basis, with differing rates for different items of capital. Relatively few, like South Africa, allow accelerated depreciation, though this appears to be the preferred tool in most modern tax regimes. The South African government grants several industry-specific incentives for textiles, automobiles, and other innovative activities. Kenya also gives industry-specific incentives to foreign direct investments.[11]

Notwithstanding recent improvements to streamline and remove obstacles to investment, the legal and fiscal frameworks for FDI in Africa have several shortcomings. There is considerable variation in FDI entry procedures and requirements across African countries. Certain sectors like tourism, petroleum, and minerals are often placed under special approval regimes. For example, in Botswana, a prospective manufacturing investor has to obtain an investment license, as well as approval from both the land board and district councils. The investment has to satisfy criteria on capital adequacy, technical skills, and the interests of the economy. Incentives can be granted only to registered companies, which are allowed only one application per 12-month period and MNCs are not allowed in activities reserved for domestic firms. In Cameroon, investment by domestic firms must have 35 percent local equity. In the Republic of Congo, investors from outside the Central African Customs and Economic Union (UDEAC) region have to deposit 1 percent of invested capital. In Gambia, investors have to go through several government departments to get their applications approved. In Kenya, multiple licenses are needed before the investor can set up a business. Some of these, like land title transfer and registration, can take from six months to eight years. Special authority is needed for oil and mineral prospecting. Mozambique reserves several activities for the public sector and encourages local equity participation, even in Export Processing Zones (EPZs). Nigeria requires approval from both the Ministry of Internal Affairs and the Ministry of Finance for new investments. In Uganda, potential investors have to establish that the project generates economic benefits like foreign exchange, employment, use of local raw materials, or technology transfer. Zambia requires a variety of different approvals by different agencies.[12]

Many countries are bringing tax rates in line with international norms, but tax systems still need to be rationalized and harmonized. Double taxation treaties have to be finalized by many countries, both within the region and elsewhere. The tax treatment of such important items as R&D, training, and new equipment purchase needs to be modernized. Provisions that carry forward losses can vary in time length, with some countries allowing three to five years, and others giving indefinite periods. When short periods are given for carryover of losses, firms may be subject to income tax, even though they have cumulative net losses (this discourages large-scale investments with long gestation periods). Withholding taxes on royalties, fees, interest payments, and dividends are similarly variable by country. EPZs in South Africa and Zimbabwe do not pay such taxes, while in other places the rates are high (Kenya imposes 20 percent on royalties) and can vary by origin of investor (e.g., Uganda and Zambia). Withholding taxes on dividends received by nonresidents can affect a company's financing decisions. If interest payments can be deducted from taxable income, foreign investors will prefer to finance themselves through debt rather than equity. Royalty and technical fee limits have been removed in most countries, but some, like Nigeria, still impose limits on such fees. Some countries levy custom duties and other taxes on imported capital goods, thus increasing the cost of investment.[13]

As mentioned above, many countries in Africa have created EPZs and maintain incentives for firms operating in them. However, with the exception of Mauritius, no other African EPZ can be regarded as successful in terms of attracting FDI or stimulating exports and employment. While the investment incentives provided are often generous, restrictive provisions and bureaucratic procedures erode their effectiveness. The cornerstone of a successful free zone program is the transparency and comprehensiveness of the incentives offered and the quick response to their application, without the need for elaborate qualifying criteria.

Other limitations in Africa include weak government bodies established to develop zones, operate zones, and regulate free zone activity. Regulatory authorities lack the basic power, autonomy, and funding to function effectively. Some lack control over their budgets and have restrictive civil service limitations on remuneration and employment conditions. In general, while the FDI regime is improving in Africa, serious deficiencies still remain.

Multinational Enterprises and Environmentally Sustainable Development in Africa

From a natural resources point of view, we can say that Africa is blessed. For example, Africa is immensely endowed with rich mineral deposits such as diamonds, bauxite, chromite, cobalt, gold, and copper. In addition, Africa is accorded with fossil fuel and other energy sources. Its mountain ranges, plains, agricultural land, timber, natural tourist attractions, oceans, and wildlife have acted as a magnet for a number of multinational enterprises, which have transformed Africa in pursuit of their monopolistic plans.

From these blessings, however, much sorrow has flowed. During the colonial era, most Africans did not benefit from the continent's resources. African economies were geared toward fulfilling the needs of the colonizers. The end of colonialism unleashed struggles for political control, social emancipation, and access to resources, but the anticipated political and economic independence have degenerated into border conflicts and interethnic wars. Retarded in their development and chaotic in their political engineering, many African countries are now on the verge of economic collapse.

Much of the blame for Africa's economic decline can be attributed to generations of opportunistic and corrupt leaders, who have done little to develop their societies and emancipate their peoples. That is why the expansion of corporate dominance has accentuated the steady descent into near economic strangulation and political chaos. Harbored by corrupt African leaders, a number of multinational enterprises have acted as economic predators in Africa, gobbling up national resources, distorting national economic policies, exploiting and changing labor relations, committing environmental despoliation, violating sovereignties, and manipulating governments and the media. In order to ensure uninterrupted access to resources, MNCs have also supported repressive African leaders, warlords, and guerrilla fighters, thus serving as catalysts for lethal conflict and impeding prospects for development and peace.[14]

In the postcolonial period, a number of African leaders have exerted dictatorial control over their societies. Through their undemocratic policies, they have spread dissatisfaction among the people, which has manifested over time in nationalistic feelings and even popular rebellions. These political tensions, in turn, have generated fierce conflicts over resource control. In response to these conflicts, many African governments have embraced collaboration with MNCs and other foreign investors. Lacking the technological capacity to harness massive reserves of oil, gold, diamonds, and cobalt, these leaders grant licenses to foreign corporations to operate in their domain, and then appropriate the resulting revenue to maintain themselves in power. For example, the late Mobutu Sese Seko of Zaire looted hundreds of millions of dollars in government funds derived from corporate revenue, stashed the money in private foreign accounts, and used it for political patronage and to silence political opponents.[15]

In turn, since the authoritarian governments in Africa are subject to corruption and economic blackmail by MNEs, they have stifled economic growth in their respective countries. Frequent changes in leadership have made it impracticable to implement development plans. Each new government comes in with new sets of policies that often undermine earlier progress by previous governments. Also, many African leaders have used revenue to reward political pals with bogus contracts for white-elephant projects that contribute nothing to development. After decades of economic mismanagement and political corruption, most African societies are in terrible shape. African unemployment rates are at crisis levels, with over 65 percent of college graduates out of work. Because manufacturing is also in a crisis, unskilled workers suffer a similar fate. Wages are also low. According to the United Nations Development Report,[16] the average unskilled worker earns about 55 cents daily, while the average white-collar employee brings home a monthly check of between US$50 and US$120. Many African societies are characterized by minimal opportunities for education and self-development, collapsed infrastructure, and a debilitating debt burden.

These conditions have made the continent even more susceptible to international financial control. Typically MNCs seek out societies with low production costs, along with abundant and easily exploitable resources, where profits can be maximized and repatriated without legal constraints. Though an apology, Nazli Choucri argues that "[s]ince multinational corporations conduct the bulk of the world's economic activity, they are the major environmental actors as producers, managers, [and] distributors. By necessity, these firms engage in a wide range of hazardous waste and pollution-intensive activities."[17] In Africa, after natural resources are excavated and extracted, various hazardous wastes, such as chemical and carbon emissions, and empty holes are left behind. The environmental degradation in the various mining centers of Africa is because MNEs are insulated from the lack of ecological codes in their overseas exploration. Also, various MNEs have used Africa as a dumping ground for hazardous-waste materials.[18] In addition, it is worth mentioning that multinational construction firms have severely degraded the flora and fauna of Africa.

The basic reason why the environment has degraded in Africa is because political leadership is weak, corrupt, and ready to cut deals with multinational enterprises. For example, governments could possibly increase the growth potential of their economies through fiscal policies (for example, through an increase or decrease of taxes) but, as Hymer states, African governments'

> ability to tax multinational corporations is limited by the ability of these corporations to manipulate transfer prices and to move their productive facilities to another country. This means that they will be attracted to countries where superior infrastructure offsets higher taxes. The government of an underdeveloped country will find it difficult to extract surplus from multinational corporations to use for long-run development programs and for stimulating growth in other industries.[19]

The globalization optimists maintain that global capital has served as a dynamic engine of growth, opening the window for diverse opportunities in terms of goods and services, creating employment, and boosting government revenues. This has been true in a few cases. In South Africa and Nigeria, for example, gold mining and oil companies respectively have brought new (though not clean) technology and made it possible for indigenous personnel to acquire skills.[20] However, any such benefits are far outweighed by activities that deplete local resources, stifle local or indigenous industry, and subvert the fragile democratic process. Africa is still confined to the role it played in the industrial revolutions: its raw materials are still being depleted without generating development.

In addition, the continent's increasing dependence on imported capital and consumer goods and services has left various sectors of the domestic economy untouched. African markets are specially targeted as dumping grounds for new and second-hand goods. Because of stiff competition from these products, infant manufacturing established earlier in Africa has quickly withered away. For example, imports of used clothing from the United States are threatening to destroy Kenya's domestic textile industry.

MNCs in Africa have promoted unsustainable technologies. As an example, for many years, the Nestlé Corporation advertised heavily in poor countries that bottle-feeding of babies is a "modern alternative" to breast-feeding. This was a disastrous and often deadly practice for poor infants, whose families are without access to clean water or funds to purchase adequate amounts of formula.[21]

Finally, as soon as the MNCs have African economies firmly in their grip, they deploy funds and patronage to manipulate the media and influence government policies. Governments, in turn, grant them the ability to sidestep labor and environmental laws. Other global institutions have contributed to the deregulation of African economies. The Generalized Agreement on Tariffs and Trade (GATT), the WTO, and the IMF all promote increased liberalization of international trade. The structural adjustment programs of the IMF require African states to freeze wages, devalue currency, remove public subsidies, and impose other austerity measures, which have brought about even greater unemployment and underutilization of productive capacity. These policies have caused considerable turmoil in Africa. In the early 1980s and 1990s, a number of African leaders were swept out of power as a result of industrial workers' and students' anti-SAP demonstrations.

In their quest to unravel the forces generating conflict in Africa, human-rights groups are closely scrutinizing MNCs. MNCs are not always responsible for the genesis of the crisis. But some of the deadliest conflicts that litter Africa's political landscape, at least in the last decade, can definitely be traced to the expansion and domination of MNCs. This is especially true in states where resources with global appeal, value, and markets are found and extracted. While the state's interest in generating revenue from these resources coincides with that of the MNCs, the latter's interest in maximizing profits conflicts with the welfare of the citizens. Thus, the state is caught between protecting a vital source of revenue and defending the rights and privileges of its citizens. Too often, the state, in order to ensure an ongoing flow of revenue, sides with the MNCs against the citizens.

For example, the oil-producing Niger Delta region is perpetually at war with the government and oil corporations. For decades, successive Nigerian governments have been beholden to the MNCs that possess the technology, technical expertise, and capital to exploit their country's oil. The exploitation has resulted in serious environmental damage, developmental neglect, human-rights abuses, economic oppression, and inequitable resource allocation. These abuses, and the need for redress, are at the heart of the conflict. In recent months, calls for secession by the oil-yielding region have grown louder. As other parts of the country caught up in oil politics fight to defend their interests, the drums of war continue to beat.

MNCs have played a major role in the Nigerian conflict. They gave their unalloyed support to the brutal military regimes of General Ibrahim Babangida and General Sani Abacha. Under Abacha, Ken Saro-Wiwa and eight other activists were hanged for crusading against the government and the oil companies. Officials at Royal Dutch Shell, which dominates the lucrative Nigerian oil industry, admitted in a press statement that the company could have stopped the hangings if it had so desired. Shell executives also confessed publicly to purchasing arms for the Nigerian State Police, who have attacked community residents and picketers. Also, in 1998, oil giant Chevron used its own helicopter to carry Nigerian soldiers, who stormed Parambe, an oil-yielding community, and killed several protesters.[22]

In Angola, meanwhile, the global trade in diamonds—widely known as "blood diamonds" or "conflict diamonds" because of their lethal consequences—has helped to perpetuate more than 20 years of civil war. With revenue from the illegal mining and sale of rough diamonds, the UNITA rebels, led by Jonas Savimbi, have been able to purchase and stockpile ammunition to prolong the war. Though fully aware of this, a number of corporations—such as American Mineral Fields (AMF), Oryx, and the world's leading diamond company, De Beers—continue to do business in the war-torn territory, where more than half a million citizens have been killed.[23]

For example, Jean-Raymond Boulle, AMF's principal shareholder, is known to have invested millions of dollars in support of corrupt African governments and rebel leaders in order to secure juicy mineral contracts. The late Congolese leader Laurent Kabila used Boulle's jet and funds to prosecute his war against Mobutu of Zaire. When Kabila came to power in 1997, AMF secured exploration rights to 600 million pounds of cobalt and 3 billion pounds of copper, among other deals. Similarly, the Foday Sankoh-led Revolutionary United Front (RUF) in Sierra Leone derives most of the funds it has used to unleash terror and mayhem on the country's people from the international trade in conflict diamonds. The RUF continues to fight a war that has claimed more than 80,000 lives, with no end in sight. According to the U.S. State Department, revenue from rough and uncut diamonds mined in conflict areas forms a large percentage of the commodity's over US$50 billion in annual sales.[24]

The conflicts that grip Africa can also be traced to a steady flow of arms by MNEs. To safeguard their economic interests, Western corporations are procuring weapons and providing arms training in areas of conflict. Embattled African leaders, anxious to defend their own interests and protect their hold on power, readily grant contracts to private security armies run by MNCs. Since the early 1990s, the growth of the corporate private security sector in Africa has been phenomenal. MNCs have become direct parties to conflicts by recruiting or hiring private security companies to help protect their installations, operations, and staff. In the process, they have connived with governments, and sometimes with rebels, whichever is most expedient, thereby instigating further conflict and perpetuating civil war. For example, in 1995, Executive Outcome (EO), a private security company, arrived in Sierra Leone. The Sierra Leonean government paid EO almost US$40 million in cash, along with mining concessions, to assist in its campaign against the RUF. The peace it secured did not last; rather, the country was plunged into deeper crisis. Executive Outcome was also in Angola, training the national army and helping to recapture lucrative mineral fields. In 1993, the Angolan state oil company, Sonangol, contracted with EO to provide security for its installations against UNITA attacks. The Angolan government also signed a three-year, US$40 million contract with EO to supply military hardware and training.[25]

In addition, J. & S. Franklin, a British supplier of military equipment, won a contract to train the Sierra Leonean military using the notorious U.S.-based Gurkha Security Guards. The Guards have carried out a series of military attacks in various mining areas to protect the activities of MNCs. J. & S. Franklin has also won supply contracts with several other African governments engaged in conflicts.[26]

Clearly, where minerals abound, MNCs find the lure irresistible. They accrue substantial profits from diamonds, which are sold in wedding rings, bracelets, and necklaces all over Europe and the United States. MNCs also profit enormously from cobalt, a vital raw material for the manufacture of jet fighters. The unbridled lust for excessive gain has deadened the senses of corporate giants like De Beers, Royal Dutch Shell, Chevron, AMF, and others to the damaging impact of their activities. These foreign investments come to Africa as result of corruption, the bribery of government officials.[27]

In conclusion, MNCs present both risks and opportunities for African nations. The risks stem from the fact that being integrated into the global economy will exacerbate inequality, at least in the short run, and raise the political costs of inequality and the social tensions associated with it. Most important, contrary to Gary Quinlivan's opinion that "multinational corporations are not committed to the destruction of the world's environment but instead have been the driving force in the spread of 'green' technologies and in creating markets for 'green products,'"[28] we argue that uncontrolled multinational enterprises are likely to expedite the rate of the ecologically unsustainable growth in Africa.

CONCLUSION

Though it is very difficult to assume that MNEs are the principal force behind globalization, it is clear that Africa's integration into the world economy would provide tremendous potential benefits. The challenge is to realize the potential benefits without incurring huge offsetting costs in the loss of the ecological basis for development and in the increase of inequality and the impoverishment of the populace. African governments and policy makers should thus cease to see globalization as an end itself, but as a means to an end. The real end is environmentally sustainable economic development for Africa. To the extent that MNEs add value to the achievement of this goal, they are very welcome. So, what can Africa do to keep the abuses of foreign investment in check as Singapore, China, and Malaysia have done? Because Africa needs to welcome MNEs in order to diversify beyond primary production and extractive industries into manufacturing, global market development, services, and new technology.[29]

In the 1980s and 1990s, the African continent was generally regarded as very hostile for MNEs because the existing foreign investments lacked symmetry between corporate objectives and the development plans of the host countries. Thus, prospective MNEs investing in Africa need to undertake a careful investigation of the existence of real or perceived concordance/discordance between corporate business goals and the socioeconomic development aspirations of the host country.[30] In order to place the direct foreign investment within the socioeconomic development plan of the African countries, the prospective MNC needs to fully understand the developmental plan of the host country.

Thus, striking a balance between corporate goals and the socioeconomic developmental targets of the African country is less likely to be risky for MNEs and may not entail unnecessary exploitation of Africa's natural resources. In short, the MNEs investing in Africa need to modify or redesign their proportional strategies to reflect local investment projects considered to be of high national priority. This approach is likely to ensure that the operations of the MNEs are in harmony with government policies and can strengthen the basis of mutual confidence between enterprises and the societies in which they operate. Furthermore, this is likely to improve the foreign investment climate and can enhance the contribution of MNEs to Africa's environmentally sustainable economic development, which seeks to ensure coherence between economic, social, and environmental goals. In other words, the multinational enterprises doing business in Africa are highly encouraged to take due account of the guidelines outlined by United Nations Centre on Transnational Corporations[31] and they need to openly disclose and make transparent their financial, structural, and performance activities. On the other hand, in order to entice environmentally sensitive MNEs, the prospective African host needs to take pains to assure prospective investors that they have adequate infrastructure, stable macroeconomic policy, transparent regulation, and efficient and honest public administration.

CHAPTER 10

TRANSFORMING AFRICA THROUGH COOPERATIVE AGRICULTURAL, EDUCATIONAL, AND ENVIRONMENTAL BUSINESS INVESTMENTS: SUMMARY AND CONCLUSION

Global capitalism, under WTO rules and the economic power of the Atlantic world, is attempting to revolutionize the developing countries' economic structure and institutions. But Africa was ill prepared to face the "international free trade imperialism" of the 1850s, and is now more unprepared to survive in the global economic order. Its economic conditions have deteriorated. About half of Africa's population lives on less than one dollar per day. Africa's share of exports in primary products has been declining and its terms of trade have declined. It is faced with a massive flight of capital and loss of skills to other lines of business. Thus Africa stands in danger of being excluded from up-to-date information technology. Why is Africa on the verge of losing its soul?

In order to understand Africa's current economic dilemmas, first, an account of African history is mapped out, along with a critical analysis of some of the most significant development paradigms it undertook in the past. Second, pragmatic strategic imperatives of people-centered, agricultural, educational, and cooperative small business investments are addressed to rescue the African continent from some of the conspicuous development malaise it is currently facing. At the outset it needs to be emphasized that the cooperative, people-centered development paradigm we are proposing for Africa's development in the twenty-first century is not intended as a move for African isolationism, but to enable the African continent to achieve sustainable development in which the African people are designers and vibrant actors in their development process.

PRE-EUROPEAN AFRICAN ECONOMIES

It is has been ascertained by anthropologists, historians, and natural scientists that Africa is the home of mankind, the cradle of civilization, and is one of the richest continents in terms of natural resources. Before the fifteenth century, Africa passed from reliance on stone technology to the domestication of plants and animals, and from farming and food production to the use of copper, bronze, and iron tools. Based on paternal or maternal common ancestry, every African was entitled to have access to land and ownership was in the hands of various kinds of collectives. The dominant activities in Africa were hunting, gathering, fishing, and agriculture. The communal villages farmed, hunted, fished, and looked after themselves. As means of exchange, what each village did not produce, they bartered for with other villages. Thus, before the fifteenth century, the family in communal Africa had a full control over land, labor, and the distribution of goods and services. As discussed by Bill Rau:

> African societies were internally self-sufficient. Political authority and legitimacy were based on economic well-being of the community and social stability, not simply on power. While technology was relatively simple by standards used in the North today, it matched and served the needs of the communities. Further, the technology was integrated to serve social needs, whether it be to control diseases or promote the cultivation of crops. Over centuries these African societies learned to utilize their environment for their own needs.[1]

In short, in ancient Africa the means of production was communally owned and the continent was self-sufficient in all basic needs. The community leadership was based on age and the legitimacy of the rulers was assured by distributing ample food for their people and by collecting grains and storing it in central storage units against periods of shortage.[2] Being self-sufficient and internally productive, most African states had minimal contact with the outside world until the fifteenth century.

INFLUENCE OF EUROPEAN CONTACT ON AFRICA'S ECONOMY: PRECOLONIAL AND COLONIAL PERIOD

With the internationalization of trade in the fifteenth century, Europe began to include the African continent in order to have access to its natural resources. From 1400 to 1600, most of the exploitation came from Portugal. "Portugal established trading posts around Africa's coasts. Gold and ivory were initially more important export items than slaves for the Portuguese. From 1492, when Columbus identified for Europe the continents of the Western hemisphere, Africa was progressively drawn into the European economic system."[3]

By the late 1500s, other European empires had eclipsed Portugal and the race of imperial colonialism had begun. The main exports in the early stages were ivory, timber, wax, and gold. However, by the mid-1600s, the slave trade became a prominent enterprise. The slave trade began to drive out all other commodities in trade. Preindustrialized Europe saw great need for cheap, disposable, manual labor, which came in the form of slaves. As various types of plantations emerged in the European colonies of South America and the Caribbean, Europe started securing slaves from Africa to work in the colonial sugar, coffee, and tobacco plantations. The slave trade not only disseminated Africa's workforce but it also contributed to the profound health and economic disaster of the continent.

After the Industrial Revolution, machines replaced raw human labor as the major source of production, and economic interest in the slave trade was replaced by a need for raw materials to be manufactured. Thus, Africa was exploited as a source of raw materials such as rubber, beeswax, ivory, gum, coffee, and palm and peanut oils. Africa has always been a source for gold, which helped expand the European economy, and later, the sphere of influence of international corporations. Perhaps this maniacal worship of gold by Europeans was unmatched by Africans, who saw a different value in these shiny rocks.

Because slavery was no longer economically viable after the Industrial Revolution and was regarded as "taboo," major European powers made a mad scramble to obtain resource rights on the continent. They were fueled by political rivalry, economic greed, and territorial ambitions. They wanted to gain a foothold on the economic base of Africa and link it to the European metropolitan economy. In 1884 and 1885, the African continent was balkanized into the European sphere of economic and political influence. With colonization, African communal living was dismantled. The policies of European colonial powers saw no remorse for the needs of the African people. African elites were forced to adopt Eurocentric cultural standards, such as language and bureaucracy. All the other less-fortunate Africans were stuck at the bottom of the social structure.

In short, prior to the "free trade imperialism" of the 1850s, *Africa was a relatively developed continent.* It had a stable economy based on tribal methods. Then, during the colonial period, the European continent continued an imperial expansion that encapsulated most of the African continent. Private ownership chopped up communal lands. Men living in rural areas were forced by the new economic situation to migrate to industrialized areas, such as mines, private farms (plantations), or urban areas. The procedures and methods of the colonial administrations worked for the benefit of European society, by providing them with gold for exchange, as well as chocolate and other epicurean delights. When World War II erupted, the European colonial powers in Africa failed to control their overseas empires, setting the stage for the period of political decolonization of the 1960s. As narrated by Rau:

> African involvement in the Second World War helped prepare the way for Africa's thrust toward independence. Over 100,000 African troops were sent to France following the fall of the Vichy regime in 1943. But more than military recruitment both Vichy and free France looked to their African colonies to supply French industries with agricultural commodities. ...The British recruited about 200,000 African soldiers, many to serve in Burma. In order to ensure a continued supply of agricultural products, the British set up agricultural marketing boards.[4]

POSTCOLONIAL ECONOMIES OF AFRICA

In the 1960s and 1970s, a number of African countries achieved political independence from colonial rule but at the cost of retaining close identification with Western models of development. In the First and Second Development Decades of the 1960s and the 1970s, the newly emerging independent states were made to pursue "industrialization by invitation." The model, though, was sponsored by the United Nations, which included it as a part of its plan to achieve economic growth. Yet *no African nation holds a seat on the U.N. Security Council.* Also, the majority of the countries in the Security Council are also the home bases for the majority of the world's largest capitalist business interests. Obviously, this again leads to European hegemony. The politically independent African states were heavily entrapped in a dependent economic system, where they had to choose against the African people's interest.

The dominant paradigm in African development strategies during the First Development Decade was based on Sir Arthur Lewis' two-sector growth model of the 1950s. As discussed earlier, this model was influenced by Lewis' investigation of Puerto Rico and the Caribbean (i.e., the British West Indies). However, when applied to Africa, the two-sector growth model was flawed because it assumed African countries needed to follow the experience of the West in order to develop. African countries such as Ghana were convinced that the most direct route for African economic transformation was through Lewis' model. It was believed that European-based companies would come to industrialize the continent if asked, the results of which would be higher living standards and a place for Africa on the world economic stage. Unfortunately, profits made by these companies were not filtered back into the infrastructure of the participating African countries. The result was a net loss of resources from Africa, with little compensation and more environmental destruction.

Nations using Lewis' method soon found that the invited foreign companies would not industrialize in Africa unless there were major concessions on the part of the African nations. This was the development method attempted by Ghana, which found that although there was a rapid building of infrastructure in the 1960s, the "invitees" never came and the whole episode resulted an economic disaster.

In short, Lewis' development model for Africa failed because the model initiated was incompatible with Africa's economic social structure. The mainstays of the African economy—agriculture and local knowledge—were assigned to play a very insignificant role in the two-sector economic model. Sadly, in Lewis' model the only role designated for the rural sector was to supply its unemployed work force to the industrial sector.

Given the fact that industrialization by invitation did not achieve the intended aims, the politically independent African states became disenchanted with other trickle-down theories of the 1970s, and began to question the efficacy and effectiveness of Western economic models. By reviewing the experience of other Third World countries and critically reviewing the root cause of social equity so rampant in Africa, most African states embarked on inward-looking industrialization and the basic needs approach to solving the problems of massive poverty and starvation.

Due to the global economic recessions of the early and late 1970s, African countries stepped up the need for the reassessment of development strategies. As a result, many African nations attempted to adopt the Lagos Plan of Action. It called for the democratization of the development process, just distribution of income, and economic integration through cooperation, among other things.

Instead of endorsing this plan, the World Bank commissioned Professor Elliot Berg to prepare a plan, which is called the Washington Consensus Economic Development model. Under the Washington Consensus, for an African nation to receive financial credit, they were forced to undertake a structural adjustment program. As discussed before, though a number of African countries adhered to the SAPs, the gross domestic product of sub-Saharan Africa fell by about 4 percent per annum. Also, agriculture, which is the backbone of the African economy, grew by 2 percent whereas the population increased by 3 percent.

The consequences of the Washington Consensus Model on Ghana were discussed as we examined the microeconomic commodity price trends for Ghana. For instance, Ghana's economic recovery under the SAPs would have been more profound if policy makers did not make some obvious errors in the application of the theory of "comparative advantage" and in the selection, timing, and sequencing of commodities for export. More specifically, Ghana was trying to expand in the cocoa market at the same time as other countries, thus creating a very large surplus and driving cocoa prices down. Other technological developments also let to great increases in surplus, such as a high-yield hybrid cocoa plant.

There is controversy over the outcome of the SAP experiment, with organizations such as the World Bank declaring success and organizations such as United Nations Economic Commission for Africa (UNECA) noting a failure. For example, Brainard and Cooper argue that trade theory, which is based on the Ricardian concept of comparative advantage, is a theoretical concept.[5] To adapt the comparative advantage model to any developing nation so that it can be used for empirical work leads to an economic fallacy. For instance, price formation of cocoa using the futures markets instead of traditional economic theory (i.e., comparative advantage) would have yielded a much better prediction method when dealing with future events. The design of the policy makers failed to take into account future trends in world cocoa prices. An increase in cocoa output in a market where world prices faced a long-run downward trend should have been curtailed. The resources devoted to rehabilitate the cocoa sector in Ghana could have been invested to produce alternative crops for export.

The lesson to be learned from the First and Second Development Decades is that the participation of dedicated representatives of the poorest groups at the grassroots level is vital to ensuring a broad and strategic approach to environmental management and sustainable development. For example, by examining the economic development status of Mauritius, we can discover some of the basic strategies used by one of the more successful African nations.

In spite its ecological fragility, Mauritius has achieved far-reaching economic reforms since its independence in 1968. It has successfully moved from being a monocrop agricultural economy to a newly diversified industrializing economy, driven by an expanding labor force, capital accumulation, and increased factory productivity. It has not only attracted considerable foreign investment, but has achieved one of Africa's highest per capita incomes. Improvements in human development have been equally impressive.

For example, Mauritius outperformed Costa Rica economically, a country of similar size and economic status. This is possible because Mauritius has attained a highly participatory democratic system based on free elections. All racial, ethnic, and religious communities have been encouraged to flourish on an equal footing. Not only has the stable political system enticed foreign direct investors, but also Mauritius' openness to the global economy has contributed to its economic growth. Given these factors, the use of export processing zones helped to facilitate growth in Mauritius. In addition, the system designed for redistributing its national income has become an effective safety net. For instance, the openness ratio (the ratio of trade in goods to GDP) increased from about 70 percent to 100 percent starting the mid-1980s.

When we compare the environmental strategies of Mauritius with Costa Rica, we notice that Mauritius has achieved more economic growth than Costa Rica. However, because there is a link between protecting the environment and a lasting economic development, the government of Mauritius has realized that environmental deterioration may arrest the gains in economic growth. For instance, the back-bone of the Mauritius economy is based on sugar plantations, textiles, and tourism. Sugar plantations are dependent on inputs such as herbicides and insecticides, and cause pollution of surface water and food products. The textile and clothing industries contribute to about 50 percent of merchandise exports, but because there is little control of land use or waste disposal (almost 82 percent of the population remains unconnected to sewerage networks and mostly use soakage pits), industrial sewage flows directly into surrounding lagoons. Most of the waste from dye manufacturing, with little or no treatment, is disposed mainly into the rivers and the sea.[6]

The tourism industry has developed in coastal zones that are fragile and has led to considerable pressure on the ecosystems. "Incipient signs of environmental degradation, including deterioration in the coral reefs, contamination of groundwater, and reduced water quality in the bays, have become evident."[7] In addition, the increasing number of vehicles on the road that don't use unleaded gasoline has resulted in pollution. Thus, the natural resources of Mauritius have become severely depleted through deforestation, land clearing, agriculture, and rural and urban infrastructure development.

Mauritius and Costa Rica have developed modest environmental mission statements and also have outlined various long-term objectives. However, unlike Costa Rica, Mauritius has a long way to go in terms of strategically designing its environmental policy goals, and then finding ways and means for achieving them. Given the fact that Costa Rica is environmentally sensitive, the most valuable lessons that Mauritius can learn from Costa Rica may include: (1) formulating comprehensive, locally based, environmentally sensitive strategic plans, (2) designing environmental education and making a blanket campaign for public awareness of the consequences of environmental education, and (3) encouraging social activities and grassroots political entrepreneurs to invest in environmental awareness programs.

CAN NEPAD REJUVENATE AFRICA'S ECONOMY IN THE TWENTY-FIRST CENTURY?

The first model designed for the twenty-first century is an economic model presented by NEPAD, a brainchild of Senegal's President Abdoulaye Wade, South Africa's President Thabo Mbeki, Algeria's President Abdelaziz Boutteflika, and Nigeria's President Olusegun Obasanjo. The NEPAD strategy, though outwardly promising, is still a strategy to obtain funds or loans from industrialized (G8) countries for Africa. As we have seen, the flaw is that these monies must be obtained under the conditions set by the World Bank and the IMF. These conditions set highly favorable terms of trade in Africa's raw materials for the G8 countries. But others have gone one step further to claim that NEPAD is a form of neocolonialism with the consent of African leaders. This is, again, the same colonial policy of resource exploitation by G8 countries on the African continent, with the ever-more involved use of African elites (who have jokingly imposed the so-called African Peer Review Mechanism to ensure progress on democracy, human rights, and good governance) to impose their will. Here is a system once more removed by name, once again altered in practice, yet the results are the same.[8]

The primary audience of NEPAD does not seem to be African citizens but Northern donors and institutions. NEPAD is neither new in its policy prescriptions nor is it Africa-driven. Rather, it has been argued that it is donor-focused and is rooted in the neoliberal macroeconomic discourse of the post-Washington Consensus Model rather than among the people the initiative is supposed to serve.[9]

Realizing that there are pros and cons concerning NEPAD, we examined whether the economic assumptions of NEPAD were valid, whether the FDI strategies of NEPAD could be implemented, and, thus, whether NEPAD could reengineer Africa's development for twenty-first century.

However, as was shown in Table 6.1, NEPAD does not seem to be independently conceived by Africans, because there seem to be linkages between NEPAD and the report prepared by the World Bank (cosigned by Africa Development Bank, UN Economic Commission for Africa, Global Coalition for Africa, and African Economic Research Consortium), entitled *Can Africa Claim the 21ˢᵗ Century?*

Moreover, most African economies currently depend on very few primary exports (which are vulnerable to world market fluctuations and most of the primary products are heavily subsidized by the industrial countries). Because diversifying into manufactured exports and demanding greater access to the G8 markets has hardly worked in the past, it is puzzling to note that NEPAD feels that a plea to the industrialized countries to open their markets to African products in the twenty-first century would work.

Because the aim of NEPAD is to make the African continent self-reliant in the twenty-first century, all Africans should feel that the sentiment behind NEPAD is a noble mission. However, upon careful evaluation, the development strategy outlined in the NEPAD document seems to be contradictory. The first section of the document pins the underdevelopment of Africa on colonialism, imperialism, and structural impediments imposed on Africa by the World Bank, IMF, WTO, and other nongovernmental institutions. The second part of the document, on the other hand, was written as an afterthought to satisfy the forged partnership (i.e., prospective Western donors) without paying attention to the diagnostic analysis in the first part of the document. Within the three years of its existence "as a vehicle for political and economic renewal in Africa, NEPAD seems shaky and unreliable. Perhaps in anticipation of the ambiguity, G8 leaders have been diplomatically supportive but have risked no significant exposure to the plan."[10]

In short, from the two-sector economic growth model of the 1960s, to the current implementation of NEPAD, we find that economic policies implemented in Africa are arising from European-based agencies and their allies in the world global market. Thus, the only real change in Africa since the 1960s is in the names and terminology used by these organizations. Their method has remained practically unaltered: exploit the resources of the African continent for the benefit of European-based companies, and later, corporations. As for the Africans, they have been treated as a source of human and natural resources during the precolonial and postcolonial periods. The current economic development strategies, which Africa has been pursuing, are to a large extent rooted in the Washington Consensus model and, with the exception of Mauritius, they have barely contributed to Africa's economic development. Therefore, to rejuvenate the African continent, we propose below culturally appropriate and people-centered, alternative, cooperative agricultural, educational, and business enterprise paradigms that could serve as viable economic strategies for Africa's redevelopment in the twenty-first century.

ALTERNATIVE STRATEGIES FOR REVITALIZING AFRICA IN THE TWENTY-FIRST CENTURY

It was documented before that the "blueprint" economic policies implemented on the African continent over the last 40 years have not benefited the African masses. On the contrary, it is Africa whose resources have been siphoned off for the benefit of foreign capitalist interests. Agriculture was viewed as a backward sector with slim prospects of becoming the motor of development. It was generally assumed that state-led industrialization could be developed in isolation from agriculture and would enable new nations in Africa to leapfrog over the agrarian stage and catch up with industrial nations by the year 2000. After independence, most African countries, following their expatriate advisors, gave low priority to agriculture because the income elasticity of food products is very low. On the other hand, industrialization was perceived to be the most expedient way of restructuring the economic system, thereby bringing about economic growth in the future. This not only went against African communal living (where communities control access to land and individuals appropriate the use of land, products, and descent rights to the land), but also never served as a feasible development strategy for an agrarian-dominated continent.

For example, as discussed in Chapter 7, in the Songor Lagoon region of Ghana, salt has been traditionally harvested by hand. Using the terms of reference used by the United Nations in analyzing the case study, we came to the conclusion that a people-centered approach is preferred by the Adangme people—that is, they want to have a say in the distribution of resources in the Ada region. Contrary to the traditional method, in which the lowest class combined the role of being producer and owner in a communal support system, the Appenteng Songor Development Strategy (ASLDS), Provisional National Defense Council (PNDC), National Defense Council (NDC), and People's National Party (PNP) generated models are based on private or state enterprise (capitalist) modes of production. The capitalist developments initiated by the ASLDS, PNDC, NDC, and PNP are oppressive because their strategies are superimposed on another mode of production to exploit or take advantage of the lowest social classes. These common people have the traditional right to claim a portion of the Songor Lagoon to collect salt. Like workers in the capitalist system, the Adangme people have lost the means of production and are open to exploitations. Therefore, we propose that the Adangme chiefs should demand that the government refrain from imposing a particular model of production on the agrarian or traditional economy of the Ada area. If the chiefs allow the New Patriotic Party (NPP) government to do this, they would condemn the traditional people to brutal exploitation by the capitalist class. The development strategy of the NPP for Ghana is based on an unadulterated capitalist model of development. They may or may not realize that by doing this, they would be imposing an oppressive mode of production on the peasants.

The NPP has assumed, without proper cost/benefit analysis, that the capitalist intensive method for developing the Songor Lagoon is the way to go. Nonetheless, our analysis showed that the traditional way of mining salt was more cost efficient than the capital-intensive strategy. Besides, the traditional method would employ more labor and income distribution, and thus would be more egalitarian. In fact, we go one step further and propose that Africa in general and the Songor Lagoon in particular should be allowed to develop cooperative enterprises to control and utilize the resources to the benefit of the African peasants and reduce rural poverty. Poverty is measured on the basis of cost of basic needs (as roughly estimated by the World Health Organization , and Food and Agricultural Organization), and thus a healthy diet includes a consumption of 2,500 calories per adult per day. The Human Development Index measures poverty in terms of life expectancy, literacy, and weighted real GDP indicators. Thus, the basic question that needs to be explored is: Do cooperative enterprises play an essential role in reducing poverty, empowering the African masses, and achieving sustainable economic development in the twenty-first century?

RESTRUCTURING AFRICA THROUGH COOPERATIVE AGRICULTURAL ENTERPRISES

Because agriculture is the backbone of Africa's economy, reengineering Africa through the transformation and expansion of its agricultural capabilities is an accepted truth. In order to redesign a workable agricultural strategy for Africa, other agricultural-related productivity studies need to be addressed. For example, the Abibirim strategy of development stresses the dynamic role reserved for the traditional economy if economic development is to take place at all in the "indigenous traditional African economies."[11] As summarized by Kofi, the philosophy behind the Abibirim strategy is based on the following premises:

1.   We cannot formulate adequate economic development theory for the indigenous African economies without a careful analysis of the role we have played and continue to play in the fulfillment of Western capitalistic goals.

2.   For viable economic development we must change our internal structures and external relations. Internally, our sociocultural milieu prevents our societies from utilizing effectively the surplus we generate to spur development. Externally, the dependent role we play in the world capitalist order inhibits our growth.

3.   The African countries should examine critically the Western capitalist economic theories, because they were developed for a different social order, and modify them, if need be, before using them.

4.   Traditional African countries should critically study and examine the socialist models, in order to adapt and use the more relevant aspects.

5.   African states must work closely together to develop and enforce development strategies and learn from each other. African unity will only make sense if a common ground is established for a development policy.[12]

The Abibirim strategy then calls for a different strategy to absorb the displaced traditional and neotraditional masses of Africa—if they are to contribute effectively to economic growth. Africa's rural and urban poor must be organized so that their needs are met. The poor cannot depend on benevolent rulers or nongovernment organizations. The poor people and the strengths of their numbers in organization could truly help them to press their demands. Thus, African governments have to relinquish their direct control over much of the community organization.

Another development strategy that Africa could learn from is the cooperative Pellervo Movement initiated by Finland from 1900 to the beginning of World War II. Requiring mass education for the Finnish society as a precondition of social progress, consumer and producer cooperative movements were established. As a result, productivity of labor and real incomes increased. The overall welfare of the population improved because internal markets expanded and the rate of unemployment was significantly reduced. Thus, the Pellervo Movement contributed to building the rural Finnish society to be based on free will and economic collaboration between citizens in the nation state. By setting up consumer and producer cooperatives, the model developed the Finnish economy via the use and expansion of internal markets. Unlike capitalist/investor-owned companies and stated-controlled enterprises, the Finnish people were able to create self-managed, democratically controlled, local cooperative enterprises (and when needed, get help from other community cooperatives) to enable them to be both consumers and producers and to provide them with the necessary goods and services.

In the field of rural development cooperatives, though initiated by the central government, Benin offers a very productive strategy. Each person in the rural development cooperatives "receives a share of the produce equivalent to the value of his (her) contribution in land and labour. Private plots, mainly for a subsistence food crop, are farmed on a common rotation basis, and the produce retained for the individual farm family. Some of the cooperatives have been combined to form large cooperative enterprises which provide basic facilities, equipment, processing, extension, and marketing services."[13]

Africa could also learn to emulate the low-input, sustainable agricultural models practiced in Cuba. This model relies on traditional and new methods of agriculture, but seeks to promote the ecological sustainability of agricultural production by replacing the dependence on heavy machinery and chemical inputs. In addition, as Cuba has shown, African countries can mobilize their high school and college seniors to temporarily give their service to the rural farm areas as part of their experiential environment education programs. By offering these education programs, African nations can integrate their school curriculum into effective rural development.

In short, over the years, Africa has been doomed at a loss when confronted with capitalist and socialist economic models of development. The complex relationship between cooperation and competition needs to be analyzed carefully, especially by African countries, which are late to industrialize and have little or no capital. The issue is finding a third way like the Pellervo Movement of Finland (which was a peaceful endeavor of peasants and those suffering from the consequences of the untrimmed competition of capitalism) in order to industrialize without being dominated by the advanced nations under capitalist (based on selfishness and creates misery and poverty for losers) or socialist (evolved to solve some of the problems created by capitalism but engenders the doom of true individualism) systems of production.

Based on the Abibirim theoretical economic model, the Finnish Pellervo cooperative strategy, the Benin rural development cooperatives, the Cuban sustainable agricultural development, and the cooperative strategy initiated by the International Labor Organization (ILO), we propose local-based decision making and integrated basic development strategies for Africa: (1) an ecologically sensitive cooperative agricultural development strategy, (2) an environmentally designed educational system, and (3) the development of small-business cooperative enterprises. These cooperative strategies will undoubtedly contribute to raising the productive forces of the agrarian people in Africa. Furthermore, it is expected that the formation of cooperative developments would strengthen the capabilities of the citizenry to undertake similar cooperative strategies so that the welfare of the agrarian people are enhanced and the marginalized groups in Africa are empowered.

It is worth noting that state-initiated and -owned cooperatives, which started in a number of African countries as the cornerstone of the governments' rural development programs, have failed to achieve the intended goals. Part of the reason is because they were ideologically oriented, excessively controlled by central governments, poorly managed (because the headquarters and top management are unknown to local members), insensitive to local conditions, and heavily dominated by the wealthier members of rural communities.[14] "To avoid a repeat of the past failed policies with respect to agricultural development, African farmers—subsistence, smallholders, medium, and/or commercial—will have to be empowered."[15] Thus, the cooperatives now operating in Africa need to scrutinize their reasons for being and have to be tailored to assert the supremacy of the producers and the purchasers. Based on consensus, the cooperatives in Africa should be in position to purchase the inputs of production economically and sell their products at their economic value so that the overall welfare of both producers and purchasers are fulfilled.

In order to salvage the continent, local communities need to be the powerhouses of development. African governments "have little choice but to diversify institutional responsibilities by encouraging local communities, elected local councils …to play a greater part in running the country."[17] Thus, the cooperative communities that we are proposing for the revitalization of Africa need to be locally owned and controlled by member-users, where local people own personal property and some tools of production. If needed, each locality can be integrated into federal cooperatives, operated under umbrella organizations. Sales of products and profits of the cooperative investments in land and capital are shared cooperatively. Each member is entitled to get a share of the produce equivalent to the value of his (her) contribution. With this strategy, each community can then have the ability to improvise and innovate.[17]

Currently, 30 percent of Africa's land area is capable of sustained production of rain-fed crops but only one-quarter of this used.[18] Land tenure arrangements could fall under communal ownership or long-term leaseholds within the framework of landownership by the state but "empirical evidence shows that more and more land is falling under *de facto* private control through formal sale and lease agreements and/or informal rental arrangements."[19] Under the cooperative arrangements we are proposing, the participants are not only the owners of land (both communal and private), but they need to participate fully in determining what form of landholding needs to be adopted. Also, members of the cooperatives, through their transparent and accountable leadership, need to be involved in creating social capital (band together to raise and solve common concerns) through planning and implementation of quality inputs and products, financing (providing access to credit), establishing infrastructure, providing storage and processing facilities, identifying competitive market environments, and teaching their youngsters using environmentally-friendly strategies. The newly formed cooperative enterprises need to be managed by a democratically elected local leadership in which members of the cooperatives are both producers and consumers (all stake holders must be involved). In short, the community cooperatives, which we are envisaging for Africa, need to be catered to meet the needs and develop the human potential of all members of the community and are likely to provide home-based development revitalization strategies for Africa's development in the twenty-first century.

As envisaged by the ILO, if properly implemented, the cooperative enterprises are likely to: (1) achieve economies of scale (reduce per unit cost), (2) attain economies of scope (reduce cost of production) as a result of joint production, (3) increase the bargaining power of producers and customers, (4) encourage self-employment and favor labor-intensive production strategies, and (5) be stable, learn from each other, and be more diversified in their activities.[20] Thus, cooperative integrative growth (both backward and forward) is to be assessed in terms of memberships, new products, services provided, net earnings, value of assets, and diversification process achieved. Concentrated diversification would occur when a cooperative enterprise adds new products or services that have technological synergies with the existing product line. Horizontal diversification requires new products or services appealing to present customers. To enter conglomeration diversification, on the other hand, local cooperatives start new product areas that are related to existing areas only with respect to managerial and functional concerns. A local cooperative achieves the conglomerate status through merger with another cooperative. Growth in this direction could lead to physical and organizational changes representing a distinct break with past business experience.[21] However, if the autonomous cooperatives are to work effectively, African governments have to relinquish their direct control-oriented strategy of development and not only empower but also provide productive assets to the local citizens.

RECREATING AFRICA THROUGH ENVIRONMENTAL-SENSITIVE EDUCATIONAL PROGRAMS

In addition to establishing diversified, cooperative, sustainable economic development in Africa, development needs to be based on educational practices, which should teach Africans about environmental and health issues. As discussed in Chapter 7, agriculture accounts for a large percentage of the labor force of the African continent. Agriculture is the mainstay of the African economy and constitutes a large percentage of exports and the GDP. The policies of the last 50 years have not emphasized the agricultural sector as a strength of the African economy. Instead, industrialization has proceeded as agricultural development has declined. The result has been catastrophic for the African condition. To revitalize the agriculture sector, in addition to mastering the basic primary-school skills, the curriculum in African schools needs to prepare students to be involved in a hands-on approach to solving environmental problems within the established cooperatives. Because Africa is dependent on its resource base for creation of wealth and has higher variability and fragility in its ecosystem, the educational system should attempt to integrate the economy with the ecosystem.

However, an analysis of the Egyptian and Kenyan educational curriculums indicates that these schooling systems are very traditional and contain almost no discussion of environmental issues. South Africa's 2005 educational curriculum goals seem to integrate economic development with environmental issues. But the implementation of the environmentally educational program in an effective manner needs to be seen.

Ghana has also incorporated environmental studies into its primary schools, but because it does not carry this type of education into the secondary and tertiary schools, it has been ineffective at combating the many environmental problems of the country, including water shortages.

Even though students, particularly in South Africa and Ghana, are made aware of the consequences of what abusing resources will do to their environment, the students need to be assigned to local communities to apply what they studied in the classrooms in order to deter environmental degradation.

Thus, we recommend first and foremost that Africa should attempt to increase enrollment and ensure quality (for example, expenditure on educational materials is less than one dollar per student per year) at the primary educational level. In addition to this, Africa's government should implement a program to give formal and informal ecoliteracy education to their citizens on the consequences of abusing natural resources. Experiential environmental education can help students to benefit by studying collaboratively on local environmental issues. In short, the environmental material that is taught to students should give them a general knowledge of their ecosystem and how to preserve and protect it. Students need to have an understanding of living things and how they survive in their natural habitat, including the survival needs of human beings and the earth's biosphere. Without this knowledge base, students will not know the importance of natural resources and the effect they have on the economy. From sustainable development perspective, it is very essential that the local cooperatives, in collaboration with the students, are actively involved in designing, implementing, and managing various environmentally sensitive short-term and long-term development projects.

Thus, the educational system in Africa should endeavor to ingrain appropriate knowledge in the minds of present and future citizens, so that they are dedicated and committed to creating cooperative management that can achieve environmentally sustainable development in twenty-first century. To this end, it is very essential that Africa create cooperative educational programs (with limited responsibilities of government) based on strong community involvement, so that adequate entrepreneurs are developed at the village and community level.

REINVIGORATING AFRICAN SELF-SUSTAINED DEVELOPMENT THROUGH ENVIRONMENTALLY SENSITIVE COOPERATIVE BUSINESS ENTERPRISES

Contrary to "Afro-pessimism" and investor perception of Africa as a "high risk" continent, NEPAD asserts that if multinational enterprises could be enticed to invest further in the continent, Africa could achieve an annual growth rate of about 7 percent, reduce by half of the proportion of Africans living in poverty by the year 2015, and achieve a sustainable long-term strategy.[22] The NEPAD argument is based on two assumptions:

1. MNCs (or MNEs) will introduce capital, technology, and other know-how skills into African countries.
2. The home governments of the MNCs could be used a source of economic support.[23]

The first assumption is simply another incarnation of Lewis' industrialization by invitation. There is no reason to assume corporations will invest in Africa, simply because they can. Foreign investors perceive Africa as politically unstable. MNCs operating in Africa have the following advantages: (1) an abundant natural capital (diamond, bauxite, chromium, cobalt, gold, silver, and the like), (2) a huge market with over 800 million people, and (3) cheap labor costs. Yet currently, the continent receives less than 3 percent of the global direct investments. Africa "should no longer have high expectations of foreign investment. Each side has been hurt by abuses of trust. International contractors have delivered shoddy products, including entire turnkey projects; corrupt or capricious African officials have milked contractors or thwarted programs. It will take time to undo this damage; investors who have been burned once will not return at the first sign of reform."[24]

The second assumption is equally flawed. The home governments of MNCs cannot be counted on for support because *the very same MNCs often economically control the home governments.*

Yet Africa is immensely endowed with rich mineral deposits such as diamonds, bauxite, chromium, cobalt, gold, and copper. These abundant natural resources have often been the source of sorrow, as exploitation by colonial and postcolonial powers has stripped Africa of many of its natural beauties. In particular, uncontrolled multinational enterprises are likely to expedite the rate of the ecological devastation in Africa. Thus, MNEs investing in Africa need to modify or redesign their proportional strategies to reflect local investment projects considered to be of high national priority.

In the 1980s and 1990s, the Africa continent had been generally regarded as very hostile for MNEs. Thus, striking a balance between corporate goals and the socioeconomic developmental targets of the African country should reduce the risk for MNEs and need not entail the unnecessary exploitation of Africa's natural resources. In other words, the MNEs doing business in Africa need to be highly encouraged to take due account of the guidelines outlined by United Nations Center on Transnational Corporations.[25] Additionally, they need to openly disclose and make transparent their financial, structural, and performance activities. On the other hand, in order to entice environmentally sensitive MNEs, the prospective African host needs to take pains to assure prospective investors that they are improving their infrastructure, while also establishing very stable macroeconomic policies, transparent regulation, and efficient and honest public administration.

The only way the existing backbone of Africa's underdevelopment can be broken and environmental sustainability can be achieved is if domestic and/or foreign investors are willing to form cooperative enterprises (both small businesses and cooperative corporations) at the local level that can create employment, wealth, and emancipate workers.

[A] cooperative enterprise, while operating within the legal framework of the orthodox conception of business does, through its
practice, challenge the conventional idea of ownership and the
employment relationship as members of a cooperative are con-
jointly both owners and employees within the organisation.
The reality of the operation of cooperatives is that despite de
jure private ownership on the part of individuals, there is a de
facto social ownership based upon democratic decision making
structures internally and strong ties with the local community
externally.[26]

Our proposal of the creation of cooperative entrepreneurship for the revitalization of Africa should not be seen as
a deviation from the norm. Throughout the world, a number
of cooperative enterprises produce goods and services for the
market:

The most renowned example of a cooperative enterprise is the
Mondragon Cooperatives Corporation (MCC). This corporation evolved from a small cooperative firm built in the economically depressed Basque lands of northern Spain, in the 1950s,
into a modern-day multinational corporation with over $8 bil-
lion in assets and $3.5 billion in sales in 1993. The MCC is
currently operated by almost 30,000 worker-owners organized
into financial, industrial, and distribution groupings. The MCC
has become a powerful force in shaping regional development
strategies and is a model of economic collaboration which is
highly respected throughout the world.[27]

Thus harnessing the energies of local communities and
private investors to form business cooperatives is the cornerstone for revitalizing Africa's self-sustained socioeconomic development. A stable political environment, the existence of
an investment code, investor confidence in the rule of law, a
relatively developed infrastructure, and conducive incentive
structures are very essential to enticing foreign investors to
Africa. However, it does not mean that Africa will not achieve
self-sustained development without foreign investment.
"[E]ven in the absence of new capital, Africa can begin to
recover and to generate new economic development because

development does not depend on capital alone. ...Small farmers, small entrepreneurs in the informal sector, and small manufacturers already possess the capacity to increase production and the demand for goods exists."[28] In addition, community-based projects in a number of African countries are based on community savings in cash or labor. For instance, the informal horticultural cultivation in Kenya, which employs more than 20 percent of the labor force, is because

> Kenya's favorable climate makes it possible to produce tropical, semitropical, and temperate fruits and vegetables. The range of products has increased steadily. More than 50 varieties of flowers are being grown. Kenya, which had almost no flower exports 15 years ago, is now the world's fourth largest exporter of flowers. ...Horticultural products go to some 30 countries, the largest single market being the United Kingdom, with a share of more than 40 percent. Middle Eastern countries are also becoming an increasingly important market.[29]

Though small enterprises are of considerable importance as sources of employment and income in sub-Saharan Africa, there are only a few government policies that might be considered as directly supportive of the growth of small firms. For example, foreign investments in Africa have generally been inefficient in resource use and have led to only minimum absorption of labor. But with judicious governmental policies and direct assistance measures (for example, by granting loans in small amounts for short periods, facilitating high repayment rates, and establishing local governments where skilled workers can function effectively), we propose that the creation of decentralized rural small enterprises and nonagricultural firms in collaboration with well-integrated, environmentally sensitive, humane, educational development strategies can create and revitalize Africa's economy in the long run.[30]

To summarize, the only way Africa can claim its development in the twenty-first century is if its development process is rooted in an African system of thought and is people-centered rather than based on Western capitalist models transplanted by apostles of external agencies. Because agriculture is the backbone of the African economy, we proposed that Africa's sustainable economic model must be largely based on integrated, environmentally sensitive, cooperative agriculture; human capital; and domestic and foreign investments. Therefore, we conclude that the linkage between agroinvestment and an environmentally sensitive educational development strategy would not only achieve growth with equity but could also collectively empower the African people to fully participate in the design and management of long-lasting development paradigms. Thus, the topics discussed in this book should help us come a long way in our understanding of how this process is going to work, and it will work, because the lives of more than 800 million Africans are at stake.

BIBLIOGRAPHY

"Adjustment Lending: An Evaluation of Ten Years of Experience," (also called the Fisher Report) in Policy Research Series 1 (Washington, DC: World Bank, December 1988).

"Cross-Border Initiatives," *Road Map for Investor Facilitation*, Paper for Fourth Ministerial Meeting in Mauritius (October 1999).

"Mauritius," in *The World Guide 1997/98*.

"Privatised Water Should At Least Flow From the Taps" (UN Integrated Regional Information Networks), accessed February 25, 2004, available at http://allafrica.com/stories/200402260008.html.

Abbey, Joe, "On Promoting Successful Adjustment—Some Lessons from Ghana" (IMF, Sept. 24, 1989), 8.

Abdullahi, S., "The Conservation of the Environment in Oil Producing Areas of Nigeria (Niger Delta Areas)" (M.Sc.

Thesis, Department of Petroleum Engineering, University of Ibadan, 1994).

Adedeji, Adebayo, "The Monrovia Strategy and the Lagos Plan of Action: Five Years After," in *Economic Crisis in Africa: African Perspectives and Development Problems and Potentials* (Boulder, CO: Lynne Rienner Publishers, 1985).

Adesina, Jimi O., "Development and Challenge of Poverty: NEPAD, Post-Washington Consensus and Beyond," a paper presented at the Conference on Africa and the Development Challenges of the New Millennium, Accra, Ghana, April 23—26, 2002.

Africa's Adjustment and Growth in the 1980's (Washington, D.C.: World Bank, 1989).

African Development Bank, *Africa Development Report: 2002* (New York: Oxford University Press, 2002).

African-Canadian Forum, Canadian Council for International Cooperation, (April 2002), "The New Partnership for Africa's Development (NEPAD): Commentary," [online] Available http://www.web.net/~iccaf/debtsap/nepadafricacdaforum.htm.

Afrique Agriculture, December 1976.

Afrique Agriculture, February 1983.

Afrique Agriculture, March 1981.

Agricultural Sector Review (World Bank, Aug. 6, 1985).

Aina, Tade Akin, "Development Theory and Africa's Lost Decade," in *Changing Paradigms in Development — South, East, and West*, ed. Margareta Von Troil (Uppsala: The Scandinavia Institute of African Studies, 1993).

Akinrinade, Olusola and J. Kurt Barling, *Economic Development in Africa* (London: Pinter Publishers, 1987).

Amako, K. Y., "The Economic Causes and Consequences of Civil Wars and Unrest in Africa," Address to the 70th Ordinary Session of the Council Ministers of the Organization of Africa Unity (Algiers, Algeria, July 8, 1999).

Amin, Samir, "A Critique of the World Bank Report, entitled 'Accelerated Development in Sub-Sharan Africa,'" *Africa Development,* Vol. 7 (Dakar, 1982).

Amin, Samir, "Underdeveloped and dependence in Black Africa: Origins and Contemporary Forms," *Journal of Modern African Studies,* no. 4 (1972).

Arreguin, Blanca, "A Model for the Future of Cuba and Agriculture" (Dominican University of California: unpublished paper, 1996).

Arthur, Len et al., "Capital Anchoring and Cooperative Ownership: The Reality of the Operation of a Cooperative Enterprise in a Globalising Economy," *Management Research News,* Vol. 24, No. 10/11 (2001).

Arvind, Panagariya and Maurice Schiff, "Commodity Exports and Real Income in Africa," in *Economic Reform in Sub-Saharan Africa*, ed. Ajay Chibber and Stanley Fischer (World Bank, 1991).

Atiemo, A., *Africa Revisited: A Journey into the Glorious Past* (Portland, OR: Alpha Production Company, 1993).

Baer, Werner, "Puerto Rico—An Evaluation of a Successful Development Programme," *Quarterly Journal of Economics,* Vol. 73, No. 4 (November, 1959).

Bakken, Henry H., *Cooperation to the FINNISH* (Madison, WI: Mimir, 1937).

Barber, Charles Victor, "Forest Resource Scarcity and Social Conflict in Indonesia," *Environment,* Vol. 40, No. 4 (May 1998).

Barbier, E., *Economics, Natural Resources, Scarcity and Development* (London: Earthscan, 1989).

Barling, J. Kurt and Olusola Akinrinade, "Editors' introduction," in *Economic Development in Africa: International Efforts, Issues and Prospects* (London: Pinter Publishers, 1987).

Barrow, C. J., *Developing the Environment,* (New York: John Wiley & Sons, 1995).

Berry, S., "Economic Change in Contemporary Africa," in *Africa,* 3rd ed. P. M. Martin and P. O'Meara, eds. (Bloomington: Indiana University Press, 1995).

Best, Lloyd, "The Caribbean Economy," *Readings in the Political Economy of the Caribbean,* N. Girran and O. Jefferson (eds.) (Jamaica: ISER/UMI, 1967).

Bowman, Larry W., *Mauritius: Democracy and Development in the Indian Ocean* (San Francisco: Westview Press, 1991).

Brainard, William C. and Richard N. Cooper, "Uncertainty and Diversification in International Trade," *Ford Research Institute Studies,* Vol. 8 No. 3 (Stanford University, 1968).

British Council, "Ghana—Country Education Profile," accessed November 21, 2003, available from http://www2.britishcouncil.org/home/learning/globalschools/globalschools-partnership/globalschools-resources-countries/globalschools-resources-countries-ghana.htm.

Brown, Michael Barratt, *Africa's Choices After Thirty Years of the World Bank* (London: Penguin Books, 1995).

Brown, Noel J. and Pierre Quilblier, *Ethics and Agenda 21* (New York: United Nations Environment Program, 1994).

Bruno, Michael, "Domestic Resource Costs and Effective Protection: Clarification and Synthesis," *Journal of Political Economy 80* (January/February 1972).

Bruton, Robert et al., "Mauritius: International Financial Services," accessed May 1, 2001, available from http://www.britannica.com.

CGIAR and The International Research Partnership for Food Security and Sustainable Agriculture, "Third System Review of the Consultative Group On International Agricultural Research" (Washington, DC: CIGAR Secretariat, October 8, 1998).

Chang, Ha-Joon, *Kicking Away the Ladder: Development Strategy in Historical Perspective* (London: Anthem Press, 2002).

Choucri, Nazli, "The Global Environment and Multinational Corporations," in *The Multinational Enterprises in Transition*, 4th ed., Phillip D. Grub and Dara Khambata (eds.) (Princeton, NJ: The Darwin Press, 1993).

Cleaver, Kevin, foreword to *Applying Environmental Economics in Africa,* by Frank J. Convery (Washington, DC: The World Bank, 1995).

CODESRIA and TWN-Africa, "The New Partnership for Africa's Development (NEPAD)," presented at the Conference on Africa and the Development Challenges of the New Millennium (Accra, Ghana April 23—26, 2002).

Coleman, Jonathan R., Takamasa Akiyama and Panos N. Varangis, "How Policy Changes Affected Cocoa Sectors in Sub-Saharan African Countries," in *Policy Research Working Papers* (WPS 1129) (April 1993).

Convery, Frank J., "Applying Environmental Economics in Africa," *World Bank Technical Paper Number 277: Africa Technical Series* (1995).

Costa Rica, *National Strategy for the Conservation and Sustainable Use of Biodiversity, Summary* (Santo Domingo de Heredia: Instituto Nacional de Biodiversidad, 1999).

Crassweller, R. D., *The Caribbean Community* (Praeger: New York, 1972).

Curtain, P. D., *The Atlantic Slave Trade: A Census* (Wisconsin: The University of Wisconsin Press, 1969).

David, Fred R., *Strategic Management: Concepts and Cases*, 7th ed., (Upper Saddle River, NJ: Prentice Hall, 1999).

DeLancey, V., "The Economies of Africa," in *Understanding Contemporary Africa*, 2nd ed. A. A. Gordon and D. L. Gordon, eds. (Boulder, CO: Lynne Rienner, 1996).

Delgado, Christopher, "Africa's Changing Agricultural Development Strategies," http://www.ifpri.org/2020/briefs/number42.htm (accessed December 9, 2004).

Demas, W. G., *The Economics of Development in Small Countries with Special Reference to the Caribbean* (Montreal: McGill University Press, 1965).

Deng, Lual A., *Rethinking African Development: Toward A Framework for Social Integration and Ecological Harmony* (Trenton, NJ: Africa World Press, 1998).

Desta, Asayehgn, *Environmentally Sustainable Economic Development* (Westport, CT: Praeger, 1999).

Desta, Asayehgn, *International Political Risk Assessment for Foreign Direct Investment and International Lending Decisions* (Needham Heights, MA: Ginn Press, 1993).

Diouf, Jacques, "The Challenge of Agricultural Development in Africa," (unpublished paper, Sir John Crawford Memorial Lecture, Washington, DC, November 2, 1989).

Driskell, B. and J. C. Motz, "Stoneworking Technology," in *Encyclopedia of Precolonial Africa,* J. O. Vogel and J. Vogel, eds. (Walnut Creek, CA: Altamira Press, 1997).

Economics of Cocoa Production and Distribution, John Simmons (ed.) (Praeger, 1976).

Eicher, Carl and John Staatz, "Agricultural Development Ideas in Historical Perspective," in *Agricultural Development in the Third World*, John Staatz and Carl Eicher (eds.) (Baltimore: John Hopkins University Press, 1984).

Eicher, Carl K. and Doyle C. Baker, *Research on Agricultural Development in Sub-Saharan Africa: A Critical Survey* (East Lansing: Department of Agricultural Economics, Michigan State University, 1982).

Eicher, Carl, "Institutions and the African Farmer," *Issues in Agriculture 14* (Consulting Group on International Agricultural Research [CGIAR], September 1999).

Elbadawi, I., "World Bank adjustment lending and economic performance in SSA in the 1980's: A comparison of early adjusters, late adjusters and nonadjusters," *Policy Research WPS,* No. 1001 (World Bank, 1992).

Energy Information Administration, "EIA Country Analysis Briefs, Egypt: Environmental Issues," accessed August 2003, available from http://www.eia.doe.gov/emeu/cabs/egypenv.html.

Evenson, Robert E. and Yoav Kislev, *Agricultural Research and Productivity* (New Haven, CT: Yale University Press, 1975).

Farrell, Alex and Maureen Hart, "What Does Sustainability Really Mean?" *Environment*, Vol. 40, No. 9 (November 1998).

Frankel, Carl, *In Earth's Company: Business, Environment and the Challenge of Sustainability* (Gabriola Island B.C., Canada: New Society Publishers).

French, Charles E. et al., *Survival Strategies for Agricultural Cooperatives.* (Ames: Iowa State University Press, 1980).

Gabre-Madhin, E. Z. and S. Haggblade, "Successes in African Agriculture: Results of an Expert Survey," *World Development*, Vol. 32, No. 5 (May 2004).

Gellar, S., "The Colonial Era," in *Africa*, 3rd ed. P. M. Martin and P. O'Meara, eds. (Bloomington, Indiana: Indiana University Press, 1995).

Georgescu-Roegen, N., "Economic Theory and Agrarian Economics," in *Oxford Economic Papers*, Vol. 12, No. 1 (February 1960).

Gerschenkron, Alexander, *Economic Backwardness in Historical Perspective: A Book of Essays*, (Cambridge, MA: Belknap Press of Harvard University Press, 1962).

Ghana 2000 and Beyond (Washington, DC: World Bank, 1993).

Ghana Education Website, The, "Education Today," accessed November 19, 2003, available from http://www.ghana.edu.gh/present/index.html.

Ghana Education Website, The, "History of Education," accessed November 19, 2003, available from http://www.ghana.edu.gh/past/index.html.

Giblin, J., "Issues in African History," 2004, http://www.uiowa.edu/~africart/toc/history/giblinhistory.html (17 September 2004).

Godfrey, M., "Trade and Exchange Rate Policy: A Further Contribution to the Debate," *Crises and Recovery in Sub-Saharan Africa*, ed. T. Rose, Development Centre of the Organization for Economic Co-operation and Development, (Paris: OECD, 1984).

Goodstein, Eban S., *Economics and the Environment* (Upper Saddle River, NJ: Prentice Hall, 1999).

Gordon, D. L., "African Politics," in *Understanding Contemporary Africa*, 2nd ed. A. A. Gordon and D. L. Gordon, eds. (Boulder, CO: Lynne Rienner, 1996).

Gordon, Robert J., *Macroeconomics* (Reading, MA: Addison Wesley, 2000).

Harrison, P., *The Third World Tomorrow*, 2nd ed. (Middlesex, England: Penguin Books, 1986).

Hassan, Comfort, Janice Olawoye, and Kent Nnadozie, "Impact of International Trade and Multinational Corporations on the Environment and Sustainable Livelihoods of Rural Women in Akwa-Ibom State, Niger Delta Region, Nigeria" (Global Development Network, September 2002).

Haynes Jr., Curtis and Jessica Gordon Nembhard, "Inner City, Economic development, Economic Growth, Cooperation," *Review of Black Economy*, Vol. 27, No. 1 (Summer 1999).

Hecht, Alan D., "The Triad of Sustainable Development: Promoting Sustainable Development in Developing Countries," *Journal of Environment & Development*, Vol. 8, No. 2 (June 1999).

Helmboldt, Niles E., Tina West, and Benjamin H. Hardy, "Private Investments and African Economic Policy," in *Strategies for African Development*, Robert J. Berg and Jennifer Seymour Whitaker (eds.) (Berkeley: University of California Press, 1986).

Hill, Polly, *Migrant Cocoa Farmers of Southern Ghana* (Cambridge: University Press, 1963).

Ho, Samuel Pao-San, "Colonialism and Development: Korea, Taiwan, and Kwantung," *The Japanese Colonial Empire*, 1985-1945, Ramon H. Myers and Mark R. Peattie (eds.) (Princeton, NJ: Princeton University Press, 1984).

Hoffman, Andrew J., *Competitive Environmental Strategy: A Guide to the Changing Business Landscape* (Washington, DC: Island Press, 2000).

Huber, Richard M. et al., "Market-Based Instruments for Environmental Policymaking in Latin America and the Caribbean," *World Bank Discussion Paper*, 381 (Washington, DC: 1998).

Hufschmidt, Maynard M. et al., *Environment, Natural Systems, and Development: An Economic Valuation Model* (Baltimore: John Hopkins University Press, 1990).

Hyden, Goran, "African Social Structure and Economic Development" in *Strategies for African Development*, Robert J. Berg and Jennifer Seymour Whittaker (eds.) (Berkeley: University of California Press, 1986).

Hymer, Stephen, "The Multinational Corporation and the Law of Uneven Development," in *Sociology of Developing Societies*, Hamza Alavi and Teodor Shanin (eds.) (New York: Monthly Review Press, 1982).

ICCO, "Study of Cocoa Production in Brazil," CS/Prod/01, 20 December 1989.

IFAD, Report No. 0105-GH, 1988.

IMF, The World Bank and the African Debt: The Social and Political Impact, The, Vol. 2, ed. Bade Onimode (London: Zed Books, 1989).

International Monetary Fund, "IMF Concludes Article IV Consultation with Mauritius," in Public Information Notices for 2002 (Washington, DC: IMF, May 22, 2001).

International Tropical Timber Organization, "Criteria for the Measurement of Sustainable Topical Forest Management," in *ITTO Policy Development Series 3* (1992).

Jamal, Amir, "Self-reliance, International Assistance, and Managing the African Economy," in Adebayo Adedeji and Timothy M. Shaw (eds.), *Economic Crisis in Africa* (Boulder, CO, 1986).

James, C. L. R., *Nkrumah and The Ghana Revolution* (London: Allison and Busby, 1977).

Jaycox, Edward V. K., "Capacity Building in Africa: Challenge of the Decade," *Capacity Building and Human Resource Development in Africa (A Report on a Roundtable Convention by the Lester Pearson Institute for International Development, Dalhousie University, September 18-19, 1989),* Alexander A. Kwapong and Barry Lesser (eds.) (Halifax, Nova Scotia, Canada: Lester Pearson Institute for International Development, Dalhousie University, 1990).

Johan, Kwesi, "The Social Impact of Ghana's Adjustment Programme 1983-1986," Paper presented to the Institute of African Alternatives, Conference on the Impact of IMF and World Bank Policies on the People of Africa, London, September 1987.

Kahn, Herman, *World Economic Development 1979 and Beyond* (New York: Morrow/Quill Papers, 1979).

Kearney, Richard C., "Mauritius and the NIC Model Redux: or, How Many Cases Make A Model?" *The Journal of Developing Areas,* Vol. 24, No. 2 (January 1990).

Keim, C. A., "Africa and Europe Before 1900," in *Africa,* 3rd ed. P. M. Martin and P. O'Meara, eds. (Bloomington: Indiana University Press, 1995).

Keller, E. J., "Decolonization, Independence, and the Failure of Politics," in *Africa,* 3rd ed. P. M. Martin and P. O'Meara, eds. (Bloomington: Indiana University Press, 1995).

Kemei, Kipchumba, "Plunder of Mau Forest a Threat to 3m People," *The East African Standard (Nairobi),* February 25, 2004.

Khumalo, Chris, "Makhaye Launches Water Irrigation Scheme," *BuaNews (Pretoria),* February 25, 2004.

Kofi, Tetteh and A. Desta, "An Alternative Strategy for Africa's Sustainable Economic Development: The Case for a Non-NEPAD Approach." Paper presented at the Third Network-Africa and the Council for the Development of

Social Research in Africa (CODESRIA), Accra, Ghana, April 23—26, 2002.

Kofi, Tetteh and Emmanuel Hanson, "Ghana, A History of an Endless Recession," *Research in Africa,* ed. Jerker Caulsson, (Uppsala: Scandinavian Institute of African Studies, 1983).

Kofi, Tetteh and James Fry, "Commodity Exchanges and Their Impact on the Trade of Developing Countries," United Nations Conference on Trade and Development (Report for UNCTAD Secretariat), TB/B/C.1/248, (1983).

Kofi, Tetteh and S. C. Drake, *Black National Cultural Ideologies and Economic Development Strategies and Problems: Africa and the Diaspora* (Stanford, CA: Food Research Institute & The African and Afro-American Studies Department, Stanford University, 1973).

Kofi, Tetteh, "A Framework for Comparing the Efficiency of Futures Markets," *American Journal of Agricultural Economics,* Vol. 55, No. 4, Part I, (November, 1973).

Kofi, Tetteh, "Development and Stagnation in Ghana: An 'Abibirim' Approach," *Universitas,* Vol. 3, No. 2 (Ghana University, March 1974).

Kofi, Tetteh, "International Cocoa Agreements," *Journal of World Trade* Law, Vol. 11, No. 1 (January/February 1977).

Kofi, Tetteh, "International Commodity Agreements and Export Earnings: Simulation of the 1968 Draft International Cocoa Agreement," *Food Research* Institute, Vol. 9, No. 2, 1972.

Kofi, Tetteh, "Market Failure and Persistent Economic Crisis in Africa: Is the US Willing and Able to Help with a

Marshall Plan" (Unpublished paper, University of San Francisco, 2001).

Kofi, Tetteh, "National Democratic Congress (NDC) Problem and New Patriotic Party (NPP) Nightmare Accumulation of Capital and the Saga of Ada Songor Lagoon," unpublished manuscript.

Kofi, Tetteh, "Peasants and Economic Development: Populist Lessons for Africa," *The African Studies Review*, Vol. 20, No. 3, 1977.

Kofi, Tetteh, "The Elites and Underdevelopment in Africa: The Case of Ghana," *Berkeley Journal of Sociology*, Vol. 17 (1972—73).

Kofi, Tetteh, "The Finnish Agrarian Development Strategy (Pellervo Cooperative Movement) Any Lessons for Africa?" mimeo, UNN-WIDER, 1994.

Kofi, Tetteh, "Vertical Price Relations in the International Coca Market and Implications for Ghana's Marketing Policies," *Economics of Cocoa Production and Marketing*, R.A. Kotey et. al (eds.) (ISSER, Ghana University, 1974).

Kruger, Jan, "Foreign Direct Investment (Part IV of XII)," *Namibia Economist,* April 6, 2001, available from http://www.economist.com.na/2001/060401/story9.htm.

La-Anyane, Seth, *Economics of Agricultural Development in Tropical Africa.* (New York: John Wiley & Sons, 1985).

Lamphear, J. and T. Falola, "Aspects of Early African History," in *Africa,* 3rd ed. P. M. Martin and P. O'Meara, eds. (Bloomington: Indiana University Press, 1995).

Lewis, W. Arthur, "Economic Development with Unlimited Supplies of Labour," *Manchester School* 22 (May 1954).

Lewis, W. Arthur, "Economic Development with Unlimited Supplies of Labor," in A. N. Agarwala and S.P. Singh, eds. *The Economics of Underdevelopment* (Oxford: Oxford University Press, 1958).

Lewis, W. Arthur, "Industrial Development in Puerto Rico," *The Caribbean Economic Review*, Vol. I, No. 1 (December 1949).

Lewis, W. Arthur, "Industrialization of the British West Indies," *The Caribbean Economic Review*, Vol. II, No. 1 (May 1950).

Lewis, W. Arthur, *Report on Industrialization in the Gold Coast* (Accra: Government Printing Department 1953).

Lewis, W. Arthur, *The Theory of Economic Growth* (London: George Allen and Unwin, 1955).

Leys, Colin, *The Rise and Fall of Development Theory* (Bloomington: Indiana University Press, 1996).

Liedholm, Carl and Donald C. Mead, "Small-Scale Industry," in *Strategies for African Development*, Robert J. Berg and Jennifer Seymour Whitaker (eds.) (Berkeley: University of California Press, 1986),.

Lofchie, Michael and Stephen Commins, "Food Deficits and Agricultural Policies in Tropical Africa," in *The Political Economy of Development and Underdevelopment*, 4th ed., Charles K. Wilber (ed.) (New York: Random House Business Division, 1988).

Loxley, John, *Ghana: Economic Crisis and the Long Road to Recovery* (Ottawa: The North-South Institute, February 1988).

Lugard, Lord, *The Dual Mandate in Tropical Africa* (Oxford: Blackwood, 1922).

Lutz, Ernst et al., "Economic and Institutional Analyses of Soil Conservation Projects in Central America and the Caribbean," World Bank Environmental Paper, No. 8, (1994).

Machpherson, W. J., *The Economic Development of Japan c. 1868-1941* (London: Macmillan, 1990).

Maizels, Alfred, *Commodities in Crisis* (Oxford: Clarendon Press, 1992).

Maizels, Alfred, Robert Bacon, and George Mavrotas, *Supply Management for Tropical Beverages*, UNU/WIDER, 1994 (mimeo, to be published by Oxford: Clarendon Press).

Mauricio, Cuesta D., "Economic Analysis of Soil Conservation Projects in Costa Rica," World Bank Environmental Paper, No. 8, (1994).

Mauritius, Ministry of Environmental and Urban and Rural Development, "Strategy Paper on Environment, 1998—2005," (memo, 1999).

McCall, J. C., "Social Organization in Africa," in *Africa,* 3rd ed. P. M. Martin and P. O'Meara, eds. (Bloomington: Indiana University Press, 1995).

McPhee, Allan, *The Economic Revolution in British West Africa* (London: George Routledge and Son Ltd., 1926).

Meadows, Donella H., *The Limits to Growth; a report for the Club of Rome's project on the predicament of mankind* (New York: Universe Books, 1972).

Media Benjamin and Peter Rosset, *The Greening of the Revolution* (Sydney, Australia: Ocean Press, 1994).

Mikreku, Ebenerzer, "Assessing Strutural Adjustment Programmes: The Case of Ghana," *IFDA Dossier* 72, July/August 1989.

Ministry of Agriculture (MOA), The, "Ghana Agricultural Policy—Action Plans and Strategies," 1984—1986.

Ministry of Economic Development and Regional Co-operation, *Vision 2020: The National Long-Term Perspective Study*, Vol. II (Port Louis, Mauritius: Silvio M Empeigne, Government Printer, 1997).

Ministry of Economic Development, Financial Services and Corporate Affairs, *Structural Transformation of the Mauritian Economy: 1960's Beyond* (2000).

Ministry of Environment and Urban and Rural Development, "Environment-Mauritius;" Mauritius, National Environment Action Plan (NEAP) I & II (memo, 1999).

Ministry of Environment and Urban and Rural Development, "Environment-Mauritius," available at http://ncb.intnet.mu/eurd/minenv/index.html.

Ministry of the Environment and Energy and the National Institute for Biodiversity (INBio), National Strategy for the Conservation and Sustainable Use of Biodiversity (Costa Rica, 1997).

Morgenstern, Oscar, *On the Accuracy of Economic Observations*, Princeton University Press, 1963.

Murphy, E. J., *History of African Civilization* (New York: Dell Publishing, 1972).

Nabli, Mustapha K. and Jeffrey B. Nugent, *The New Institutional Economics and Development: Theory and Application to Tunisia*.

Nigerian Structural Adjustment Programme: Policies, Impact, and Prospects, The, (Washington, DC: World Bank, December 1988).

O'Toole, T., "The Historical Context," in *Understanding Contemporary Africa,* 2nd ed. A. A. Gordon and D. L. Gordon, eds. (Boulder, CO: Lynne Rienner, 1996).

Ohde, Thorsten, *Finland: Nation of Cooperators* (Williams and Nargate Ltd., 1931).

Okigbo, Bede N., "Towards Sustainable Environmental and Resource Management Futures in Sub-Saharan Africa," in *Sustaining the Future,* George Benneh et al. (eds.) (Tokyo: The United Nations University, 1996).

Organisation for Economic Cooperation and Development (OCED), *Towards Sustainable Development: Environmental Indicators* (Paris: OECD Publications, 1998).

Oshima, Harry T., Economic Growth in Monsoon Asia—A Comparative Survey (Tokyo, 1987).

Panayotou, T., "Empirical Tests and Policy Analysis of Environmental Degradation at Different Stages of Economic Development," World Employment Programme Research Working Paper, WEP 2-22/W.

Pariser, Harry S., *Adventure Guide to Costa Rica,2nd ed.,* (Edison, NJ: Hunter Publishing, 1994).

Persson, Annika and Mohan Munasinghe, "Natural Resources Management and Economywide Policies in Costa Rica: A Computable General Equilibrium (CGE) Modeling Approach, The World Bank Environmental Department and Economic Development Institute," *The Greening of Economic Policy Reform,* Vol. II: Case Studies (Oxford: Oxford University Press, 1997).

Pigato, Miria, "The Foreign Investment Environment in Africa: The Incentive Framework for Foreign Investment in Africa," Africa Region Working Paper Series, No. 15 (April 2001).

Poole, B.L., *The Caribbean Commission* (Columbia: University of South Carolina Press, 1951).

Potholm, C. P., *The Theory and Practice of African Politics* (Englewood Cliffs, NJ: Prentice-Hall).

Prebisch, Raul, *The Economic Development of Latin America and Its Principal Problems* (New York: United Nations, 1950).

Quinlivan, Gary M., "Multinational Corporations: Myths and Facts," *Religion and Society*, Vol. 10 No. 6 (November and December 2000).

Randriamaro, Zo, "The NEPAD, Gender, and the Poverty Trap" [online] Available http:www.web.net/~iccaf/debtsap/nepadgera.htm (2004).

Ranis, Gustav, "The Role of Institutions in Transition Growth: The New Asian Newly Industrializing Countries," *World Development*, Vol. 17, No. 9 (1989).

Rau, Bill, *From Feast to Famine: Official Cures and Grassroots Remedies to Africa's Food Crisis* (London: Zed Books Ltd., 1990).

Reynolds, L. G. and Peter Gregory, *Wages, Productivity and Industrialization in Puerto Rico* (Homewood, IL: Irwin, 1965).

Rhee, Yung Whee, and Therese Belot, "Export Catalysts in Low Income Countries: a Review of 11 Success Stories," World Bank Discussion Paper 72 (Washington, DC, 1990).

Robert, Karl-Henrik et al., *A Compass for Sustainable Development*, International Journal of Sustainable Development and World Ecology (March 26, 1997).

Robinson, Joan, *Economic Philosophy* (New York: Anchor Books, 1962).

Robinson, William and Jerry Harris, "Towards a Global Ruling Class: Globalization and the Transnational Capitalist Class," *Science and Society*, Vol. 64, No. 1 (Spring 2000).

Rodney, W., *How Europe Underdeveloped Africa* (Washington, DC: Howard University Press, 1974).

Role of Institutions in Economic Development, The, World Development Special Issue, Vol. 17, ed. I. Adelman and E. Thorbecke (September 1989).

Ruf, F., "Will Côte d'Ivoire Give Up Its Position of World Leading Cocoa Producer to Indonesia?" *The Cacao Cafe*, Vol. 37 No. 3, July-Sept. 1993.

Russo, Rosemaria, Jumping from the Ivory Tower: Enhancing Environmental Education through Service Learning and Community Involvement (San Francisco: Argosy University, 2004).

Ruttan, Vernon, "Models of Agricultural Development," in *Agricultural Development in the Third World,* Carl Eicher and John Staatz (eds.) (Baltimore: John Hopkins University Press, 1984).

Sadler, Barry, "Climb Down from the Earth Summit," *Ecodecision*, 24 (Spring 1997).

Said, Swafiya, "A Discussion of the Link Between the Preschool Curriculum and the 8-4-4 Standard One Curriculum in Kenya" (Madrasa Resource Centre, Mombasa, Kenya), accessed 2004, available from www.worldbank.org/children/africa/pdffiles/va1albpa.pdf.

SAPRIN, "Executive Summary, The Policy Roots of Economic Crisis and Poverty, A Multi-Country–Participatory Assessment of Structural Adjustment, November 2001."

Schick, K. D., "Prehistoric Africa," in *Africa*, 3rd ed. P. M. Martin and P. O'Meara, eds. (Bloomington: Indiana University Press, 1995).

Schlemmer, Lawrence, "Getting Real About Democracy in Africa: NEPAD and the Challenge of Good Governance," a paper presented at an international colloquium on Cultures, Religions and Conflicts, Mzaar, Lebanon. Ministry of Culture, September 18—21, 2002.

Schotter, Andrew, *The Economic Theory of Social Institutions* (Cambridge: Cambridge University Press, 1981).

Sede-Bonilla, "Dependence as an Obstacle to Growth in Puerto Rico"; Edwin Carrington, "Industrialization by Invitation in Trinidad since 1950," *New World Quarterly*, Vol. 4, No. 2 (1968).

Seers, Dudley and G. R. Ross, *Report on Financial and Physical Problems of Development in The Gold Coast* (Accra: Office of Government Statisticians, 1952).

Seers, I. D., "The Limitations of the Special Cases," *Bulletins of Oxford Institute of Economics and Statistics* (May 1963).

Sen, A. K., *Choice of Techniques* (Oxford: Clarendon Press, 1960).

Singer, Hans W., "The Distribution of Gains Between Borrowing and Investing Countries," *American Economic Review 40* (May 1950).

Steel, William F. and Jonathan W. Evans, Industrialization in Sub-Saharan Africa: Strategies and Performance (Washington, DC: World Bank, 1984).

Stephen Younger, "Economic Recovery Program – A Case Study of Stabilization and Structural Adjustment in Sub-Saharan Africa," in *World Bank EDI Policy Case Studies, Analytical Case Studies No. 1,* (1989).

Stiglitz, Joseph E., *Globalization and Its Discontents* (New York: W.W. Norton, 2002).

Subramanian, Arvind and Devesh Roy, "Who Can Explain the Mauritian Miracle: Meade, Romer, Sachs, or Rodrik?" in IMF Working Paper, WP/01/116 (International Monetary Fund, 2001).

Tandon, Yash, NEPAD and Foreign Direct Investments (FDIS): Symmetries and Contradictions (online) Available http://www.web.net/~iccaf/debtsap/nepadfdid.htm.

Thirlwall, A. P., *Growth and Development* (Boulder, CO: Lynne Rienner, 1994).

Thorbecke, Eric, "The Employment Problem: A Critical Evaluation of Four ILO Comprehensive Country Reports." *International Labour Review,* Vol. 107, No. 5 (May 1973).

Todaro, Michael P., *Economic Development,* 6th ed. (New York: Addison-Wesley, 1996).

Toynbee, Arnold J., *A Study of History,* Abridgement of Volumes 1—6, D.C. Somervell (ed.) (New York and London: Oxford University Press, 1956).

Trivedi, Pravin K. and Tamamasa Akiyama, "A Framework for Evaluating the Impact of Pricing Policies for Cocoa and Coffee in Cote d'Ivoire," *The World Bank Economic Review,* Vol. 6, No. 2, May 1992.

Tsakok, Isabella, *Agricultural Price Policy: A Practitioner's Guide to Partial Equilibrium Analysis* (Cornell University Press, 1990).

UNCTAD, "Prospects for the World Cocoa Market until the Year 2005," UNCTAD/Com/r, 1991.

UNDP, "United Nations Programme of Action for African Economic Recovery," Report 5132, Statistical Study on Trends on Evaluation, 1994—1995.

UNDP, *Human Development Report* (Oxford: Oxford University Press, 1990).

US Congress (Committee on Foreign Affairs, U.S. House of Representatives), Structural Adjustment in Africa: Insights from the Experiences of Ghana and Senegal (Report of a Staff Study Mission to Great Britain, Ghana, Senegal, Côte d'Ivoire and France, Nov. 29—Dec. 20, 1988) (Washington, DC: U.S. Government Printing Office, March 1989).

Utting, Peter, "Deforestation in Central America: Historical and Contemporary Dynamics," *Sustainable Agriculture in Central America* (New York: St. Martin's Press, 1997).

Vaal EduNet Project (South Africa), "Curriculum, 2005," accessed November 19, 2003, available from http://www.edunet.co.za/html/curriculum_2005.html.

Victor, David G. and Eugene B. Skolnikoff II, "Translating Intent into Action: Implementing Environmental Commitments," *Environment*, Vol. 41, No. 2 (March 1999).

Wallace, David, *Sustainable Industrialization* (London: Earthscan Publications, 1996).

Weaver, James H., *Achieving Broad-Based Sustainable Development* (West Hartford, CT: Kumarian Press, 1997).

Williams, Eric, foreword, The Caribbean Economic Review, Vol. 1, Nos. 1 and 2 (December 1949).

Wood, G. A. R. and R. A. Lass, *Cocoa*, 4th ed. (Harlow, Essex: Longman Scientific and Technical, 1985).

World Bank Group, The, "Can Africa Claim the 21st Century," 2002, http://wbln0018.worldbank.org/AFR/afr.nsf/ d f b 6 a d d 1 2 4 1 1 2 b 9 c 8 5 2 5 6 7 c f 0 0 4 c 6 e f 1 / 9d48d6dce826ccd0852568f1006dbf2e?OpenDocument (September 17, 2004).

World Bank Group, The, "Ghana," accessed March 21, 2004, available from http://www.worldbank.org/afr/.

World Bank Group, The, "S. Africa," accessed March 21, 2004, available from http://www.worldbank.org/afr/.

World Bank, The, "Entering the 21st Century," in *World Development Report 1999/2000* (Oxford: Oxford University Press).

World Bank, The, "Institutions for Environmental Stewardship," Jose I. dos R. Furtado and Tamara Belt, eds., with Ramachandra Jammi (Washington, DC: WBI Learning Resources Series, 2000).

World Bank, The, "Mauritius: Technology Strategy for Competitiveness" (September 22, 1994).

World Bank, The, *Can Africa Claim the 21st Century?* (Washington, DC: The World Bank Press, 2000).

World Bank, The, *Sub-Saharan Africa: From Crisis to Sustainable Growth* (Washington, D.C.: The World Bank, 1989).

Bibliography

World Bank, The, *The East Asian Miracle, Economic Growth and Public Policy* (New York: Oxford University Press, 1993).

World Bank, The, *World Development Report 1992* (New York: Oxford University Press, 1992).

World Commission on Environment and Development, *Our Common Future* (Oxford: Oxford University Press, 1987).

World Guide 1997/98, The, (Oxford: New Internationalist Publications, 1997).

World Resource Institute, *Environmental Almanac* (Boston: Houghton Mifflon Company, 1992).

NOTES

INTRODUCTION

1. Council for Development of Social Science Research in Africa (CODESRIA) and Third World Network (TWN-Africa), "The New Partnership for Africa's Development (NEPAD)," 23rd—26th April. See also, The World Bank, *Can Africa Claim the 21st Century?* (Washington, D.C: The World Bank Press, 2000).
2. The World Bank Group, "Can Africa Claim the 21st Century," 2002, http://wbln0018.worldbank.org/AFR/afr.nsf/dfb6add124112b9 c852567cf004c6ef1/9d48d6dce826ccd0852568f1006dbf2e? OpenDocument (September 17, 2004).
3. See note 1 above.
4. T. Kofi and A. Desta, "An Alternative Strategy for Africa's Sustainable Economic Development: The Case for a Non-NEPAD Approach." Paper presented at the Third Network-Africa and the Council for the Development of Social Research in Africa (CODESRIA), Accra, Ghana, April 23—26, 2002.
5. See, for example, W. Arthur Lewis, "Economic Development with Unlimited Supplies of Labour," *Manchester School* 22 (May 1954).

CHAPTER 1

1. Michael Barratt Brown, *Africa's Choices After Thirty Years of the World Bank* (London: Penguin Books, 1995), 3.

2. T. O'Toole, "The Historical Context," in *Understanding Contemporary Africa,* 2nd ed. A. A. Gordon and D. L. Gordon, eds. (Boulder, CO: Lynne Rienner, 1996), 24.

3. Albert Churchward cited in A. Atiemo, *Africa Revisited: A Journey into the Glorious Past* (Portland, OR: Alpha Production Company, 1993).

4. Ibid., pp. 39-40.

5. W. Rodney, *How Europe Underdeveloped Africa* (Washington, DC: Howard University Press, 1974), 34—35.

6. K. D. Schick, "Prehistoric Africa," in *Africa,* 3rd ed. P. M. Martin and P. O'Meara, eds. (Bloomington: Indiana University Press, 1995), 50.

7. See note 2 above.

8. J. Lamphear and T. Falola, "Aspects of Early African History," in *Africa,* 3rd ed. P. M. Martin and P. O'Meara, eds. (Bloomington: Indiana University Press, 1995), 73.

9. Schick, "Prehistoric Africa," 63.

10. B. Driskell and J. C. Motz, "Stoneworking Technology," in *Encyclopedia of Precolonial Africa,* J. O. Vogel and J. Vogel, eds. (Walnut Creek, CA: Altamira Press, 1997), 103.

11. E. J. Murphy, *History of African Civilization* (New York: Dell Publishing, 1972), 16.

12. Ibid., p. 16.

13. Schick, "Prehistoric Africa," 70.

14. Rodney, *How Europe Underdeveloped Africa,* 36.

15. J. C. McCall, "Social Organization in Africa," in *Africa,* 3rd ed. P. M. Martin and P. O'Meara, eds. (Bloomington: Indiana University Press, 1995), 180.

16. Rodney, How Europe Underdeveloped Africa, 36.

17. Ibid., p. 40.

18. C. A. Keim, "Africa and Europe Before 1900," in *Africa,* 3rd ed. P. M. Martin and P. O'Meara, eds. (Bloomington: Indiana University Press, 1995), 115.

19. Rodney, *How Europe Underdeveloped Africa,* 76.

20. Murphy, *History of African Civilization,* 263.

21. J. Giblin, "Issues in African History," 2004, http://www.uiowa.edu/~africart/toc/history/giblinhistory.html (17 September 2004). Also see T. A. Kofi and S. C. Drake, *Black National Cultural Ideologies and Economic Development Strategies and Problems: Africa and the Diaspora*

(Stanford, CA: Food Research Institute & The African and Afro-American studies Department, Stanford University, 1973); and P. D. Curtain, *The Atlantic Slave Trade: A Census* (Wisconsin: The University of Wisconsin Press, 1969).

22. Curtain, *The Atlantic Slave Trade*, 116.
23. Murphy, *History of African Civilization*, 272.
24. V. DeLancey, "The Economies of Africa," in *Understanding Contemporary Africa*, 2nd ed. A. A. Gordon and D. L. Gordon, eds. (Boulder, CO: Lynne Rienner, 1996), 91.
25. Ibid., p. 124.
26. Ibid., p. 127.
27. D. L. Gordon, "African Politics," in *Understanding Contemporary Africa*, 2nd ed. A. A. Gordon and D. L. Gordon, eds. (Boulder, CO: Lynne Rienner, 1996), 55.
28. Ibid., p. 151.
29. S. Amin, "Underdeveloped and Dependence in Black Africa: Origins and Contemporary Forms," *Journal of Modern African Studies,* no. 4 (1972): 503-521.
30. S. Gellar, "The Colonial Era," in *Africa,* 3rd ed. P. M. Martin and P. O'Meara, eds. (Bloomington, Indiana: Indiana University Press, 1995), 115.
31. Gordon, "African Politics."
32. DeLancey, "The Economies of Africa," 95.
33. C. P. Potholm, *The Theory and Practice of African Politics* (Englewood Cliffs, NJ: Prentice-Hall), 38.
34. O'Toole, "The Historical Context."
35. Potholm, *The Theory and Practice of African Politics,* 39.
36. Ibid., p. 40.
37. Ibid., p. 41.
38. Ibid., p. 154.
39. E. J. Keller, "Decolonization, Independence, and the Failure of Politics," in *Africa,* 3rd ed. P. M. Martin and P. O'Meara, eds. (Bloomington: Indiana University Press, 1995), 160.
40. T. Kofi, "Market Failure and Persistent Economic Crisis in Africa: Is the US Willing and Able to Help with a Marshall Plan" (Unpublished paper, University of San Francisco, 2001).
41. S. Berry, "Economic Change in Contemporary Africa," in *Africa,* 3rd ed. P. M. Martin and P. O'Meara, eds. (Bloomington: Indiana University Press, 1995), 363.
42. Ibid., p. 306.

CHAPTER 2

1. The Implementation Committee of NEPAD comprises the heads of state of Algeria, Egypt, Nigeria, Senegal, South Africa, and ten others, that is, two from each of the Organization of African Unity's five regions. The NEPAD secretariate is located in South Africa and is primarily responsible to coordinate activities and source funds for its operations.

2. W. Arthur Lewis, *The Theory of Economic Growth* (London: George Allen and Unwin, 1955).

3. Ibid.

4. W. Arthur Lewis, "Industrial Development in Puerto Rico," *The Caribbean Economic Review*, Vol. I, No. 1 (December 1949).

5. W. Arthur Lewis, "Industrialization of the British West Indies," *The Caribbean Economic Review*, Vol. II, No. 1 (May 1950).

6. W. Arthur Lewis, *Report on Industrialization in the Gold Coast* (Accra: Government Printing Department 1953).

7. W. Arthur Lewis, "Economic Development with Unlimited Supplies of Labor," in A. N. Agarwala and S.P. Singh, eds. *The Economics of Underdevelopment* (Oxford: Oxford University Press, 1958).

8. B.L. Poole, *The Caribbean Commission* (Columbia: University of South Carolina Press, 1951).

9. L. G. Reynolds and Peter Gregory, *Wages, Productivity and Industrialization in Puerto Rico*, Ch. 1 (Homewood, IL: Irwin, 1965).

10. Lloyd Best coined the phrase Industrialization by Invitation (IBI) in his article "The Caribbean Economy," *Readings in the Political Economy of the Caribbean*, N. Girran and O. Jefferson (eds.) (Jamaica: ISER/UMI, 1967). Best used the phrase to describe Lewis' (1950) development strategy devised for the British West Indies.

11. R. D. Crassweller, *The Caribbean Community* (Praeger: New York, 1972).

12. Ibid.

13. Eric Williams, foreword, *The Caribbean Economic Review*, Vol. 1, Nos. 1 and 2 (December 1949).

14. Ibid.

15. Ibid.

16. Joan Robinson, *Economic Philosophy* (New York: Anchor Books, 1962).

17. Lewis, "Industrial Development in Puerto Rico"

18. Ibid.

19. Ibid.

20. Lewis, "Industrialization of the British West Indies"

21. Ibid., p. 16.

22. Ibid., p. 18.

23. Ibid., p. 18.

24. Ibid., p. 19.

25. A. K. Sen, *Choice of Techniques* (Oxford: Clarendon Press, 1960).

26. W. G. Demas, *The Economics of Development in Small Countries with Special Reference to the Caribbean* (Montreal: McGill University Press, 1965).

27. Lewis, "Industrialization of the British West Indies," 31.

28. Ibid., pp. 44—45.

29. Ibid., p. 50.

30. Ibid., p, 53

31. See, for example, Lewis, *The Theory of Economic Growth.*

32. Michael P. Todaro, *Economic Development,* 6th ed. (New York: Addison-Wesley, 1996), 76.

33. Olusola Akinrinade and J. Kurt Barling, *Economic Development in Africa* (London: Pinter Publishers, 1987), 4.

34. Ibid.

35. William F. Steel and Jonathan W. Evans, *Industrialization in Sub-Saharan Africa: Strategies and Performance* (Washington, DC: World Bank, 1985), 2.

36. Lewis, *The Theory of Economic Growth,* 9.

37. Todaro, *Economic Development,* 80.

38. Lual A. Deng, *Rethinking African Development: Toward a Framework for Social Integration and Ecological Harmony* (Trenton, NJ: Africa World Press, 1998), 32.

39. Lewis, "Report on Industrialization and the Gold Coast," 1953.

40. Dudley Seers and G. R. Ross, *Report on Financial and Physical Problems of Development in The Gold Coast* (Accra: Office of Government Statisticians, 1952).

41. Lewis, "Report on Industrialization and the Gold Coast."

42. Please note that the numbers in parentheses refer to sections of "Report on Industrialization and the Gold Coast" (Lewis 1953).

43. Sede-Bonilla, "Dependence as an Obstacle to Growth in Puerto Rico"; Edwin Carrington, "*Industrialization by Invitation in Trinidad since 1950,*" *New World Quarterly,* Vol. 4, No. 2 (1968); L. G. Reynolds and Peter Gregory, *Wages, Productivity and Industrialization in Puerto Rico* (Homewood, IL: Irwin, 1965); and Werner Baer, "Puerto Rico—An Evaluation of a Successful Development Programme," *Quarterly Journal of Economics,* Vol. 73, No. 4 (November, 1959), 645—671.

44. Eric Thorbecke, "The Employment Problem: A Critical Evaluation of Four ILO Comprehensive Country Reports." *International Labour Review,* Vol. 107, No. 5 (May 1973), 393—423.

CHAPTER 3

1. Raul Prebisch, who was then the head of the United Nations Commission for Latin America, developed this argument. For details, please refer to Raul Prebisch, *The Economic Development of Latin America and Its Principal Problems* (New York: United Nations, 1950), and Hans W. Singer, "The Distribution of Gains Between Borrowing and Investing Countries," *American Economic Review 40* (May 1950), 473-485.

2. William F. Steel and Jonathan W. Evans, *Industrialization in Sub-Saharan Africa: Strategies and Performance* (Washington, DC: World Bank, 1984), 14.

3. Michael P. Todaro, *Economic Development* (New York: Longman, 1994), 459.

4. Ibid., pp. 469-470.

5. Colin Leys, *The Rise and Fall of Development Theory* (Bloomington: Indiana University Press, 1996), 108.

6. Steel and Evans, *Industrialization in Sub-Saharan Africa,* 10.

7. See, for example, P. Harrison, *The Third World Tomorrow,* 2nd ed. (Middlesex, England: Penguin Books, 1986), 25-42. According to Tade Akin Aina, "Development Theory and Africa's Lost Decade," in *Changing Paradigms in Development – South, East, and West,* ed. Margareta Von Troil (Uppsala: The Scandinavia Institute of African Studies, 1993), 21-22, empowerment in Latin American countries has been achieved through a kind of social mobilization known as conscientization, a process of consciousness raising that constitutes a basis for grassroots social movements. It is a democracy of direct involvement and concrete choices rather than a formal democracy of indirect representation and programmed choices. It can also reduce the incessant problems of the breach of human rights.

8. Aina, "Development Theory and Africa's Lost Decade," 21.

9. Lual A. Deng, *Rethinking African Development* (Trenton, NJ: Africa World Press, 1998), 31.

10. J. Kurt Barling and Olusola Akinrinade, "Editors' introduction," in *Economic Development in Africa: International Efforts, Issues and Prospects* (London: Pinter Publishers, 1987), 10-11.

11. Adebayo Adedeji, "The Monrovia Strategy and the Lagos Plan of Action: Five Years After," in *Economic Crisis in Africa: African Perspectives and Development Problems and Potentials* (Boulder, CO: Lynne Rienner Publishers, 1985), 15.

12. Ibid., p. 23.

13. See Asayehgn Desta, *Environmentally Sustainable Economic Development* (Westport, CT: Praeger Publishers, 1999).

14. Deng, *Rethinking African Development,* 44-45.

15. I. Elbadawi, "World Bank adjustment lending and economic performance in SSA in the 1980's: A comparison of early adjusters, late adjusters and nonadjusters," Policy Research WPS, No. 1001 (World Bank, 1992), 1.

16. Deng, *Rethinking African Development,* 53.

17. Ha-Joon Chang, *Kicking Away the Ladder: Development Strategy in Historical Perspective* (London: Anthem Press, 2002).

18. The IMF, *The World Bank and the African Debt: The Social and Political Impact,* Vol. 2, ed. Bade Onimode (London: Zed Books, 1989), 2.

19. Ibid.

20. *Financial Times* (London), September 1, 1993, p. iii.

21. Ibid.

22. Jonathan R.Coleman, Takamasa Akiyama and Panos N. Varangis, "How Policy Changes Affected Cocoa Sectors in Sub-Saharan African Countries," in *Policy Research Working Papers* (WPS 1129) (April 1993); Panagariya Arvind and Maurice Schiff, "Commodity Exports and Real Income in Africa," in *Economic Reform in Sub-Saharan Africa,* ed. Ajay Chibber and Stanley Fischer (World Bank, 1991); Stephen Younger, "Economic Recovery Program – A Case Study of Stabilization and Structural Adjustment in Sub-Saharan Africa," in *World Bank EDI Policy Case Studies, Analytical Case Studies No. 1, (*1989); *Africa's Adjustment and Growth in the 1980's* (Washington, D.C.: World Bank, 1989); UNDP, *Human Development Report* (Oxford: Oxford University Press, 1990); The Nigerian Structural Adjustment Programme: Policies, Impact, and Prospects (Washington, D.C.: World Bank, December 1988); and "Adjustment Lending: An Evaluation of Ten Years of Experience," in *Policy Research Series* 1 (World Bank, December 1988), 1. (Also called the Fisher Report).

23. US Congress (Committee on Foreign Affairs, U.S. House of Representatives), Structural Adjustment in Africa: Insights from the Experiences of Ghana and Senegal (Report of a Staff Study Mission to Great Britain, Ghana, Senegal, Côte d'Ivoire and France, Nov. 29—Dec. 20, 1988) (Washington, DC: U.S. Government Printing Office, March 1989).

24. Joe Abbey, *On Promoting Successful Adjustment—Some Lessons from Ghana* (IMF, Sept. 24, 1989), 8.

25. Ibid., p. 15.

26. John Loxley, *Ghana: Economic Crisis and the Long Road to Recovery* (Ottawa: The North-South Institute, February 1988), 22.

27. IFAD, Report No. 0105-GH, 1988.

28. Ebenerzer Mikreku, "Assessing Strutural Adjustment Programmes: The Case of Ghana," *IFDA Dossier* 72, July/August 1989. See also, Kwesi Johan, "The social Impact of Ghana's Adjustment Programme 1983-1986," Paper presented to the Institute of African Alternatives, Conference on the Impact of IMF and World Bank Policies on the People of Africa, London, September 1987.

29. Younger, "Economic Recovery Program;" Abbey, *On Promoting Successful Adjustment*; Loxley, *Ghana: Economic Crisis and the Long Road to Recovery*.

30. Oscar Morgenstern, *On the Accuracy of Economic Observations*, Princeton University Press, 1963.

31. Ibid.

32. Samir Amin, "A Critique of the World Bank Report, entitled 'Accelerated Development in Sub-Sharan Africa,'" Africa Development, Vol. 7 (Dakar, 1982).

33. The Ministry of Agriculture (MOA), "Ghana Agricultural Policy—Action Plans and Strategies," 1984—1986.

34. Michael Bruno, "Domestic Resource Costs and Effective Protection: Clarification and Synthesis," *Journal of Political Economy 80* (January/February 1972), 16-33.

35. Isabella Tsakok, Agricultural Price Policy: A Practitioner's Guide to Partial Equilibrium Analysis (Cornell University Press, 1990).

36. *Agricultural Sector Review* (World Bank, Aug. 6, 1985), ix.

37. Ibid., p. 9.

38. Ibid., pp. 10-12.

39. Ibid., p.13.

40. William C. Brainard and Richard N. Cooper, "Uncertainty and Diversification in International Trade," *Ford Research Institute Studies,* Vol. VIII No. 3 (Stanford University, 1968).

41. Ibid., p. 260.

42. Bruno, "Domestic Resource Costs and Effective Protection," 16-17.

43. Brainard and Cooper, "Uncertainty and Diversification in International Trade," 277.

44. *Agricultural Sector Review* (World Bank, Aug. 6, 1985), 9.

45. Bruno, "Domestic Resource Costs and Effective Protection," 16.

46. *Agricultural Sector Review* (World Bank, Aug. 6, 1985), 14-15.

47. Tetteh Kofi and Emmanuel Hanson, "Ghana, A History of an Endless Recession," *Research in Africa*, ed. Jerker Caulsson, (Uppsala: Scandinavian Institute of African Studies, 1983).

48. ERPII, in National Programme for Economic Development, 10.

49. Younger, "Economic Recovery Program," 171.

50. Robert E. Evenson and Yoav Kislev, *Agricultural Research and Productivity* (New Haven, CT: Yale University Press, 1975), 11.

51. G. A. R. Wood and R. A. Lass, *Cocoa*, 4th ed. (Harlow, Essex: Longman Scientific and Technical, 1985).

52. ICCO, "Study of Cocoa Production in Brazil," CS/Prod/01, 20 December 1989, 64.

53. Ibid., p. 66—67.

54. *Afrique Agriculture*, March 1981, 22-54.

55. *Afrique Agriculture*, December 1976, 24-65.

56. *Afrique Agriculture*, February 1983, 52.

57. Polly Hill, *Migrant Cocoa Farmers of Southern Ghana* (Cambridge: University Press, 1963).

58. F. Ruf, "Will Côte d'Ivoire Give Up Its Position of World Leading Cocoa Producer to Indonesia?" *The Cacao Cafe*, Vol. 37 No. 3, July-Sept. 1993.

59. Ibid., p. 247.

60. UNCTAD, "Prospects for the World Cocoa Market until the Year 2005," UNCTAD/Com/r, 1991, 14.

61. Alfred Maizels, *Commodities in Crisis* (Oxford: Clarendon Press, 1992).

62. Tetteh Kofi and James Fry, "Commodity Exchanges and Their Impact on the Trade of Developing Countries," United Nations Conference on Trade and Development (Report for UNCTAD Secretariat), TB/B/C.1/248, (1983).

63. Allan McPhee, *The Economic Revolution in British West Africa* (London: George Routledge and Son Ltd., 1926).

64. Tetteh Kofi, "Vertical Price Relations in the International Coca Market and Implications for Ghana's Marketing Policies," *Economics of Cocoa Production and Marketing*, R.A. Kotey et. al (eds.) (ISSER, Ghana University, 1974); See also, Tetteh Kofi, "Development and Stagnation in Ghana: An Abibirim Approach," Universitas, University of Ghana Publication, Vol. 3 No. 3. (March 1974).

65. For a historical review of the agreements see Tetteh Kofi, "International Cocoa Agreements," *Journal of World Trade* Law, Vol. 11, No. 1 (January/February 1977). See also, *Economics of Cocoa Production and Distribution*, John Simmons (ed.) (Praeger, 1976).

66. Tetteh Kofi, "International Commodity Agreements and Export Earnings: Simulation of the 1968 Draft International Cocoa Agreement," *Food Research* Institute, Vol. 9, No. 2, 1972, 177—201.

67. Kofi and Hanson, "Ghana, A History of an Endless Recession," 1983.

68. M. Godfrey, "Trade and Exchange Rate Policy: A Further Contribution to the Debate," *Crises and Recovery in Sub-Saharan Africa*, ed. T. Rose,

Development Centre of the Organization for Economic Co-operation and Development, (Paris: OECD, 1984).

69. Panagariya and Schiff, "Commodity Exports and Real Income in Africa," 170-171.

70. Coleman et al., "How Policy Changes Affected Cocoa Sectors."

71. Panagariya and Schiff, "Commodity Exports and Real Income in Africa."

72. Coleman et al., "How Policy Changes Affected Cocoa Sectors."

73. Pravin K. Trivedi and Tamamasa Akiyama, "A Framework for Evaluating the Impact of Pricing Policies for Cocoa and Coffee in Cote d'Ivoire," *The World Bank Economic Review*, Vol. 6, No. 2, May 1992.

74. Coleman et al., "How Policy Changes Affected Cocoa Sectors," 40.

75. W. J. Machpherson, *The Economic Development of Japan c. 1868-1941* (London: Macmillan, 1990), 33.

76. Panagariya and Schiff, "Commodity Exports and Real Income in Africa," 171.

77. Ibid., p. 180.

78. Tetteh Kofi, "Peasants and Economic Development: Populist Lessons for Africa," *The African Studies Review*, Vol. 20, No. 3, 1977; Kofi, "International Commodity Agreements and Export Earnings," 1972; and Kofi, *Economics of Cocoa Production and Distribution*, 1976.

79. Kofi, "International Commodity Agreements and Export Earnings," 1972; and Kofi, *Economics of Cocoa Production and Distribution*, 1976.

80. Gill and Duffus, *Cocoa Market Report*, No. 33, March 1989.

81. Tetteh Kofi, "A Framework for Comparing the Efficiency of Futures Markets," *American Journal of Agricultural Economics*, Vol. 55, No. 4, Part I, (November, 1973), 584.

82. Alfred Maizels, Robert Bacon, and George Mavrotas, *Supply Management for Tropical Beverages*, UNU/WIDER, 1994 (mimeo, to be published by Oxford: Clarendon Press).

83. Alfred Maizels, *Commodities in Crisis* (Oxford: Clarendon Press, 1992), 15.

84. Ibid., p. 16.

85. Ibid., p. 17.

86. Tsakok, 1990.

87. Ibid., p. 123-124.

88. Brainard and Cooper, "Uncertainty and Diversification in International Trade," 267.

89. *Ghana 2000 and Beyond* (Washington, DC: World Bank, 1993).

90. Rhee, Yung Whee, and Therese Belot, "Export Catalysts in Low Income Countries: a Review of 11 Success Stories," World Bank Discussion Paper 72 (Washington, DC, 1990).

91. N. Georgescu-Roegen, "Economic Theory and Agrarian Economics," in *Oxford Economic Papers*, Vol. 12, No. 1 (February 1960), 1-40.

92. World Bank, *The East Asian Miracle, Economic Growth and Public Policy* (New York: Oxford University Press, 1993).

93. *The Role of Institutions in Economic Development*, World Development Special Issue, Vol. 17, ed. I. Adelman and E. Thorbecke (September 1989).

94. Mustapha K. Nabli and Jeffrey B. Nugent, *The New Institutional Economics and Development: Theory and Application to Tunisia.*

95. Tetteh Kofi, "The Finnish Agrarian Development Strategy (Pellervo Cooperative Movement) Any Lessons for Africa?" mimeo, UNN-WIDER, 1994.

96. Harry T. Oshima, *Economic Growth in Monsoon Asia—A Comparative Survey* (Tokyo, 1987).

97. Samuel Pao-San Ho, "Colonialism and Development: Korea, Taiwan, and Kwantung," *The Japanese Colonial Empire, 1985*-1945, Ramon H. Myers and Mark R. Peattie (eds.) (Princeton, NJ: Princeton University Press, 1984).

98. Ibid., p. 349.

99. Lord Lugard, *The Dual Mandate in Tropical Africa* (Oxford: Blackwood, 1922).

100. Gustav Ranis, "The Role of Institutions in Transition Growth: The New Asian Newly Industrializing Countries," *World Development*, Vol. 17, No. 9 (1989).

101. Ibid., p. 1447.

102. Andrew Schotter, *The Economic Theory of Social Institutions* (Cambridge: Cambridge University Press, 1981), p. 2.

103. Tetteh Kofi, "The Finnish Agrarian Development Strategy," 1994.

104. Ibid.

105. Thorsten Ohde, *Finland: Nation of Cooperators* (Williams and Nargate Ltd., 1931).

106. Ibid.

107. Henry H. Bakken, *Cooperation to the FINNISH* (Madison, WI: Mimir, 1937), 203.

108. Edward V. K. Jaycox, "Capacity Building in Africa: Challenge of the Decade," *Capacity Building and Human Resource Development in Africa (A Report on a Roundtable Convention by the Lester Pearson Institute for International Development, Dalhousie University, September 18-19, 1989)*, Alexander A. Kwapong and Barry Lesser (eds.) (Halifax, Nova Scotia, Canada: Lester Pearson Institute for International Development, Dalhousie University, 1990), 113.

CHAPTER 4

1.   See for example, Asayehgn Desta, *Environmentally Sustainable Economic Development* (Westport, CT: Praeger, 1999).

2.   Kevin Cleaver, foreword to *Applying Environmental Economics in Africa,* by Frank J. Convery (Washington, DC: The World Bank, 1995), xvii.

3.   The World Bank, "Mauritius: Technology Strategy for Competitiveness" (September 22, 1994), 1.

4.   Arvind Subramanian and Devesh Roy, "Who Can Explain the Mauritian Miracle: Meade, Romer, Sachs, or Rodrik?" in IMF Working Paper, WP/01/116 (International Monetary Fund, 2001), 6.

5.   International Monetary Fund, "IMF Concludes Article IV Consultation with Mauritius," in Public Information Notices for 2002 (Washington, DC: IMF, May 22, 2001), 1–5.

6.   Ibid., p. 7.

7.   Eban S. Goodstein, *Economics and the Environment* (Upper Saddle River, NJ: Prentice Hall, 1999), 448.

8.   Larry W. Bowman, *Mauritius: Democracy and Development in the Indian Ocean* (San Francisco: Westview Press, 1991), 8.

9.   Ibid., p. 9.

10.   Ibid., p. 10.

11.   Ibid., p. 22.

12.   *The World Guide 1997/98*, (Oxford: New Internationalist Publications, 1997), 386.

13.   Ibid.

14.   Robert Bruton et al., "Mauritius: International Financial Services," accessed May 1, 2001, available from http://www.britannica.com.

15.   Available from http://memory.loc.gov.

16.   See, for example, Asayehgn Desta, *International Political Risk Assessment for Foreign Direct Investment and International Lending Decisions* (Needham Heights, MA: Ginn Press, 1993), 36.

17.   "Mauritius," in *The World Guide 1997/98,* 386.

18.   Bowman, *Mauritius*, 116.

19.   Ibid., p. 77.

20.   Ibid., p. 81.

21.   *The World Guide 1997/98*, 387.

22.   Ministry of Economic Development and Regional Co-operation, *Vision 2020: The National Long-Term Perspective Study,* Vol. II (Port Louis, Mauritius: Silvio M Empeigne, Government Printer, 1997), p. 4.12.

23.   Ibid., p. 68.

24.   Ibid.

25. See, for example, Robert J. Gordon, *Macroeconomics* (Reading, MA: Addison Wesley, 2000).

26. Ministry of Economic Development and Regional Co-operation, *Vision 2020*, p. 4.13.

27. Bowman, *Mauritius*, 103.

28. Ibid., p. 104.

29. Richard C. Kearney, "Mauritius and the NIC Model Redux: or, How Many Cases Make A Model?" *The Journal of Developing Areas*, Vol. 24, No. 2 (January 1990), 199.

30. The World Bank, "Mauritius: Technology Strategy for Competitiveness," i.

31. Bowman, *Mauritius*, 114.

32. Ibid., p. 131.

33. Ibid., p. 132.

34. Herman Kahn, *World Economic Development 1979 and Beyond* (New York: Morrow/Quill Papers, 1979), 350.

35. Bowman, *Mauritius*, 115–16.

36. World Bank, "Mauritius: Technology Strategy for Competitiveness," 18.

37. Bowman, *Mauritius*, 116.

38. Ibid., 126–130.

39. World Bank, "Mauritius: Technology Strategy for Competitiveness," 3.

40. Kearney, "Mauritius and the NIC Model," 208.

41. Subramanian and Roy, "Who can Explain the Mauritian Miracle," 7.

42. Ministry of Economic Development and Regional Co-operation, *Vision 2020*, p. 4.23.

43. Ibid., p. 4.24.

44. Ministry of Economic Development, Financial Services and Corporate Affairs, *Structural Transformation of the Mauritian Economy: 1960's Beyond* (2000).

45. See, for example, James H. Weaver, *Achieving Broad-Based Sustainable Development* (West Hartford, CT: Kumarian Press, 1997), 26.

46. World Bank, "Entering the 21st Century," in *World Development Report 1999/2000* (Oxford: Oxford University Press), 238.

47. Subramanian and Roy, "Who can Explain the Mauritian Miracle," 13.

CHAPTER 5

1. Donella H. Meadows, *The Limits to Growth; a report for the Club of Rome's project on the predicament of mankind* (New York: Universe Books, 1972).

2.   World Commission on Environment and Development, *Our Common Future* (Oxford: Oxford University Press, 1987), 6—7.

3.   Alex Farrell and Maureen Hart, "What Does Sustainability Really Mean?" *Environment*, Vol. 40, No. 9 (November 1998), 7.

4.   Noel J. Brown and Pierre Quilblier, *Ethics and Agenda 21* (New York: United Nations Environment Program, 1994), 6.

5.   Carl Frankel, *In Earth's Company: Business, Environment and the Challenge of Sustainability* (Gabriola Island B.C., Canada: New Society Publishers), 179.

6.   Ibid., pp. 180—181; Karl-Henrik Robert et al., *A Compass for Sustainable Development*, International Journal of Sustainable Development and World Ecology (March 26, 1997), 12—15.

7.   Frankel, *In Earth's Company*.

8.   Barry Sadler, "Climb Down from the Earth Summit," *Ecodecision*, 24 (Spring 1997), 28.

9.   David Wallace, *Sustainable Industrialization* (London: Earthscan Publications, 1996), 2.

10.   David G. Victor and Eugene B. Skolnikoff II, "Translating Intent into Action: Implementing Environmental Commitments," *Environment*, Vol. 41, No. 2 (March 1999), 17.

11.   See, for example, Maynard M. Hufschmidt et al., *Environment, Natural Systems, and Development: An Economic Valuation Model* (Baltimore: John Hopkins University Press, 1990), 6.

12.   Alan D. Hecht, "The Triad of Sustainable Development: Promoting Sustainable Development in Developing Countries," *Journal of Environment & Development*, Vol. 8, No. 2 (June 1999), 128.

13.   Farrell and Hart, "What does Sustainability Really Mean," 7.

14.   Ibid. Also please refer to Organisation for Economic Cooperation and Development (OCED), *Towards Sustainable Development: Environmental Indicators* (Paris: OECD Publications, 1998), 109.

15.   OCED, *Towards Sustainable Development*, 107.

16.   The World Bank, "Institutions for Environmental Stewardship," Jose I. dos R. Furtado and Tamara Belt, eds., with Ramachandra Jammi (Washington, DC: WBI Learning Resources Series, 2000), 41.

17.   Ibid., p. 42.

18.   Ibid.

19.   Ibid.

20.   Charles Victor Barber, "Forest Resource Scarcity and Social Conflict in Indonesia," *Environment*, Vol. 40, No. 4 (May 1998), 5—6. Also see for example, Peter Utting, "Deforestation in Central America: Historical and Contemporary Dynamics," *Sustainable Agriculture in Central America* (New York: St. Martin's Press, 1997), 17.

21. International Tropical Timber Organization, "Criteria for the Measurement of Sustainable Topical Forest Management," in *ITTO Policy Development Series 3* (1992).

22. See, for example, C. J. Barrow, *Developing the Environment*, (New York: John Wiley & Sons, 1995) 194.

23. Environmental Stresses in Mauritius, accessed 2002, available from http://www.int.mu/iels/stresses_mau.htm.

24. Ministry of Economic Development and Regional Co-operation, *Vision 2020: The National Long-Term Perspective Study*, Vol. II, p. 8.94.

25. Ibid., p. 8.93.

26. Harry S. Pariser, *Adventure Guide to Costa Rica,2nd ed.,* (Edison, NJ: Hunter Publishing, 1994), 88—89.

27. Annika Persson and Mohan Munasinghe, "Natural Resources Management and Economywide Policies in Costa Rica: A Computable General Equilibrium (CGE) Modeling Approach, The World Bank Environmental Department and Economic Development Institute," *The Greening of Economic Policy Reform*, Vol. II: Case Studies (Oxford: Oxford University Press, 1997), 4—5.

28. For example, see Peter Utting, "Deforestation in Central America," 11.

29. World Resource Institute, *Environmental Almanac* (Boston: Houghton Mifflon Company, 1992), 528.

30. Ibid., pp. 147—148.

31. T. Panayotou, "Empirical Tests and Policy Analysis of Environmental Degradation at Different Stages of Economic Development," World Employment Programme Research Working Paper, WEP 2-22/W, p. 238.

32. World Bank, *World Development Report 1992* (New York: Oxford University Press, 1992), 50.

33. Ibid.

34. World Bank, *World Development Report 1992*, 124.

35. Ibid., p. 126—127.

36. Mauritius, Ministry of Environmental and Urban and Rural Development, "Strategy Paper on Environment, 1998—2005," (memo, 1999).

37. See, for example C. J. Barrow, *Developing the Environment*, 89.

38. Environmental Stresses in Mauritius.

39. Frank J. Convery, "Applying Environmental Economics in Africa," *World Bank Technical Paper Number 277: Africa Technical Series* (1995), 122.

40. Ibid.

41. Cuesta D. Mauricio, "Economic Analysis of Soil Conservation Projects in Costa Rica," World Bank Environmental Paper, No. 8, (1994) 40—41; Ernst Lutz et al., "Economic and Institutional Analyses of Soil

Conservation Projects in Central America and the Caribbean," World Bank Environmental Paper, No. 8, (1994) 40—41.

42. Ministry of the Environment and Energy and the National Institute for Biodiversity (INBio), "National Strategy for the Conservation and Sustainable Use of Biodiversity" (Costa Rica, 1997), 7.

43. Fred R. David, *Strategic Management: Concepts and Cases*, 7th ed., (Upper Saddle River, NJ: Prentice Hall, 1999), 5—6.

44. Ministry of Environment and Urban and Rural Development, "Environment-Mauritius," available at http://ncb.intnet.mu/eurd/minenv/index.html.

45. Costa Rica, *National Strategy for the Conservation and Sustainable Use of Biodiversity, Summary* (Santo Domingo de Heredia: Instituto Nacional de Biodiversidad, 1999), 11—18.

46. Ibid., 20.

47. Ibid.

48. David, *Strategic Management,* 176—177.

49. Costa Rica, *National Strategy for the Conservation and Sustainable Use of Biodiversity,* 21.

50. See, for example Ministry of Environment and Urban and Rural Development, "Environment-Mauritius;" Mauritius, National Environment Action Plan (NEAP) I & II (memo, 1999).

51. Ibid.

52. Ibid., p. 13.

53. Ibid., pp. 14—15.

54. Costa Rica, *National Strategy for the Conservation and Sustainable Use of Biodiversity,* 22—34.

55. Andrew J. Hoffman, *Competitive Environmental Strategy: A Guide to the Changing Business Landscape* (Washington, DC: Island Press, 2000), 10.

56. Richard M. Huber et al., "Market-Based Instruments for Environmental Policymaking in Latin America and the Caribbean," *World Bank Discussion Paper,* 381 (Washington, DC: 1998), 11.

CHAPTER 6

1. Council for Development of Social Science Research in Africa (CODESRIA) and Third World Network (TWN-Africa), The New Partnership for Africa's Development (NEPAD) (April 3—26, 2002). See also The World Bank, *Can Africa Claim the 21st Century?* (Washington, D.C: The World Bank Press, 2000).

2. Ibid.

3. Zo Randriamaro (2004). "The NEPAD, Gender, and the Poverty Trap" [online] Available http:www.web.net/~iccaf/debtsap/nepadgera.htm.

4. William Robinson and Jerry Harris, "Towards a Global Ruling Class: Globalization and the Transnational Capitalist Class," *Science and Society*, Vol. 64, No. 1 (Spring 2000), 27, quoted by Ian Taylor in "The New Partnership for Africa's Development (NEPAD) and the Global Political Economy: Towards a False Start," a paper presented at the Conference on Africa and the Development Challenges of the New Millennium, Accra, Ghana, April 23—26, 2002, p. 6.

5. Jimi O. Adesina, "Development and Challenge of Poverty: NEPAD, Post-Washington Consensus and Beyond," a paper presented at the Conference on Africa and the Development Challenges of the New Millennium, Accra, Ghana, April 23—26, 2002.

6. Ibid., p. 27.

7. African-Canadian Forum, Canadian Council for International Cooperation, (April 2002), "The New Partnership for Africa's Development (NEPAD): Commentary," [online] Available http://www.web.net/~iccaf/debtsap/nepadafricacdaforum.htm.

8. Ibid.

9. NEPAD.

10. Ibid., p. 8.

11. Ibid.

12. Zo Randriamaro, "The NEPAD, Gender and the Poverty Trap," 2.

13. The World Bank, *Can Africa Claim the 21st Century?* (Washington, D.C: The World Bank Press, 2000), 92.

14. Amir Jamal, "Self-reliance, International Assistance, and Managing the African Economy," in Adebayo Adedeji and Timothy M. Shaw (eds.), *Economic Crisis in Africa* (Boulder, CO, 1986), 134.

15. NEPAD, pp. 29—32.

16. See, for example, Asayehgn Desta, *International Political Risk Assessment for Foreign Direct Investment and International Lending* (Needham Heights, MA: Ginn Press, 1993).

17. CODESRIA and TWN-Africa, The New Partnership for Africa's Development, (paragraphs 86—92). See also Yash Tandon (26-29 April, 2002), NEPAD and Foreign Direct Investments (FDIS): Symmetries and Contradictions (online) Available http://www.web.net/~iccaf/debtsap/nepadfdid.htm.

18. Tandon, "NEPAD and Foreign Direct Investments."

19. Ibid., p.16.

20. Ibid., p. 2.

21. SAPRIN, "Executive Summary, The Policy Roots of Economic Crisis and Poverty, A Multi-Country–Participatory Assessment of Structural Adjustment, November 2001," in Tandon, p.16.

CHAPTER 7

1. Tetteh Kofi, "The Elites and Underdevelopment in Africa: The Case of Ghana," *Berkeley Journal of Sociology*, Vol. 17 (1972—73), 96—101.

2. Carl Eicher and John Staatz, "Agricultural Development Ideas in Historical Perspective," in *Agricultural Development in the Third World*, John Staatz and Carl Eicher (eds.) (Baltimore: John Hopkins University Press, 1984), 4.

3. Carl Eicher, "Institutions and the African Farmer," *Issues in Agriculture 14* (Consulting Group on International Agricultural Research [CGIAR], September 1999), 1—2.

4. Hirschman cited in Ibid.

5. A. P. Thirlwall, *Growth and Development* (Boulder, CO: Lynne Rienner, 1994), 89.

6. Schultz cited in Vernon Ruttan, "Models of Agricultural Development," in *Agricultural Development in the Third World,* Carl Eicher and John Staatz (eds.) (Baltimore: John Hopkins University Press, 1984), 42.

7. Christopher Delgado, "Africa's Changing Agricultural Development Strategies," http://www.ifpri.org/2020/briefs/number42.htm (accessed December 9, 2004), paragraph 11.

8. Ibid.

9. Eicher, "Institutions and the African Farmer," 10—12.

10. CGIAR and The International Research Partnership for Food Security and Sustainable Agriculture, "Third System Review of the Consultative Group On International Agricultural Research" (Washington, DC: CIGAR Secretariat, October 8, 1998).

11. Michael Lofchie and Stephen Commins, "Food Deficits and Agricultural Policies in Tropical Africa," in *The Political Economy of Development and Underdevelopment,* 4th ed., Charles K. Wilber (ed.) (New York: Random House Business Division, 1988), 306.

12. I.D. Seers, "The Limitations of the Special Cases," *Bulletins of Oxford Institute of Economics and Statistics* (May 1963), 83—84.

13. Jacques Diouf, "The Challenge of Agricultural Development in Africa," (unpublished paper, Sir John Crawford Memorial Lecture, Washington, DC, November 2, 1989), 6.

14. Abibirim is an Akan word that has philosophical connotations implying "Blackness" or "being Africanized." Colloquially, it means "inside Africa," "belonging to Africa," or "the Blackman." By this strategy it is intended to drive home the need to build institutions to solve the problem of "structural imbalances" in the economy.

15. Tetteh Kofi, "Development and Stagnation in Ghana: An 'Abibirim' Approach," *Universitas*, Vol. 3, No. 2 (Ghana University, March 1974).

16. C. L. R. James, *Nkrumah and the Ghana Revolution* (London: Allison and Busby, 1977).

17. Ibid.

18. For details, please see Asayehgn Desta, *Environmentally Sustainable Economic Development* (Westport, CT: Praeger Publishers, 1999).

19. See for example, Kofi, "Development and Stagnation in Ghana: An 'Abibirim' Approach."

20. Tetteh Kofi, "National Democratic Congress (NDC) Problem and New Patriotic Party (NPP) Nightmare Accumulation of Capital and the Saga of Ada Songor Lagoon," unpublished manuscript.

21. See for example, Kwame Boafo-Arthur, "Chieftaincy and Politics in Ghana Since 1982," *West Africa Review*, Vol. 3, No. 1, 2001.

22. For instance, Kofi explained how African nations can learn from Finland. See a short article in the University of San Francisco newspaper, *Foghorn*, April 10, 1995, entitled "African Countries Can Learn from Finland".

23. This section of the paper is taken from Kofi, "National Democratic Congress (NDC) Problem and New Patriotic Party (NPP) Nightmare Accumulation of Capital and the Saga of Ada Songor Lagoon," 37—40.

24. See for example, Alexander Gerschenkron, *Economic Backwardness in Historical Perspective: A Book of Essays*, (Cambridge, MA: Belknap Press of Harvard University Press, 1962); see also Arnold J. Toynbee, *A Study of History*, Abridgement of Volumes 1—6, D.C. Somervell (ed.) (New York and London: Oxford University Press, 1956).

25. See, for example, Blanca Arreguin, "A Model for the Future of Cuba and Agriculture" (Dominican University of California: unpublished paper, 1996).

26. E. Z. Gabre-Madhin and S. Haggblade, "Successes in African Agriculture: Results of an Expert Survey," *World Development,* Vol. 32, No. 5 (May 2004), 753.

27. Media Benjamin and Peter Rosset, *The Greening of the Revolution* (Sydney, Australia: Ocean Press, 1994), 15.

28. Ibid., p. 48.

29. Gabre-Madhin and Haggblade, "Successes in African Agriculture," 761.

CHAPTER 8

1. This chapter is based on the conceptual model described by Asayehgn Desta, *Environmentally Sustainable Economic Development* (Westport, CT:

Praeger, 1999), 125—134; and was written with the assistance of Cassandra Mann and Giuliana Silvestri, all of Dominican University of California, San Rafael.

2. Swafiya Said, "A Discussion of the Link Between the Preschool Curriculum and the 8-4-4 Standard One Curriculum in Kenya" (Madrasa Resource Centre, Mombasa, Kenya), accessed 2004, available from www.worldbank.org/children/africa/pdffiles/va1albpa.pdf.

3. Ibid.

4. Ibid.

5. Kipchumba Kemei, "Plunder of Mau Forest a Threat to 3m People," *The East African Standard (Nairobi)*, February 25, 2004.

6. Vaal EduNet Project (South Africa), "Curriculum, 2005," accessed November 19, 2003, available from http://www.edunet.co.za/html/curriculum_2005.html.

7. Ibid.

8. The World Bank Group, "S. Africa," accessed March 21, 2004, available from http://www.worldbank.org/afr/.

9. Chris Khumalo, "Makhaye Launches Water Irrigation Scheme," *BuaNews (Pretoria)*, February 25, 2004.

10. The Ghana Education Website, "History of Education," accessed November 19, 2003, available from http://www.ghana.edu.gh/past/index.html.

11. The Ghana Education Website, "Education Today," accessed November 19, 2003, available from http://www.ghana.edu.gh/present/index.html.

12. British Council, "Ghana—Country Education Profile," accessed November 21, 2003, available from http://www2.britishcouncil.org/home/learning/globalschools/globalschools-partnership/globalschools-resources-countries/globalschools-resources-countries-ghana.htm.

13. Ibid.

14. The World Bank Group, "Ghana," accessed March 21, 2004, available from http://www.worldbank.org/afr/.

15. allafrica.com, "Privatised Water Should At Least Flow From the Taps" (UN Integrated Regional Information Networks), accessed February 25, 2004, available at http://allafrica.com/stories/200402260008.html.

16. Ibid.

17. me-schools.com, "Egypt," accessed November 24, 2003, available from http://www.me-schools.com/countries/egypt.htm.

18. Ibid.

19. Ibid.

20. Energy Information Administration, "EIA Country Analysis Briefs, Egypt: Environmental Issues," accessed August 2003, available from http://www.eia.doe.gov/emeu/cabs/egypenv.html.

21. Ibid.

22. Rosemaria Russo, *Jumping from the Ivory Tower: Enhancing Environmental Education through Service Learning and Community Involvement* (San Francisco: Argosy University, 2004), 14.

CHAPTER 9

1. CODESRIA and TWN-Africa, "The New Partnership for Africa's Development (NEPAD)," presented at the Conference on Africa and the Development Challenges of the New Millennium (Accra, Ghana April 23—26, 2002), 29—31.

2. This chapter was funded by the Compton Foundation and written with assistance of Chettapon Paiboonvarakit of Dominican University of California.

3. For a discussion on FDI in Africa, please refer to Jan Kruger, "Foreign Direct Investment (Part IV of XII)," *Namibia Economist,* April 6, 2001, available from http://www.economist.com.na/2001/060401/story9.htm.

4. See for example, Gary M. Quinlivan, "Multinational Corporations: Myths and Facts," *Religion and Society,* Vol. 10 No. 6 (November and December 2000), 1—6.

5. E. Barbier, Economics, Natural Resources, Scarcity and Development (London: Earthscan, 1989).

6. Stephen Hymer, "The Multinational Corporation and the Law of Uneven Development," in *Sociology of Developing Societies,* Hamza Alavi and Teodor Shanin (eds.) (New York: Monthly Review Press, 1982).

7. "A Legacy of Colonialism and Imperialism," available at http://www.tlio.org.uk/issues/legacy/leg_1.html.

8. Bilateral treaties are aimed to promote investment between two contracting parties. They could refer to national laws for standards of treatment and protection in accord with international law, national treatments, most favored nations (MFN), fair and equal treatment of investments, accommodation of specific country concerns such as liberation of restrictions to entry and establishment of FDI, and harmonization of investment incentives.

9. African countries participating in the Cross Border Initiative are: Burundi, Comoros, Kenya, Madagascar, Malawi, Mauritius, Namibia, Rwanda, Seychelles, Swaziland, Tanzania, Uganda, Zambia, and Zimbabwe.

10. "Cross-Border Initiatives," *Road Map for Investor Facilitation*, Paper for Fourth Ministerial Meeting in Mauritius (October 1999).

11. Miria Pigato, "The Foreign Investment Environment in Africa: The Incentive Framework for Foreign Investment in Africa," Africa Region Working Paper Series, No. 15 (April 2001).

12. Ibid.

13. Ibid.

14. K. Y. Amako, "The Economic Causes and Consequences of Civil Wars and Unrest in Africa," Address to the 70th Ordinary Session of the Council Ministers of the Organization of Africa Unity (Algiers, Algeria, July 8, 1999).

15. S. Abdullahi, "The Conservation of the Environment in Oil Producing Areas of Nigeria (Niger Delta Areas)" (M.Sc. Thesis, Department of Petroleum Engineering, University of Ibadan, 1994).

16. UNDP, "United Nations Programme of Action for African Economic Recovery," Report 5132, Statistical Study on Trends on Evaluation, 1994—1995.

17. Nazli Choucri, "The Global Environment and Multinational Corporations," in *The Multinational Enterprises in Transition*, 4th ed., Phillip D. Grub and Dara Khambata (eds.) (Princeton, NJ: The Darwin Press, 1993), 509.

18. Bede N. Okigbo, "Towards Sustainable Environmental and Resource Management Futures in Sub-Saharan Africa," in *Sustaining the Future*, George Benneh et al. (eds.) (Tokyo: The United Nations University, 1996), 146.

19. Hymer, "The Multinational Corporation and the Law of Uneven Development," 143.

20. See, for example, Quinlivan, "Multinational Corporations: Myths and Facts."

21. Eban S. Goodstein, *Economics and the Environment* (Upper Saddle River, NJ: Prentice Hall, 1995), 479.

22. Comfort Hassan, Janice Olawoye, and Kent Nnadozie, "Impact of International Trade and Multinational Corporations on the Environment and Sustainable Livelihoods of Rural Women in Akwa-Ibom State, Niger Delta Region, Nigeria" (Global Development Network, September 2002).

23. Ibid.

24. Ibid.

25. Ibid.

26. Amoako, "The Economic Cause and Consequences of Civil Wars."

27. Joseph E. Stiglitz, *Globalization and Its Discontents* (New York: W.W. Norton, 2002), 72.

28. Quinlivan, "Multinational Corporations," 4.

29. See for example, Stiglitz, *Globalization and Its Discontents,* 73—74.

30. This approach draws upon the analytical model described by Asayehgn Desta, *International Political Risk Assessment for Foreign Direct Investment and International Lending Decisions* (Needham Heights, MA: Ginn Press, 1993), 27-39.

31. For details see Asayehgn Desta, *Environmentally Sustainable Economic Development* (Westport, CT: Praeger, 1999), 160.

CHAPTER 10

1. Bill Rau, From Feast to Famine: Official Cures and Grassroots Remedies to Africa's Food Crisis (London: Zed Books Ltd., 1990,), 12.

2. Ibid., p. 25.

3. Ibid., p. 15.

4. Ibid., p. 50.

5. William C. Brainard and Richard N. Cooper, "Uncertainty and Diversification in International Trade," *Ford Research Institute Studies, Stanford University,* Vol. 8, No. 3, 1968.

6. Frank J. Convery, "Applying Environmental Economics in Africa," *World Bank Technical Paper Number 277: Africa Technical Series* (1995), 122.

7. Ibid.

8. See, for example, Lawrence Schlemmer, "Getting Real about Democracy in Africa: Nepad and the Challenge of Good Governance," a paper presented at an international colloquium on Cultures, Religions and Conflicts, Mzaar, Lebanon. Ministry of Culture, September 18—21, 2002, p. 1.

9. Jimi O. Adesina, "Development and Challenge of Poverty: NEPAD, Post-Washington Consensus and Beyond," a paper presented at the Conference on Africa and the Development Challenges of the New Millennium, Accra, Ghana, April 23—26, 2002.

10. Schlemmer, "Getting Real About Democracy in Africa," p. 1.

11. See Chapter 7, note 14 for an explanation of Abibirim.

12. Tetteh Kofi, "Development and Stagnation in Ghana: An 'Abibirim' Approach," in *Universitas,* Vol. 3, No. 2 (Ghana University, March 1974).

13. Seth La-Anyane, *Economics of Agricultural Development in Tropical Africa.* (New York: John Wiley & Sons, 1985), 46.

14. See, for example, Carl K. Eicher and Doyle C. Baker, *Research on Agricultural Development in Sub-Saharan Africa: A Critical Survey* (East Lansing: Department of Agricultural Economics, Michigan State University, 1982).

15. Lual A. Deng, *Rethinking African Development: Toward A Framework for Social Integration and Ecological Harmony* (Trenton, NJ: Africa World Press, 1998), 173.

16. Goran Hyden, "African Social Structure and Economic Development" in *Strategies for African Development*, Robert J. Berg and Jennifer Seymour Whittaker (eds.) (Berkeley: University of California Press, 1986), 72.

17. Ibid.

18. See, for example, The World Bank, *Sub-Saharan Africa: From Crisis to Sustainable Growth* (Washington, D.C.: The World Bank, 1989), 89.

19. African Development Bank, *Africa Development Report: 2002* (New York: Oxford University Press, 2002), 212.

20. International Labour Organization, "How Cooperatives Create Jobs," updated April 18, 2005, <http://www.ilo.org/dyn/empent/empent.portal?p_docid=CREATION&p_prog=C&P_SUBPR...

21. Charles E. French et al., *Survival Strategies for Agricultural Cooperatives*. (Ames: Iowa State University Press, 1980), 134.

22. CODESRIA and TWN-Africa, "The New Partnership for Africa's Development (NEPAD)," presented at the Conference on Africa and the Development Challenges of the New Millennium, Accra, Ghana, April 23—26, 2002), 29—31.

23. Ibid.

24. Niles E. Helmboldt, Tina West, and Benjamin H. Hardy, "Private Investments and African Economic Policy," in *Strategies for African Development*, Robert J. Berg and Jennifer Seymour Whitaker (eds.) (Berkeley: University of California Press, 1986), 337.

25. For details see Asayehgn Desta, *Environmentally Sustainable Economic Development* (Westport, CT: Praeger Publishers, 1999), 160.

26. Len Arthur et al., "Capital Anchoring and Cooperative Ownership: The Reality of the Operation of a Cooperative Enterprise in a Globalising Economy," *Management Research News,* Vol. 24, No. 10/11 (2001); ABI/INFORM Global.

27. Curtis Haynes Jr. and Jessica Gordon Nembhard, " Inner City, Economic development, Economic growth, cooperation," *Review of Black Economy*, Vol. 27, No. 1 (Summer 1999), 27—47.

28. Helmboldt, West, and Hardy, "Private Investments and African Economic Policy," 332.

29. The World Bank, *Sub-Saharan Africa*, 92.

30. Carl Liedholm and Donald C. Mead, "Small-Scale Industry," in *Strategies for African Development*, Robert J. Berg and Jennifer Seymour Whitaker (eds.) (Berkeley: University of California Press, 1986), 319—326.

INDEX

N

O

P

R